HIGHER
FACULTIES

HIGHER FACULTIES

A Cross-National Study of
University Culture

Adam Podgórecki

 Westport, Connecticut
London

Library of Congress Cataloging-in-Publication Data

Podgórecki, Adam.
Higher faculties : a cross-national study of university culture /
Adam Podgórecki.
p.   cm.
Includes bibliographical references (p.   ) and index.
ISBN 0–275–95616–4 (alk. paper)
1. Education, Higher—Cross-cultural studies. 2. Learning and
scholarship—Cross-cultural studies. 3. Intellectual life—Cross-
cultural studies. 4. Scholars—Interviews. I. Title.
LB2322.2.P64   1997
378'.001—dc20   96–26876

British Library Cataloguing in Publication Data is available.

Library of Congress Catalog Card Number: 96–26876
ISBN: 0–275–95616–4

First published in 1997

Praeger Publishers, 88 Post Road West, Westport, CT 06881
An imprint of Greenwood Publishing Group, Inc.

Printed in the United States of America

Copyright Acknowledgments

The author and publisher gratefully acknowledge permission to reprint extracts from Paul
R. Gross and Norman Levitt. 1994. *Higher Superstition: The Academic Left and Its
Quarrels with Science*. Baltimore, Md.: Johns Hopkins University Press.

Every reasonable effort has been made to trace the owners of copyright materials in this
book, but in some instances this has proven impossible. The author and publisher will be
glad to receive information leading to more complete acknowledgments in subsequent
printings of the book and in the meantime extend their apologies for any omissions.

Contents

Acknowledgments

I thank the following scholars for their kindness in sharing with me their experiences of diverse scholars and their social determinants. At Stanford University, Preston Cutler (former deputy director of the Center for Advanced Study in the Behavioral Study, Stanford), Alex Inkeles (Hoover Institution), James March, Lawrence Friedman, Robert Gordon, John Merryman, Henry Taube (Nobel Prize winner), Kenneth Arrow (Nobel Prize winner), Arthur Schawlow (Nobel Prize winner), Mauro Cappelletti, Walter Zawojski (physicist and artist), and Cindy Stewart (student) At the University of California, Robert Kagan, Jerome Skolnick, Guy Benveniste, John Coons, Sheldon Messinger, Martin Trow, Robert Post, Philippe Nonet, David Matza, Melvin Calvin (Nobel Prize winner), Jeremy Waldron, Neil Smelser (then at the University of California), Glenn Seaborg (former chancellor and Nobel Prize winner), Laura Nader, Gregory Grossman, Clark Kerr (former chancellor and president), Martin Jay, and Eva Morawska (University of Pennsylvania). I also thank Robin Farquhar, former president of Carleton University for his remarks.[1]

Jan Gorecki and Jan Klimowski offered many penetrating remarks concerning Chapter 2, and some of their suggestions have been used. Thanks are also due to Neil Smelser and Frank Vallee for their insightful comments on an earlier draft of the book and for permission to use those comments.

   Special thanks go to Paul Pedersen from the University of Alabama at Birmingham and to Nick Street from Greenwood Press for their insightful and helpful comments regarding the earlier draft of the manuscript.

   My thanks to Claire Gigantes for her most impressive, imaginative, and meticulous editorial work; Dru Claar-Thompson for her highly competent in-house editing; Ellen Dorosh for her efficiency in guiding the overall production process; Dian Smithers and Olga Cada for transcribing the interviews conducted at Stanford University and the University of California at Berkeley; and, finally, Carleton University for the grant enabling me to transcribe part of these interviews.

Introduction

This study attempts to determine the current role of scholars and scholarship and their impact outside the academic realm. Because scholars are a diverse species with diverse understandings of their function and purpose, I have devised a typology, proposed in Chapter 3, to classify different types of scholars, identify the psychological determinants that incline scholars to the scholarly life, discern what types flourish in what kinds of social systems, and assess the contribution of scholars to sociopolitical change.

This tentative classification addresses what "is." Because the scholarly world is a peculiar mixture of descriptive and normative issues, it seems appropriate to consider what constitutes the ideal scholar and, thereby, distinguish between "is" and "ought." Accordingly, an ideal scholarly paradigm is presented in Chapter 1, followed by a sketchy and selective review of the existing literature on the issues of scholarship and creativity in Chapter 2. Scholarly creativity is a narrower issue than creativity in general. Scholarly, artistic, and literary creativity may overlap, but the important question here is what is unique to scholarly ingenuity (if there are enough empirical data to make such an inquiry).

Chapter 4 focuses on different university cultures, international centers of scholarship and scientific creation, specifying the links among various types of scholars as classified here and the types of social structure in which they function. Different social milieux assimilate different categories of scientific researchers. Of course, because there are, as yet, no comparative descriptions of the "scientific ethos" that characterizes different societies, what is presented here is largely anecdotal and possibly misleading and should be treated as preliminary to more reliable and comprehensive analyses that may emerge. The general lack of comparative research data should not act as a deterrent to subsequent investigation.

Chapter 5 presents, to substantiate better those observations, interviews conducted in April and May 1994 with scholars from Stanford University and the University of California at Berkeley (one of the most advanced academic communities in the world). These particular universities provide ample opportunity for empirical observation of leading academic figures as well as leading figures in the contemporary world of science. The basis for the interviews was the original draft of the typology, which was used as a springboard for conversation on a range of issues. Thus, tested against perceptions other than my own, the typology was refined — on the strength of feedback from these scholars as well as ongoing research — into the version proposed here.

It is one thing to design an ideal typology of scholars and to propose that these types are produced by different social systems or the institutions operating within them and to claim that specified types of scholars satisfy certain needs of those systems. However, it is another thing to demonstrate that these ideal scholarly models describe reality and that they are, indeed, produced by social processes. As Max Weber observed: "An ideal type is formed by the one-sided accentuation of one or more points of view and by the synthesis of a great many diffuse, discrete, more or less present and occasionally absent concrete individual phenomena, which are arranged according to those one-sidedly emphasized viewpoints into a unified analytical construct. . . . In its conceptual purity, this mental construct . . . cannot be found empirically anywhere in reality" (Weber 1949: 90).

Weber's general thesis is borne out in Chapter 6, which contains highly one-sided, often anecdotal "case studies" of several real scholars, who are treated here as representatives of types in themselves. However, both the natural and social sciences have, by now, developed such remarkable constructive and destructive potentials that they cannot be allowed to function anonymously, divorced from the "real world."[1] Those working within them have become public figures and, as such, must undergo public scrutiny. These case studies confront prevalent opinion with the existing academic praxis. The reactions they incur may, in some cases, be controversial, but they should not be construed as personal attacks. As public figures, scientists must accept scrutiny on the basis not only of their accomplishments but also of their internal motives. In this new and necessary atmosphere of generalized cognitive control, scientists (as politicians) may, and must, become transparent to the public eye.

Finally, the results of the study are summarized and generalized in Chapter 7.

When I was conducting my empirical research on scholars in California, Preston Cutler, a former deputy director of the Center for Advanced Study in Behavioral Sciences at Stanford, suggested that it might be helpful to those who are interested in the results of this investigation for me to reveal my academic "credentials." More specifically, he suggested that, as a specialist in the sociology of law, I should provide some background to my interest in the social role of scholars. Therefore, I tried to disclose my theoretical background. Among other things, this exercise would acquaint the reader with the scope of my scientific experience and with my necessary biases. Here again, because a comparative perspective in studies of scholars of different backgrounds is *in statu nascendi* and empirical material is still lacking, personal experience plays a crucial role. Although the use of personal experience as a valid source of data is a departure from traditional scholarship and although it perhaps invites criticism on the grounds of partiality or personal bias, it seems reasonable to make full disclosure of all of one's strengths and weaknesses.

1

The Ideal Scholar

Scholars are not purely empirical beings; they are determined by a variety of factual circumstances, and they themselves influence (as teachers, experts, specialists, and so on) different material situations and social realities. However, they also are normatively oriented human beings. Therefore, in order to analyze them, one has to take their axiological dimensions. These have been cultivated through centuries of philosophical, practical, experiential, and other causes. Hence, it is not enough to analyze scholars sociologically; various sociologically relevant dimensions must be taken into consideration as well.

It is necessary to stress that there are "ideal" (Weberian) types of scholars, but there also are types of scholars as they are normatively shaped. This ideal-normative image of scholars must be included in an analysis of the typology of real categories of scholars because their normative image seriously influences the models of scholars as they exist in reality; in this way, the normative ingredient penetrates into the factual reality of scholars as they appear on the academic scene.

Generally speaking, one may say that the ideal type of scholar is a synthesis of the following essential elements: the general ethos of the human being interested in gnoseological matters (oriented toward disinterested knowledge), the scientific ethos of those who deal with scientific matters, and individual creative potential. In dealing with scientific matters, the gnoseological ethos must be well-developed. This means several things. One should have certain beliefs that have developed out of one's life experience. One should be open to new arguments that may ultimately modify one's beliefs. The beliefs themselves should be resistant to outside oppression, that is, they should be unresponsive to pressures alien to their gnoseological content; they should be changed only when the arguments for doing so are logically sufficient and compelling. Nevertheless, in the last instance, beliefs should be tested against the personal integrity of their holders, who should be ready to defend their beliefs with all their personal values and assets. Finally, a gnoseologically oriented person should be an eager and open witness of the epoch's problems and ideas.

Because it is not enough to internalize and represent these features, other characteristics are necessary to the scholarly ethos. Scholars should be consistent. They should be dedicated to solving certain problems and should not abandon a given problem without sufficient cause. Certainly, they should never abandon their integrity for any gains they might make by doing so. The scholarly attitude should not change because a scholar's personal preferences have shifted; these attitudes have an autotelic value. A scholarly mind should be dedicated to the intricacies of spiritual or material reality and to their exploration and explication. A scholar should exhibit an "academic seriousness" (he or she should not approach the scholarly endeavor with less than a solemn dedication). The specific links between the general human ethos and the scholarly ethos must be acknowledged.

This dry list of basic ethical and scholarly characteristics demands further elaboration.

ETHICAL FEATURES

Everyone looks at social reality from his or her own point of view. This point of view is determined, in general, by the observer's life span and, especially, social position, life story, interpretation of his or her own personal experiences, ability to analyze these experiences individually or collectively, inclination to various theories that might explain the experiences, and so on. For all the variables, there are certain common denominators by which diverse points of view can, nonetheless, be compared; there are also certain norms that link these experiences into a more general hierarchy. Diversity of experience has many positive features; in particular, it enables individuals to reach generalizations that surpass the social and intellectual horizons of an individual observer. Those who are unable to understand the individual and social experiences of others lack the proper tools to develop a comprehensive scholarly outlook.

Because a person's field of observation is, of necessity, limited, one must be open to the life observations and generalizations of others. Hence, the *Weltanschauung* of those who are alert to knowledge should be additive (receptive to and willing to accept the wisdom generated by others). If the ethos of an individual is autocratic and authoritarian (the sort of ethos generated mainly by authoritarian social systems), then that individual will tend not to be cognitively open. This "reverse socialization" could occur not only because of the limitation imposed by a narrow purview but also because of the pressure of external features that do not allow the sharing of experiences and wisdom on the academic "free market."

Everyone living in a social system is exposed to pressures to conform. Some are more ready than others to internalize these pressures, believing and behaving accordingly. The more ready people are to accept the general values of society, the less they are able to see material and social reality in a nonprescribed way. One may roughly divide the pressures operating in society into those based on physical stress, attempts to induce people to change their social behavior by giving them a different role to perform, and persuasion (logical argumentation or emotional guidance). A person who changes beliefs only under physical pressure is not a good candidate to be a scholar; he or she is too rigid.

On the market of social experiences and cognitive wisdom, it is not just rational arguments that circulate; quite often, derivations (rationalizations, justifications, or spurious explanations) predominate. It can be quite difficult to distinguish rational arguments from prefabricated ones, because derivations are produced, as a rule, by sophisticated centers of mass confusion (in this respect, the mass media play an important role); however, they are often deliberately produced in order to disorient or mislead. Excessive resistance to a change of attitude in the face of rational argumentation indicates that a given person lacks the proper features to be a scholar.

In social intercourse, it is very difficult to prove something irrefutably. In social exchange, subjective perceptions interfere with the precise use of argumentation to test ideas or beliefs against objective criteria. In consequence, subjectivity and divergent points of view must be accepted as legitimate components. In social intercourse, the subjective features of individual integrity assume importance as a methodological factor. Individuals who are not ready to support their beliefs with their own integrity are not equipped to be scholars in the social sciences and humanities.

Under social or political pressure, individuals should be ready to pay a price (sometimes painful and humiliating) in defense of their personal beliefs. Willingness to stand firm against irrational external pressures indicates whether a given individual is internally prepared to be a scholar. Again, these kinds of pressures are often encountered in modern authoritarian systems.

Scholars should be alert to the subtlest symptoms and trends of their epoch. They should be the most sensitive witnesses of their time, seeking the hidden drifts of meaning behind technological and social change and the nuanced substructures it creates in society. The scholarly psyche is best developed by those who, by nature or curiosity, are most attentive to their times.

These features can be elaborated further. Scholars should be internally consistent, that is, they should be guided mainly by logic and formally congruous methodology. Because scholars are not artists, they cannot be swayed by changeable moods, a diversity of vision, or their own powers of empathy. Their primary goal is to deliver an adequate picture of material or spiritual reality as they perceive it, according to methods that they are ready to apply. It is impossible to free oneself of *all* value judgments, but it is possible to perceive and disclose to oneself those values that function more or less as hidden agendas. Scholars who depart from the requirement of logical coherence are scholarly traitors, and their hidden agendas should be closely scrutinized. In addition, their scholarly integrity should be seriously questioned.

Scholars confront a permanent problem. Their duty is to describe issues of the day in terms that are accepted in their discipline. The task is to make this description optimally adequate. They have to create a new terminology if the existing academic vocabulary appears insufficient. They also have a duty to state whether the methodological apparatus they use belongs to the traditional epistemological orientation or whether a new epistemology has to be developed for the elaborated diagnosis; eventually, the elaborated description (diagnosis) diverges from an ontologically reliable picture of analyzed reality. Scholars also have a duty to try to explain existing reality and to test the solidity of this explanation. Their primary duty is to explore existing explanations and, where appropriate explanatory hypotheses do not exist, to develop new ones. Because an explanation is one side of the task, the second and corresponding side is to discuss possible strategies to solve the problem under investigation.

Scholars are not allowed to abandon their task without sufficient reason. If they are unable to solve the problem, then they must suspend their efforts until such time as they have renewed potential to deal with it. If they unexpectedly confront a problem of a higher rank, then they must postpone their work until metaquestions have been settled. The scholar who abandons a problem for reasons that are not inherent to the requirements of the task demonstrates an instrumental (pragmatic-opportunistic) approach to the scholarly endeavor.

Scholars should not depart from the demands of their inquiry in order to profit elsewhere from their methodological capacities or the confidence placed in them. In this respect, a scholar should be like a monk; if a monk uses the respect he has gained through his ascetic life for private interests rather than scientific pursuits, he betrays the rudimentary imperatives of his vocation. He not only deceives his own vocation (as eloquently described by Max Weber) but he deceives the trust it traditionally inspires. However, a scholar is not a saint. Paraphrasing Robert Merton, Harriet Zuckerman says: "The ethos of science has it that scientists should derive their prime gratification from doing research and contributing new knowledge. Scientific honours should not be sought but should come as a byproduct. At the same time, the drive for recognition is also built into the ethos of science since recognition by knowledgeable peers is valued as the chief symbol that scientists have done their jobs well" (Zuckerman 1977: 209).

The scholarly ethos has peculiar autotelic value: it is independent from outside factors. This ethos is autonomous. What characterizes it is that, although someone's political or social values may change (under the influence of existential conditions), a real scholarly ethos would remain constant. If a scholar abandons his or her scientific ethos for reasons other than a change of cognitive paradigm, it becomes clear that certain outside factors have gained the upper hand. It also becomes obvious that the purity of scientific inquiry is soiled by values existing outside the academic realm. The study of totalitarian regimes abundantly illustrates when and how these regimes are able to impose their totalitarian political values on their "scientific workers"; certain totalitarian systems also have been very effective in inculcating into the brains of their subjects the false ideological claim that the political values of the regime have the upper hand over "sterile" scientific values.

The scholarly mind should be constantly vigilant of existing reality in order to comprehend it adequately and explain it fully — or, rather, to keep continued watch for transformations in a changeable reality, because complete description and final explanation are never possible. The scholarly mind should be aware both that it cannot give a final diagnosis of reality *hic* and *nunc* and that it cannot fully explain reality as it exists *hic* and *nunc*.

Scholars should exhibit an "academic seriousness" in their scholarly pursuits. The stereotype of the old-fashioned German scholar — a scholar of deadly sincerity, of closed and inward-looking concentration, notoriously absentminded in regard to other than scholarly matters, and evidently humorless when it comes to his academic quest — nevertheless describes the scholarly fate: utter dedication to a self-centered attempt to analyze, uncover, and elaborate what is hidden behind the curtain. This demands not only full concentration but also personal sacrifice, sometimes total, of one's freedom and private pleasures. There is something deeply ironic in the expression, "He devoted himself to scientific work." It should be said, rather, that "he wanted to ennoble himself by scientific work."

There are some specific links between the general human ethos of an individual oriented toward knowledge and a scholarly, gnostic ethos. Glasses help those eyes that wear them. If a human psyche is oriented toward contemplation of beauty, then it seeks reinforcement of its task through experience of enchantments, grace, and charm. The self that is oriented toward goodness concentrates on altruism and benevolence. A human psyche that is interested in truth looks for ways of seeing reality more clearly. A particular version of the human self tries to reinforce its task by finding a subself that helps it to fulfil the main assignment.

With these considerations in mind, the following section outlines existing typologies of scholars built on axiological and psychological premises by Florian Znaniecki, Merton, Johann Galtung, Magoroh Maruyama, and O. J. Harvey.

TYPOLOGIES BASED ON AXIOLOGICAL AND PSYCHOLOGICAL PREMISES

Znaniecki

Using axiological and psychological criteria without specifying them, Znaniecki proposes an elaborated typology of scholars. Analytical definitions of "scholar" reveal what people usually understand by this term. Thus, the 1980 *Webster's Dictionary* defines a scholar as "a specialist in a particular branch of learning." The 1981 *Webster's* describes a scholar as "one who has done advanced study in a special field." Taking all previous understandings into account, one might suggest a synthetic definition of scholar should be understood as "one who contributes something new to the existing body of knowledge." In this book, creativity is regarded as a crucial scholarly characteristic. One should note that Znaniecki's classification is based on the developmental view of scholarly history. His hidden assumption is that the role of the scholar is continually evolving, dividing its main branches, once mature enough, into new scholarly subroles. Over and above this basic thesis, the classification is designed to provide an abstract typology of different categories of scholars.

Znaniecki distinguishes the following types of scholars:

The technological scholar, whose task is to define situations and make plans for technicians to execute (Znaniecki 1940: 38)[1];

Sages, who, like technologists, sometimes go beyond their role of justifying and rationalizing to create "higher," more comprehensive and exhaustive standards of valuations and norms of conduct (Znaniecki 1940: 76);

The religious scholar, whose main role is strictly determined by the task of the sacred school — the perpetuation of sacred lore (Znaniecki 1940: 100);

The discoverer of truth, who is preoccupied with finding a new standard of theoretical validity that can successfully compete for social recognition not only with the prestigious prophet of the sacred school but also with men who have specialized in the cultivation of absolute knowledge (Znaniecki 1940: 119);

The systematizer, who, according to Znaniecki, probably has too extensive and difficult a task: "to test the total knowledge of his epoch and civilization or . . . the total existing knowledge about a certain field of reality and to organize into a system the truths that stand the test" (Znaniecki 1940: 124);

The contributor, whose highest achievement is to make one or more discoveries that show that the scientific systems of his or her predecessors have been inadequate and that, with the help of those discoveries, one can construe a more adequate scientific system (Znaniecki 1940: 135);

The fighter for truth, who, according to Znaniecki, wants logical victory for a system that he or she believes is superior to other systems of truth (Znaniecki 1940: 138);

The eclectic scholar and the historian — the former collects knowledge impartially, and the latter reconstructs and interprets the theories of the past (Znaniecki 1940: 148–49);

The disseminator of knowledge, who spreads exoteric knowledge among the lay population (Znaniecki 1940: 140);

The explorers, or "individual scientists who specialize, so to speak, in doing the unexpected," who are "seeking in the domain of knowledge for new ways into the unknown" (Znaniecki 1940: 165).

Znaniecki distinguishes two categories of explorers: the discoverer of facts and the discoverer of problems.

There are several weak points in this classification. One might object to the distinction between the discoverers of truth and the explorers (the discoverers of fact or problems). Against the very notion of the "discovery of facts," one might argue that, quite often, if not as a rule, one is not discovering "the fact" but is construing it and that, only after construction of a fact, which is supposed to "describe" or make the fact more familiar to our current cognitive apparatus, is it incorporated into the general body of sciences. It also should be suggested as a general epistemological hypothesis that no one reality exists, corresponding to one exclusive truth, but that various realities exist, being at the same time simultaneously connected with their own appropriate truths. One might add that the whole area of the "pathology of scholarly life" and important problems of scientific subculture are entirely omitted.[2] Nonetheless, Znaniecki's pioneering work definitely opened many new avenues for further investigation.

Merton

Merton's typology seems to be the most general (Merton 1968: 606–15). He distinguishes four sets of institutional imperatives: universalism, "communism," disinterestedness, and organized scepticism.

Science is universalistic because its generalizations do not depend on the personal or social attributes of its protagonists and are verified on the basis of objective procedure. Science, thus, has an international, impersonal, and virtually anonymous character. Because democracy is tantamount to the progressive elimination of restraints upon the cultivation of socially appreciated faculties and because it is essential for the development of disinterested criteria that determine accomplishment, democracy provides the proper scope for the universalistic criteria in science.

Merton also accentuates the element of "communism" in science. Communism in this sense emerges when a society ensures that a scientific law or theory does not remain in the exclusive possession of the inventor or his or her heirs (or participants of his or her mafia) but becomes a common legacy of the whole society. In this context, Merton refers to Newton's well-known remark, "If I have seen further, it is by standing on the shoulders of giants" (Merton 1995).

Although Merton does not directly identify disinterestedness, he proposes that "it is . . . a distinctive pattern of institutional control over the wide range of motives which characterize the behaviour of scientists." Absolute disinterestedness does not exist; disinterestedness at best is tempered by various supervisory arrangements that serve as checks on one another.

According to Merton, organized scepticism involves, *inter alia*, a latent questioning of certain grounds of established routine, authority, vested procedures, and the realm of the "sacred" in general. It follows that the totalitarian state, closing itself against penetration by scientific inquiries, tends to restrict the scope provided for scientific inquiry (Merton 1968: 614–15).

Galtung

Galtung proposes a sort of metatypology.[3] He is constructing a much more general typology of scholars, based less on the psychological characteristics of those who are engaged in scholarly pursuits as on more general sociocultural features. He distinguishes the Teutonic theory-building orientation, supported by abstract notions that disregard empirical data; the Anglo-Saxon approach, characterized mainly by empirical generalizations and weakness in theory building; the Gallic approach, which is basically similar to the Teutonic but enriched by substantial elements of wit; and the Nipponic approach, based mainly on seniority (Galtung 1981). Galtung (1981: 823) summarizes his observations in the following table:

	Saxonic	Teutonic	Gallic	Nipponic
Paradigm analysis	Weak	Strong	Strong	Weak
Descriptions:				
proposition production	Very strong	Weak	Weak	Strong
Explanations:				
theory formation	Weak	Very strong	Very strong	Weak
Commentary on				
other intellectuals	Strong	Strong	Strong	Very strong

Once more he summarizes his observations in this way (1981: 838):

Saxonic style	How do you operationalize it: (U.S. version) How do you document it? (UK version)
Teutonic style	Wie konnen Sie das zuruckfuhren — ableiten? (How can you trace this back — deduce it from basic principles?)

Gallic style	Peut-on dire cela en bon francais? (Is it possible to say it in French?)
Nipponic style	Donatano monka desuka? (Who is your master?)

Maruyama and Harvey

Maruyama goes further; he proposes a much broader characterization that tries to take into account not only national and individual characteristics but also various important epistemological differences. As he notes, this typology has many features in common with Harvey's classification presented below. Maruyama divides his typology mainly on the basis of cognitive characteristics (Maruyama 1991: 3):

H Type	I Type	S Type	G Type
homogenist	heterogenist	heterogenist	heterogenizing
universalist	individualist	mutualist	mutualizing
hierarchical	isolationist	interactive	interactive
classifying	randomizing	contextual	contextualizing
eternal	temporary	pattern maintenance	pattern generation
sequential	no order	simultaneous	simultaneous
competitive	uniquing	cooperative	cogenerative
zero-sum	negative-sum	positive-sum	positive-sum
unity by similarity	independence	mutual gain by diversity	mutual gain by diversity
identity	identity	relation	relating
specialization	specialization	convertibility	convertibility
opposition	separation	absorption	absorption
tension	indifference	continuity	flow
extension	caprice	stability	development
one truth	subjectivity	polyocular	polyocular

Dealing with similar matters and drawing mainly on personality characteristics, Harvey presents four types of scientific approaches (which he calls "systems"):

System I: high absolutism and closeness of beliefs; high evaluativeness; high positive dependence on representativeness of institutional authority; high identification with social roles and status position; high conventionality; high ethnocentrism.

System II: deep feelings of uncertainty, distrust of authority, rejection of the more socially approved guidelines to action accompanied by lack of alternative referents; psychological vacuum; rebellion against social prescriptions; avoidance of dependency on God and tradition.

System III: manipulating people through dependency on them; fairly high skills in effecting desired outcomes in his world through the techniques of having others do it for him; autonomous internal standards, especially in social sphere; some positive ties to the prevailing social norms.

System IV: high perceived self-worth despite momentary frustrations and deviations from the norm; highly differentiated and integrated cognitive structure; flexible, creative, and relative in thought and action; internal standards that are independent of external criteria, in some cases coinciding with social definitions and in others not. (Harvey in Maruyama 1991: 12)

It is interesting to note that Maruyama's types H, I, and G are quite similar to Harvey's types I, II, and IV.

The investigation of various types of scholars indicates that the typology based on personal characteristics is appropriate when applied inside larger social bodies; then, personal differences decide, within broader frameworks, why these or other types of scholars are inclined to behave in this or another way. When scholars are studied in a more general way, the cognitive structures (like those specified by Galtung, Maruyama, or Merton) seem to be especially worthwhile as grounds for an adequate classification. Nonetheless, the typology based first on sociological and later on psychological features appears to be the most comprehensive.

Clearly, the scholarly model not only must take into consideration the chief characteristics of a general human ethos and of human individuality but also should include broader cognitive structures. The scholar's individual potential to create something is of a different epistemological character: it is not based on the normative imperative or on cognitive perspectives; it is shaped by the given features of creative capability. Thus, from a gnoseological point of view, a scholar is a peculiar mixture: a normative-cognitive and factual aggregate.

Definitions of Connected Concepts

It remains in this chapter to place the notion of scholars in its proper context. Although, with three basic notions involved (intellectual, intelligentsia, and scholar), the matter does not appear to be too complicated, those addressing it have managed to distort it to a considerable degree. To do this, there must be some discussion of general and confusing terms, such as "intellectual,"[4] "intelligentsia," and "scholar." In recent discussions of intellectuals and scholars, for example, few remember that the intelligentsia as a phenomenon was specific only to Poland and Russia.[5] A clarification of these terms is, therefore, needed.

Indeed, some writers understand intellectuals as something distinct from the intelligentsia.[6] Others comprehend intellectuals as a new class. It was Karl Mannheim who first triggered sociological discussion of this matter. Mannheim described intellectuals as "a relatively classless stratum which is not too firmly situated in the social order." He reminds us that the term "socially unattached intelligentsia" (which later was attributed to Mannheim) was coined by Alfred Weber (1920). Historically speaking, according to Mannheim, the intelligentsia has had two courses of action. First, united as it was only by a single constant — education — this group could engage in providing a diagnostic synthesis of the existing sociopolitical situation. Second, members of the intelligentsia could engage in "the quest for the fulfilment of their mission as the predesigned advocate of the intellectual interests of the whole" (Mannheim 1936: 158). Later, scholars accentuated the intellectual content of this "socially unattached group" and analyzed mainly intellectuals,[7] while others accentuated the "mission in the interests of the whole" and primarily analyzed the intelligentsia in a strict sense. After Isaiah Berlin and Aleksander Gella, however, it should be clear that the concept of intelligentsia should belong in the second category — those who are dedicated to the "mission in the interests of the whole."

In an effort to synthesize various understandings of intellectuals, Eva Etzioni-Halevy (1985: 9) offered this definition: "Following Lipset and Dobson (1972: 137) and Brym (1980: 12), intellectuals are here defined as persons who are professionally engaged in the creation, elaboration and dissemination of theoretical knowledge, ideas and symbols. This would include the overlapping categories of members of university faculties (i.e., academics), scientists, social scientists, journalists and writers. People who only, or chiefly, disseminate theoretical knowledge and ideas (such as schoolteachers) are not included."

In an earlier, influential book, *The Future of Intellectuals and the Rise of the New Class*, Alvin Gouldner (1979) distinguishes the following as the most essential features of this "new class": it is a benign group of technocrats; it is a master class (because it uses education rather than exploitation); it is composed of professionals who work for the old (monied) class; it may be viewed as subservient to the old monied class; and it is a new, flawed, universal class whose power is constantly growing. One may doubt whether Gouldner's perception of intellectuals is accurate. The experience of communism, its later demise, and the precursory faith invested in it by many top Western intellectuals, as well as their subsequent disenchantment, seriously shattered the belief in intellectuals. Raymond Aron understands the intelligentsia in his own (apparently incorrect) way:

One might perhaps conveniently borrow a definition from the late Louis Bromfield, one of the most intellectual of anti-intellectuals. A person of spurious intellectual pretensions, often a professor or the protege of a professor. Fundamentally superficial. Over-emotional and feminine in reactions to any problem. Supercilious and surfeited with conceit and contempt for the experience of more sound and able men. Essentially confused in thought and immersed in a mixture of sentimentality and violent evangelism. A doctrinaire supported of Middle-European socialism as opposed to Greco-French-American ideas of democracy and liberalism. Subject to the old-fashioned philosophical morality of Nietzsche which frequently leads him into jail or disgrace. A self-conscious prig, so given to examining all sides of a question that it becomes thoroughly added while remaining always in the same spot. An anaemic bleeding heart. (Aron 1957: 230)

Before the fall of communism in 1989, the concept of intellectual was associated by some with the political left wing. Robert Brym summarizes this point of view in the following way: "I was able to claim — reasonably I think — that intellectuals are more likely to align themselves with the left, the more left-wing (1) the class or group from which they originate, (2) the class or group which effectively controls the educational institutions through which they pass and (3) the class or group to which they become occupationally and politically tied during early adulthood" (Brym 1980: 73).

After the collapse of communism, the left wing no longer associated itself as strongly with the left. One might have expected, after this historic event, that at least some of those who participated in building international communism would regard it as their *first* duty to explain the unique processes involved in systematic and cumulative oppression under the Communist version of the totalitarian system and their own role in this system.[8] However, nothing like that happened.

After the unique historic experience of the demise of the Soviet bloc, Communist intellectuals (not so much the Western ones, who had no first-hand experience of Communist totalitarianism), emerged as a band of sickly victims rather than as benign individuals, victims deprived of a sense of responsibility. They seem not to understand that they have an obligation to undo the evils that they accomplished. At best, they think that they have a responsibility to denounce the system they once helped to create. Moreover, with their denunciations, they reap remarkable gains, as firsthand experts, in the very countries that were previously engaged in a cold war with those now being denounced.[9]

It is clear that the subject of intellectuals is highly politicized. This does not help to clarify their position in society, what society expects of them, or their own visions and value preferences. Noam Chomsky once highlighted the loaded political understanding of the role of intellectuals thus: "those who are concerned about unemployment for intellectuals need not worry too much, I believe. Under circumstances such as these [American counterrevolutionary intervention in the Third World], there should be considerable need and ample opportunity for the secular priesthood" (Chomsky 1978: 37). Ahmad Sadri looks at the problem from a different, but also from a normative, point of view. According to him, "Weber reminded his audience once more of the irrationality of the world and the tragedy of having to act in it as though it were otherwise." Sadri concludes that "acting courageously in a polytheistic world calls for the ethics of a hero" (Sadri 1992: 103).

The introduction of a normative dimension could lead to various consequences. What is valid in connection with a sociologist also could be significant for any nonintellectual. Aleksander Matejko and Guy Germain point to the potential consequences of the activities of the intellectual in the following way:

The critical role of sociology is socially beneficial as long as sociologists are themselves aware of the limits of their competence and the weakness of their generalizations. Unfortunately, the need for grants and fame (not necessarily in that order) pushes sociologists to promise more than they are actually able to deliver. In addition, sociology remains more oriented to the distribution of goods and services than to the growth of them. It is quite irresponsible from the position of citizen to stimulate exaggerated mass expectations without oneself contributing enough to growth, enabling societies to improve their general standards. (Matejko and Germain 1993: 93–94)

The problem of intellectuals versus values is an important one, especially the question to what extent intellectuals behave as agents of their own class or society. Structuralist, postmodernist, feminist, and poststructuralist discourses introduce several interesting metaperspectives, but, unfortunately, they bring nothing tangible to the problem.[10]

In conclusion, it might tentatively be proposed that all scholars should be considered as intellectuals, whereas not all intellectuals are scholars (some are executives, diplomats, artists, politicians, and so on), and that the intelligentsia constitutes an entirely different social stratum that may (or may not) overlap with intellectuals or scholars.

2

Scholarly Creativity

The features of scholarly creativity[1] are even more complicated and unpredictable than an axiological analysis of the "ideal model" of scholars. The phenomenon of creativity is difficult to comprehend, and its causes are highly indeterminate. Artistic creativity is difficult to determine because of its multifacetedness, but the scientific determinants of creativity are also difficult to grasp. Therefore, it is necessary to look in some detail at the psychological, social, and cultural factors and interactions that stimulate or hamper creative forces as they function in the scientific arena.

There are multiple understandings of creativity[2] and many more or less penetrating works on this subject. The *Index of Scientific Writings on Creativity* (Rothenberg and Greenberg 1974) lists 9,968 titles of articles and books dealing exclusively with this matter. Yet, the tale of an unknown Chinese philosopher may reveal more about creativity than some of these volumes:

"Si-tien, do you regard Lin Jiu, the author of a fascinating book which immediately brought him universal fame, as a creative scholar?" asked the student Sie. "It isn't bad to be a beginner," replied Si-tien. After a few years, the student Sie approached Si-tien again, "Master, do you regard Lin Jiu, who just produced a book opening fascinating panoramas of ideas, as a creative scholar?" "It isn't bad to be a beginner," answered Si-tien. The student Sie asked his master, after several more years, "Teacher, do you regard the scholar Lin Jiu, who recently wrote an illuminating book which will survive, undoubtedly, through many centuries, as a creative person?" Si-tien replied, "It isn't bad to be a beginner." The student Sie inquired again, "So, Master, when can we regard a person as creative?" Si-tien replied, "When he is happily oppressed by an inner force." (Podgórecki 1993)

In a little-known thesis, Lewis Feuer summarizes his ideas concerning creativity in the following way:

I shall try to show that the scientific intellectual was born from the hedonist-libertarian spirit which, spreading through Europe in the sixteenth and seventeenth centuries, directly nurtured the liberation of human curiosity. Not scepticism, but satisfaction; not guilt, but joy in the human status; not self-abnegation, but self-affirmation; not original sin, but original merit and worth; not gloom but merriment; not contempt for one's body and one's senses, but delight in one's physical being; not the exaltation of pain, but the hymn of pleasure — this was the emotional basis of the scientific movement of the seventeenth century. (Feuer 1963: 7)

Although Feuer and Si-tien, the Chinese philosopher, seem to be correct in their observation that creativity is strongly associated with an element of joy, if not ecstasy, they appear to mistake the result for its cause. Indeed, discoveries, creations, and inventions may be associated with exhilarating bliss. Yet, this bliss is likely the result of an accumulated élan vital that suddenly erupts after a prolonged and sometimes painful process of search and examination.

Without any doubt, creativity seems to be the most elusive of all human phenomena. Some thinkers connect creativity with harmony, some with anxiety, some with some elements of madness, and some with exceptionally strong motivation.[3] Yet, all these approaches can be criticized. The achievement of harmony can result in a dull environment that dampens all attempts to produce something original; anxiety may freeze creativity as dormant ideas strive to erupt; madness may produce things that are comprehensible only to a lunatic; and even the strongest motivation may not suffice to solve the puzzle of the *perpetuum mobile*. Hence, it might be prudent to offer a panorama of the various understandings of creativity put forth by the current specialists on the subject and later confront them with the basic ideas in this study.

DIFFERENT FORMS OF CREATIVITY

Specialists in creativity assume the existence of different types of creativity. Although creativity seems to be the result of a specific type of sociocultural activity, it currently is perceived mainly as the individual potential. Consequently, psychological insights are brought to bear on the problem, and social psychology or sociology enters the debate only when psychological potentialities appear to be failing. Generally speaking, it can be observed that prerequisites of individual creativity constitute a *necessarius condicione* (necessary condition), whereas the prerequisites of social psychology or sociology constitute *conditione sine qua non* (sufficient condition) for scientific creativity.

CONDITIONS OF CREATIVITY INDIVIDUALLY GENERATED

Frank Barron (1965), one of the authorities on creativity (although currently regarded by some as outdated), conducted several empirical inquiries in order to analyze individual originality. In a study of military officers, he summarized his findings as follows (the brackets contain the number of cases out of 25 to which the adjectives were applied by impartial judges; high scores are listed first, then low scores):

Wide Interests (12-1)	Logical (9-2)
Clever (9-1)	Rational (9-2)
Imaginative (9-1)	Shrewd (9-2)
Playful (9-1)	Civilized (8-2)
Poised (11-2)	Loyal (8-2)
Resourceful (12-3)	Mature (8-2)
Reflective (9-3)	Versatile (7-0)
Quick (9 3)	Efficient (14-3)
Enterprising (11-4)	Initiative (13-3)
Energetic (10-4)	Organized (10-4)
Determined (10-2)	Fair-minded (13-6)
Talkative (10-2)	

Barron also made an illuminating observation about the ability to "jump" from rational to fantastic modes of thought. As he explained: "The effectively original person may be characterized above all by the ability to regress very far *for the moment* while being able quite rapidly to return to a high degree of rationality, bringing with him the fruits of his regression to primitive and fantastic modes of thought. . . . Perhaps when the cortex is most efficient, or intelligence greatest, the ego realizes that it *can afford to allow* regression — because it can correct itself" (Barron 1968: 218,

223). He expressed this same idea more succinctly: "Thus the creative genius may be at once naive and knowledgable, being at home equally to primitive symbolism and to rigorous logic" (Barron 1968: 224).

Barron's study of writers led him to the conclusion that:

Creative writers are persons whose dedication is to nothing less than a quest for ultimate meanings, or perhaps it is not so much that they are dedicated as they understand themselves as to have been elected and have accepted the office. What is enjoined upon them then is to listen to the voice within and to speak out. What they speak is to be the truth, but it need not be everyone's truth, or even anyone else's. In these essentials, omitting writing as the specific form, I believe writers are no different from creative individuals in all walks of life, including those whose business is to be silent. (Barron 1968: 249)

In 1960, Maria Manturzewska studied all the entrants to the Chopin Competition, a prestigious international piano competition held in Warsaw every four years. Her study led her to the following conclusions: "Among external conditions the most important role is played by the family's musical traditions, socio-economic status of the family, and parental attitudes toward musical studies and the career of the competitor. . . . Technology in individual education also plays a substantial role. . . . Time devoted to exercise seems to be crucial. . . . 4–5 hours per day is the norm for a modern, outstanding pianist" (Manturzewska 1969: 124).

Gudmund Smith and Ingegerd Carlsson concluded their own astute study of creativity as follows:

To the general reader and to the artist or art historian, the most impressive outcome of this study might be the affirmation that real creativity is dependent on a fair level of harmony — by no means complete but sufficient for control and efficacy. Moreover, creativity does not seem to function without a certain measure of anxiety which the artist must tolerate so as not to dodge crucial steps in the artistic process. Severe mental burdens can inhibit creativity — there is no reason to uphold the old romantic notion of extremely fruitful creation on the verge of despair or madness. On the other hand, a lack of conflict-laden or deep experiences may result in tame arts products, even if they are "genuine." (Smith and Carlsson 1990: 209–10)

Seidler, in his study on the crisis of creativity, attached great importance to the hidden work of the unconscious.[4] He held the view that "creativity is the inner life of man himself, a life within a life. This life manifests itself in a type of 'adaptation' which goes beyond the more

immediate and day-to-day concerns of man to a new, original, and stimulating fulfillment of his future" (Seidler 1995: 170).

The problem of evaluating the final goals of creativity tends to get lost
behind the various attempts to define the phenomenon. So, what is, or
what should be, the final aim of individual discovery, and why should it be
pursued at all? The answer seems to be that it should contribute to the
general process of discovering truth and raise possibilities for using this
truth to implement the ideas of global ethics.[5]

At the conclusion of their attempt to synthesize problems related to
individual creativity, Tardif and Sternberg indicate that "It is generally
acknowledged that people are creative within a particular domain of
endeavour, even though people who are creative in different domains may
share common traits." The authors also note that commonly associated
with creativity are

General features like, relatively high intelligence, originality, articulateness,
verbal fluency and good imagination, cognitive abilities like, theoretical thinking,
flexibility and skill in making decisions, independence of judgement, ability to
cope well with novelty, skills of logical thinking, ability to visualize internally,
ability to escape perceptual sets and entrenchment in particular ways of thinking,
and finding order in chaos, ability to recognize "good" problems in their fields,
tolerance for the ambiguity, capability to have impact on others in their immediate surroundings. (Sternberg 1988: 433)

In their synthesis, Tardif and Sternberg summarize the findings of the
other contributors to their study. They list the following features as links
to creativity:

being a firstborn,

having survived the loss of one or both parents early in life, experiencing unusual
     situations;

being reared in a diversified, enriching, and stimulating home environment;

being exposed to a wide range of ideas,

being happier with books than with people and liking school and doing well there,

developing and maintaining excellent work habits,

having many hobbies,

being a compulsive reader,

being able to form distinct and closely knit peer groups, but yet being able to
     survive in marginality. (Sternberg 1988: 433–37)

THE SOCIAL CONDITIONS OF CREATIVITY

Rothenberg recapitulates his lengthy studies on creativity in a short and provocative statement: "All my writers and scientists had one parent, who, altogether a business executive or a homemaker or brother, told stories, wrote poetry or diaries, or else was interested in tinkering with puzzles or problems and pursuing scientific activities. The creative person, in other words, strives to fulfill a parent's *implicit, unrealized* yearnings" (Rothenberg 1990: 13).

This statement is interesting not merely because of its content, but because of the emphasis on background and environment. Otherwise put, each creative person strives to fulfill the expectations of their significant others. Although individual (psychological) features seem to be necessary for arriving at new discoveries, the internal dynamics of the creative milieu should be regarded as an even more decisive element. In fact, it could be claimed that each discovery is preceded by the work of several supporting people who remain in the background as substantial contributors.[6] Traditionally, discovery has been regarded not only as the sometimes protracted work of an individual mind but also as the result of a collaborative interaction of the relevant creative "subculture." This subculture, in order to fulfil its task, has to be able, first, to discern when a problem is ripe for fresh scrutiny and new, imaginative solutions; then, to work collectively toward a solution; next, to develop a creative environment conducive to finding a suitable solution and capable of generating such a solution; and finally, to synthesize the various attempts into a coherent whole.

With the current drive to professionalize the sciences, humanities, and social sciences, the situation becomes much more complicated. There are several reasons for this. Sensing a scholarly problem is not an easy task. The majority of scholars are socialized to adopt preexisting ideas; consequently, only those who are not conformists, who are marginals or deviants, try to deal with new problems. The recognition of the validity and nature of the problem can take various forms. Empathy, for example, may be required to recognize that certain issues are ready for new explanation. Thus, at the end of the nineteenth century, Sigmund Freud gained recognition because he was able to sense that the upper class of the bourgeoisie had reached a point of saturation with material goods and that it was ready for new avenues of gratification, and sex was the undiscovered gratification at hand.

Usually, an exciting movement, religious inspiration, sect, or innovative institution is needed to develop a collective search for an imaginative solution. Although universities present an ideal framework for such attempts, they are, as a rule, governed by the current breed of conformists. Consequently, to conquer territories that officially belong to universities, one needs to get around the coterie of ruling conformists. Leaders with new ideas or charismatic inventors have to start their projects with a new type of scientific discourse (or establish a new paradigm). Currently, great scientific minds tend not to surface in the United States or in Europe;[7] instead, they are drowned out by a variety of peculiar sociocultural movements and pseudoscientific mass movements generated by the groupies of Marxism, feminism, neo-Marxism, structuralism, poststructuralism, deconstructionism, and other prevailing intellectual winds (in fact, they are personifications of artificial great scientists). In this atmosphere, genuine impulses toward scientific creativity virtually do not exist.

To create a scientific school, the following elements appear to be necessary: a continuous seminar, a climate of challenge and cooperation, and an atmosphere of horizontally balanced connections. Presently, where atomistic, professional, and competitive scientific milieux are predominant, the chances of building a scientific school of this type, especially in the "soft" sciences, are minimal.

Additionally, an attempt to motivate diverse sets of scholars who are heterogeneous in their orientations and not united by a common goal (they are guided, instead, by the exigencies of individual career paths) infringes on the functioning of a scholarly leader, a creator of a new scientific school. Because the ideas of a continuous seminar and a scientific school have evaporated, the rules of building such a school are not known, and the possibility of establishing the necessary rules is minimal. Hence, attempts to organize a creative scholarly center even informally are practically nonexistent.

If this diagnosis is correct, then the possibility that a synthesis of work from dispersed researchers and teachers can be prepared also is nil, because the common links between various researchers have not been established (except those that endure for technical reasons), and the possibility that their research findings will be treated as the independent sets of primary data necessary for such a synthesis does not exist.

LARGE AND SMALL DISCOVERIES

These conditions cumulatively minimize the chances of making any significant discoveries and increase the probability that small findings will emerge. This tends to be overlooked because the public focus is on "large" discoveries, while the "small" ones are disregarded. However, small discoveries may include new paradigms (such as establishing basic patterns in the structure and understanding of reality and in the perception and interpretation of its structure through, for example, idealism, realism, or pragmatism), new theories (for example, the creation of novel and general hypotheses explaining the body of existing middle-range hypotheses from a more universal perspective), and new "factual" inventions (for example, factual inventions that are pregnant with subsidiary discoveries that emerge from lower orders of generality).

Nonetheless, the sum of small discoveries constitutes the main body of science. The majority of large discoveries in the sciences (in mathematics, chemistry, biology, and physics) are made by young men or women, whereas the bulk of those who make small discoveries are older men or women. In fact, older people in "soft" sciences (like politics) use experience, routine, and knowledge to organize their teamwork, which serves as the basis for their creativity. This approach is especially useful for the following kinds of small discoveries:

discoveries of fact (for example, a statement that the nineteenth- and twentieth-century Polish population is characterized by punitive tendencies);

new interpretations (for example, an observation that the predominant task of highly developed countries in the twentieth century consists not so much in the production of goods as in the generation and distribution of services);

new explanations (for example, that the bulk of human behavior is regulated not by the inclination to gain more but by a disposition to conform to the strictures imposed by law, especially intuitive and living law);

exemplifications of a new type (for example, that humans descended not from one particular branch of apes but from several branches);

discoveries connected with "situational" validity (for example, the geographical discoveries of the eighteenth and nineteenth centuries, which indicated that human life styles comprised a multiplicity of ethics governing human behaviors, or the fact that, in Canada, the decline in traffic deaths in the 1970s and 1980s can be attributed to the use of seat belts and air bags);

new links between facts, explanations, interpretations, or theories (for example, the employment of a new type of microelectronic chip allows for much faster and more precise interpersonal communication);

new classifications of social phenomena (currently, crimes in Africa reflect religious and tribal allegiances);

newly extended chains of logical or factual consequences (for example, the supposition that the incest taboo is not so much generated by biological or physiological factors as imposed by the tendency to strengthen the socializing power of parents);

new scientific perspectives (for example, various efforts to find the cause of
cancer and its cure); and

scientific forecasts (for example, the supposition that Catholic doctrine supporting population growth unintentionally helps to share sociopolitical
infrastructure that is prone to new conflicts on a global scale).

It must be taken into consideration that the main bulk of innovative
scholarly work consists of small discoveries and that these largely remain
anonymous. It is easy to attribute them to somebody else. This situation
triggers a tendency to intellectual theft on a large scale: to attribute a small
discovery to another person is not too complicated a task in a general
atmosphere of anonymity.[8] The newly emerging paradigms (instrumentality, slyness, "alliances of mediocrity"), schools of thought ("schools" like
Marxism,[9] post-Marxism,[10] poststructuralism,[11] and postmodernism
[with the exception of a partially justified criticism of the narrow-minded-
ness of neopositivism]) drastically change traditional attitudes toward
knowledge. Because the new professional scholars bear the basic burden
of scientific activity, they appear to be, and in consequence are, the main
producers of the existing body of scientific knowledge. One may hypoth-
esize that taking into consideration their "low" professional ethic (instrumentalism or slyness), their relative anonymity, their newly generated
paradigms of mediocre alliances, and their desperate need to survive
inside the academic market, they are responsible for many unidentified
scientific frauds. Thus, the rapidly developing professionalism of sciences,
humanities, and social sciences leads, contrary to existing professional
ideology and expectations, directly to its own opposite: the creation of a
formalized subculture of scientific swindling.

CONCLUSION

It must be stressed that the problems connected with scholarly creativity pertain to all human activities that try to construct something new.
What is specific to scholarly activities, and what distinguishes them from
artistic creativity? Scholarly activities are oriented not toward beauty or
goodness but toward truth. In the case of beauty, subjective tastes are
employed to decide whether a particular product is art; a given
phenomenon is deemed "good" if it fits into the accepted value system.

The situation is different in the case of scholarly creativity. In some
areas, mainly in the sciences, objective measures are available. In the
humanities and social sciences, the situation is much more complicated,
and it is possible to mistake false truth for truth. This possibility makes it

difficult to perceive and differentiate between the creative scholar and his
or her derivatives. Hence, devising a typology, usually a dull and unin-
spiring method of analysis, may be useful. A typology of scholars helps to
separate those who are genuinely creative from those who are not.

The creative scholar should, thus, be the target of a complex investigation if one intends to investigate the specificity of academia adequately.
How the modern creative scholar relates to other categories of scholars
has to be scrupulously elucidated.

Currently, the professional (career) scholar in the sciences, especially
in the humanities and social sciences, concentrates on small discoveries,
treating them not as constructive elements in a more comprehensive
picture of natural or human reality but as steps up a personal career ladder.
Thus, he or she does not regard these discoveries as autotelic, as having a
value in themselves, but as heterotelic, having an outside value.

Additionally, functioning inside the vast ocean of learned professionals, an isolated scholar feels lost. He or she perceives academia, his or her
natural habitat, as a heterogeneous territory where everyone is prepared to
fight with everyone else. The scholar's level of insecurity is high; support
for those who are learning is designed mainly as a defensive strategy for
him- or herself, not as sustenance for them; he or she mistrusts, a priori, all
scholarly approaches made in his or her direction.

For this scholar, homogeneous *alliances of mediocrity*, although
composed almost exclusively of "obscurities," have obvious advantages.
Their constituents serve as mutual supports: they boldly attack those
whom they consider to be outsiders; they pretend to supply their adherents
with an artificial paradigm purporting to explain all the complexities of
the human condition; they construct a jargon and call it a "new epistemology"; they are quick to find academic openings on all continents and grab
them; they are of a homogeneous type.[12]

Roughly speaking, academia currently consists of four groups of scholars: a relatively small group of innovative scholars; a larger but bold arriviste body of mediocre scholars; a large heterogeneous assembly of
professionals; and a decomposing and defensive corps of traditional
scholars.

These considerations lead to the conclusion that the creative scholar —
now gradually disappearing — is the most precious of the academic
assembly. Therefore, to analyze academia as a whole, one must study
mainly the creative (innovative) scholar. Paradoxically, scholarly creativity is a unique form of human endeavor in that it despises equality;[13]
moreover, it depends not only on unprecedented originality of thought
and output in certain areas of reality but also, unlike the arts or various

interhuman activities, on explaining why its point of view constitutes the most adequate understanding of the data pertaining to whatever aspect of reality with which it is concerned. Innovative scholars should, thus, be selected as the target of exhaustive investigation.

It seems clear that, at the present moment, the central, mainly psychological, problem of scholarly creativity cannot be resolved exclusively by means of existing methods. A cruder sociological approach might be more appropriate; paradoxically, the forthcoming analysis of scholarly social settings might help to clarify the problem. At least in the area of musical creativity, psychologists seem to be aware of the need for such an approach. As one leading psychologist says:

In the light of our analyses of biographical material, one of the fundamental conditions for the development of artistic activity and for the development of the creativity of musical talent in all stages of life seems to be the "musical dialogue" with someone who believes in the talented individual's potential, who understands his or her musical ideas and accepts them, who supports the musician emotionally in his/her endeavours and helps to overcome the stress of life. Absence of such person at any stage of the artist's life appears disadvantageous to his/her functioning and further development. (Manturzewska 1995: 334)

3

A Typology of Scholars

THE PROBLEM

In recent decades, the panorama of those who represent "academia" drastically departed from the model of a wise man deeply sunk in thought, absentminded, disinterested in his own personal affairs, immersed in books — an erudite man. Presently, there exists a large kaleidoscope of women and men who deal, more or less ingeniously, and more or less professionally, with scientific matters.[1,2]

There are numerous contributory studies dealing with the psychological and social determinants of scientists,[3] but instead of focusing on what others have already done, I will attempt to approach the matter from a new perspective. The following is a new tableau of scholars based on my own encounters with men and women of science from many different cultures, disciplines, and countries.[4]

CLASSIFICATION

During a field study in March and April 1994 at Stanford University and the University of California at Berkeley, an extended typology of scholars was developed by the author:

scholar innovators (innovators of new paradigms, generators of new ideas or new theories or patterns of applicability);

indirect innovators (innovators through the accumulation of many addable elements);

scholar innovators who plant new ideas (maieutic "mentors");

scholar innovators motivated by the idea of moral or social justice;

professional scholars (repetitors, interpreter-commentators, fans, analysts, the erudite, classifiers, devoted teachers, the metawise or escapists, disseminators) or career scholars;

institutional builders, and ideas systematizers;

gatekeepers (peer evaluators, evaluators of publications, administrators [board members, deans, presidents]);

collective scholars (task oriented, "Troyan cohorts" [scholars who are commissioned to destroy certain ideas]);

instrumental scholars (implementors of dogmas, self-promoting [shrewd, clever, bordering on crooked dealings — networkers]);

spectacular scholars;

sensationalists and "neutralizers";

operators;

deviants: (disenchanted, vicious shockers, walking "cadavers" [not only physiologically old — "age is, of course, a fever chill that every physicist must fear. He's better dead than living still when once he's past his thirtieth year" said Nobel Prize winner P.A.M. Dirac (Zuckerman 1977: 164), but also old in spirit], prestidigitators-acrobats [scholastic or talmudic duelists]).

From this typology were distilled the following categories of scholars:

innovators (or "creators") (discoverers of truth, creators of illuminating explanations, masters in the construction of new understandings of social reality), including creators of new paradigms;

potential innovators;

collective innovators;

builders;

professional scholars (repetitors, interpreter-commentators, fans, analysts, the erudite, collectors, classifiers);

disenchanted scholars;

instrumental (sly) scholars;

spectacular scholars (those who inadvertently become prominent);

gatekeepers;

operators.

This classification is built, of course, on the overlapping of various roles. For example, an instrumental scholar, when oriented toward his or her own gain, also could be understood as an operator (he or she is also, as a rule, a professional scholar). There are also different motives for pursuing "scientific work"; it might be undertaken in order to seek truth or to gain recognition. The social functions of certain scientific roles could have entirely different effects: "gatekeepers," for example, might try to preserve the "purity" of the sciences, or they might use their gatekeeping function against other scholars, particularly their own competitors, in order to hamper the others' careers.

INNOVATORS

"Ideas occur to us when they please, not when it pleases us" (Max Weber, 1946)

One of the best descriptions of the concept of innovator comes from La Piere. It is summarized by William M. Cross in the following way: "Innovation may occur in the realm of ideas, organizations or technology. There is natural resistance to innovation because new ideas and combinations of material usually threaten powerful elements of the *status quo*. The innovator tends to be asocial, sensitive, courageous, unimpressed by authority and wealth, and hypermotivated. The social context of innovation tends to be one of considerable permissiveness, e.g. social disorganization or urbanization" (Cross 1985: 1).

The category of innovators is elusive. However, "quite contrary to the twin stereotypes that scientists, especially the better ones, are loners and that important scientific contributions are the products of individual imagination, . . . the majority of investigations honoured by Nobel awards have involved collaboration" (Zuckerman 1977: 176). It is very difficult to isolate a single feature that can be said to characterize all creative scholars.[5] He or she who currently is regarded by peers as a charlatan, a possessed man or woman, someone with an unbalanced personality, may appear tomorrow as someone gifted with the necessary insight to see matters in unorthodox and creative ways.

Many innovators are uncooperative. Because they are endowed with an ability to see matters at a "deeper" level than others, they are task oriented and not adjusted to the requirements of public relations etiquette. Innovators create many unnecessary tensions with those who are "slower," more methodical, or less visionary and scrupulous. Innovators rarely respond to others' demands for further explication or clarification.

They are internally motivated to push forward and to trace the consequences of their discovery. Innovators are not, as a rule, more intelligent:
they simply seem to be more stubborn. By repeatedly coming back to the
same problem, they analyze it from all possible angles, trying to specify
all imaginable ramifications and consequences of the idea. Sometimes
they may appear narrow-minded, and in certain respects, they are. Their
work usually gains recognition after they have lost interest in their discovery or when they are gone from the scene. The truism "you recognize
them by the fruits of their labors" certainly applies to innovators.

Innovators in the sciences tend to differ from those in the humanities.
In the sciences, they are antiauthoritarian, open-minded, easygoing, without accumulated insecurities, and, to some extent, humorous. Paradoxically,
in the humanities, they are authoritarian, insecure, closed-minded, humorless, and ill at ease in social relations. Stiffness does not help in the
sciences, where it is relatively easy to prove whether one is correct or not.
In the humanities, however, where proof depends so much on an individual's persuasiveness, some authoritarian traits may be helpful.

Because innovators are so preoccupied with their pursuits, they are
easy to rob; they are not suspicious and attach little importance to whatever use is made of their ideas and by whom. Hence, they often remain
unrecognized while others enjoy the benefits of their ingenuity. Some
become embittered when they find that others have appropriated their
discoveries. There is within the general type of creative scholar a quite
peculiar subcategory, the sage-scholar. These are scholars who have
already proven their ability to discover a new idea and present it in a
manner that satisfies all methodological requirements. Original in their
own areas and able to take one or more important steps toward the illumi-
nation of existing reality (natural or social), they also are masters in the
methodological subtleties involved in their specialties. Yet, while satisfy-
ing all necessary methodological standards, they also are able to recognize
the advantages and shortcomings of the epistemology they use. Therefore,
sage-scholars are able to reach a higher cognitive point of view that allows
them to see their specialty from a panoramic metapoint. They are sages
not only in the sense that they can see the advantages of their own scholarly outlook but also because they are aware of its limitations. The difference between a sage-scholar and a scholar is that the sage can both
conduct research in a manner appropriate to an academic specialist in a
given area and evaluate the gnoseological value of this type of scientific
conduct. An additional difference is that sages not only seek a synthesis in
a certain area but also treat their findings, and the findings of others, as
necessary elements in a larger theoretical perspective. Daniel Bell, Robert

K. Merton, and Neil Smelser are examples of sage-scholars in the social sciences.

Generally speaking, innovators can be divided into three basic categories: pure theoreticians, pure technicians, and sages equipped with technical knowledge.

The ranks of pure technicians are growing rapidly, while those of sage-technicians are rapidly diminishing. The fragmentation of the social sciences and the accumulation of empirical studies within each branch create such a mass of information that it becomes practically impossible to oversee one's own field of study.[6] Fields of competence are shrinking, and competence is shrinking accordingly. It now is easier to become qualified in a small area of scholarship than to produce synthetic knowledge in a field. Communication among different fields and subfields of study has become increasingly arduous. This situation leads to the creation of artificial "monopolies" on areas of study, which, in turn, makes the situation at the metalevel more demanding.

Sage technicians are losing ground in their own areas of competence. They face an increasing number of aggressive "epistemologists";[7] they also have the task of shaping various data into a coherent entity (or theory) and the responsibility of comparing these entities with those in other fields within the social sciences. In the end, they simply do not have the time or the habits to come up with general synthetic overviews, nor are they expected to.

As a result, inside this enormous heterogeneous domain called "the social sciences," the tendency to understand social reality as a whole gives way to a phenomenon in which various "fiefdoms," with or without gnostic goals, are built to establish professional empires of existence. In effect, wisdom and its tendency to understand and generalize is being replaced by a cognitively neutral professionalism.

The charismatic scholar is another subcategory of innovative scholars. A charismatic scholar not only develops an idea but also spreads it. An idea lives inside such scholars and is transmitted to others. Charismatic scholars do not respect the individuals with whom they are confronted but cherish the thoughts they proclaim. They regard themselves as messengers of ideas, and ideas may be given more or less potency depending on the scholar's performance.

Charismatic scholars can be dangerous in that they may attach special importance to an idea that is worthless and manage, nonetheless, to capture the minds (if not the souls) of their students, transforming them into vessels (or personal vassals) through whom the particular idea can be spread. The charismatic scholar often inspires; one almost always finds a charismatic scholar attached like a figurehead to a "scientific school." One might say that German philosophy and the social sciences have been built by charismatic scholars thus defined.

POTENTIAL INNOVATORS

Potential innovators are of crucial importance to any social system. They are the ones who deal with the problems that plague these systems. Because they exist predominantly as dormant creators, actual creators are difficult to trace. The difficulty increases when the category of innovator-imposter comes into the picture. Innovators are human beings, capricious and difficult to deal with, and certain shrewd individuals, playing on these ambiguities, are able to sneak into the creators' category.

Most outstanding innovators have been exposed to unusual and often difficult human experiences. For example, World War II gave rise to an enormous amount of literature, poetry, technical innovation, and music; yet, the war was a deeply shattering experience. No one would reasonably suggest that human beings should be subjected to such man-made pain in order to "produce" innovators. Nevertheless, it is under such circumstances that many new technical and existential ideas have been born.

Thus, as a general rule, it can be suggested that any type of holistic revolution may enhance the possibility of changing a given type of personality into a creative one. An artistic revolution evidently transgresses the cognitive boundaries of the conventional world. It acquaints one with a new type of experience and shows that the status quo is not always appropriate. Similarly, industrial revolutions open the door to new possibilities. All milieux that generate refined subcultures should be regarded as potential "schools" for innovators. Furthermore, if a social system needs more innovators, it should sow its educational establishment with artistic seeds.

COLLECTIVE INNOVATORS

Innovators need a frame of reference suitable for comparison. They cannot appear from nowhere. For their development, they need fresh and vigorous stimuli. In this regard, there exists the phenomenon of "collective innovators." These are scholars whose ideas are compatible in some areas but who differ from one another in methods of construction and in basic assumptions, scholars who, aware of the complexity of modern knowledge, accept a cumulative approach to scientific matters. Many scholars are aware that, through mutual cooperation and competition, something new is added to their own individual ingenuities. In an atmosphere of reciprocal stimulation and continuous methodological-theoretical challenges, these scholars may solve problems, step by step, that exceed their own individual potential. Characteristically, they plant the internal dynamics of their own scientific research into the common soil of a creative subculture. Recognizing that innovative geniuses are a rare commodity, research laboratories, investigative teams, and task-solving groups opt for this type of scientific cooperation. The reason for this is obvious: the current complexity of ongoing research, study, and investigation is too vast for one individual to assimilate.

It is interesting to note that in the former Communist countries, this piecemeal approach was encouraged (if not demanded) in order to enhance control over what went on in the ivory towers of academia and to prevent one individual from setting up a fiefdom in a given scientific area, becoming a "star." In order to win the battle with "capitalist-oriented sciences," it was useful to find, select, and employ a group of young scholars who, lured by attractive inducements, could fight with independent-minded scholars of the traditional breed. On the other hand, in capitalist countries, the cautious economic approach dictates that it is not prudent to invest too much in one individual, no matter how impressive he or she may appear; it is much better to support a project.

Thus, one might predict that the dynamics of empirical investigation, the need for gathering data, and the imperative of adequate theoretical generalization will systematically shift the development of sciences toward a collective type of inventiveness in academic work.

BUILDERS

Real scholars should also be regarded as builders.[8] They help to generate the conditions required for creative activities. They do this as engineers who change physical reality or as social engineers who try to influence social reality. Builders are understood here as guardians on whom one can rely. From one point of view, they are altruistic; their lack of egoism is well-tested. From another point of view, they are motivated by an imperative to dominate others.

Builders exist in many walks of life. There are, of course, builders of cathedrals or ships; there are those who want to build shelters for others and those who want to serve God. Physicians are, or should be, builders: they build or rebuild the physiological defense systems of organisms, and they are, or should be, happy when these redesigned defense mechanisms work. Practicing economists are builders as well: they try to design a functional, efficient economic order and are satisfied when this order is not transformed into chaos.

Some scholars are also megabuilders. They are happy to help build a new and just society by reliable, scientific means. Just as they are happy to construct a more efficient computer, so they are satisfied to draw up a plan for a more harmonious society. They are pleased to build an organic entity that functions not only for its own purposes or for the needs of the community but also, and perhaps above all, for the universal community of academics. A good dean protects his or her faculty, takes care of all who work there, has a vision of developing trends, understands the faculty's weak and strong points, and, above all, is able to inspire those who are eaten by self-doubt.

Real builders are scholars who combine an authentic need to serve others with theoretical, technical, and material knowledge. They want to assist others, and they know how to do it. As innovators in the sciences want to add something to the atlas of existing knowledge, so builders in the social sciences strive toward the enlargement of our wisdom by providing others with new or additional avenues of inquiry. Builders are innovators in facilitation.

Scholar-builders can be divided into two important categories: institution builders-facilitators and scientific systematizers.

In the social sciences, systematizers occupy a special position. It is impossible to be a totally new innovator in these sciences. Therefore, a systematizer of empirical data or "middle range" social theories plays a role that originally belonged to the innovators in "hard" sciences. Systematizers may build a new social reality on the basis of accessible social data, especially when it is fashionable to speak both about theory building and about the social construction of reality. The novel manner of speaking is less important here; rather, it is essential to stress the building, construction approach.

PROFESSIONAL SCHOLARS

Most of those currently working in the sciences are professional scholars. They consist of repetitors, interpreters, groupies, analysts, people of erudition, collectors, and classifiers.

Repetitors are the least "ambitious" among scholars. They simply repeat what has already been achieved in a given scientific area. They tend to transmit the data that students are supposed to memorize. There is an inverse proportion between the number of repetitors and the level of development evident in the country's higher education: a greater number of repetitors among scholars is associated with a less-developed higher education system, and a greater number of creators is associated with a more highly developed system of higher education. Nonetheless, one should remember that this type of scholar is, as a rule, highly appreciated by students in some countries (for example, the United States and Canada). They provide students with "hard" information that has to be remembered, and, thus, give them what they need to pass examinations (preferably multiple choice). Because students are there mainly to get good marks and enter the job market as quickly as possible, they are not very interested in the development of deeper theoretical problems; they are motivated by the system to be career oriented.

Interpreters (or commentators) explain the meaning behind the ideas of others. They try to translate complicated ideas into language that is accessible to those who want to absorb it. These scholars usually furnish examples of how this knowledge relates to the current sociopolitical context. Because they undertake to use their own small inventiveness to bring something new to the existing pool of knowledge, they have to be placed on a level higher than repetitors.

There are also interpreters who merely analyze material created by others because they are unable to contribute anything more. These analysts can find the "hidden agenda" behind various scientific assumptions and reveal its treasures to others. Thus, they can be useful in that they occasionally reveal unexpected implications of certain assumptions and obtain a peculiar hermeneutic ability to read a text or suppositions contained in given ideas.

Groupies comprise a more developed category of professionals. Subjectively, they are aware that they do not have creative capacities and that they progress by jumping on someone else's bandwagon. Sometimes they are able to add something to the development of an idea that they perceive as attractive. They also may join somebody else's scientific school because they are convinced that the ideas in question need practical help to be developed further, that they have hit on a "profitable" track, that the ideas are "right" and "just" and overturn a "false cognitive consciousness," or they are under the spell of these ideas. Certain Marxists, feminists, postmodernists, and poststructuralists represent this type of scientific orientation.

Groupies are not always dogmatic; they may try to test the validity of the ideas to which they adhere. This adherence may create an "enlarged scientific school" that can display a larger perspective and richness through newly introduced ideas. Yet, if they steadfastly cling to these ideas for emotional, political, religious, or conformist reasons, they essentially depart from the model of a professional scholar.[9]

Erudite scholars are "living libraries," those who not only can supply the proper reference but can briefly summarize the essential points of the information in question. Usually, they are so burdened with knowledge that they fall very low on the scale of creativity. Nonetheless, in an academic community, they can be quite valuable if they are willing to share their intellectual treasures.

Collectors and classifiers belong to a different class. They accumulate new data (and sometimes theories) and keep them in predesigned categories. They are valuable not only in botany or astronomy but also in economics or literature. Although some are "resourceful" people whose expertise pertains not to debatable explanations but to reliable information, there also are those who are able to locate whatever data are needed to test or disprove certain diagnostic or theoretical conceptions. Sometimes, those who are indeed resourceful are labeled as exclusively resourceful; their originality is, thus, denied, and they are restricted artificially to this subsidiary role.

All these categories of scholars (repetitors, interpreters, groupies, analysts, the erudite, collectors, and classifiers) are linked by their professionalism. They do not regard science as a vocation but as a job, one job among many. Because they work in a specific branch of the social division of labor, they perform their duties according to the standards required there. They do this well. They are expected to put their souls into their work, although most do not.

Generally speaking, professional scholars revolutionized the business of "manufacturing reputations." They discovered that, in the social sciences, in which the criteria of the pecking order are rather loose, the crucial academic value is attached to the enigmatic notion of reputation, and they use whatever tactics and strategies are necessary to enhance their own. They do not care that the best way to gain a good reputation is to produce creative work; they concentrate instead on administrative tricks or measures that will help them to climb the ladder to become presidents, directors, editors, members of boards, vice-presidents, members of the editorial boards, even secretaries. (These positions, indeed, enhance "reputation"; the members of the board of the Research Committee of Sociology of Law, part of the International Sociological Association, currently comprise mainly former public-oriented directors or officials of the international institute earlier established by the Research Committee to promote the development of the sociology of law.)

DISENCHANTED SCHOLARS

In one of the Eastern countries, there lived a poet who said to his Maker, "My God, you gave me talent, but too little." This also is the destiny of the disenchanted scholar. Disenchanted scholars are interested in scientific matters; they have achieved a certain amount in the past; they still are regarded by some as authorities. However, they realize that there is a boundary that they will never be able to cross. After a struggle with the inherent limits of their inventiveness and after some internal battles pertaining to their self-image, such scholars eventually rebel not only against gnoseological restrictions but also, if not mainly, against their total scientific environment.

Disenchanted scholars then attack outside reality and blame it for their own failings. In a totalitarian system, they may attack the system, saying (to their narrow circle of trusted friends only) that communism or fascism is bad as such. They may further assert that, because of the inherent injustices of the system, they were deprived of the proper means to develop their abilities and denied access to the places where they could have displayed their capacities to the fullest.

The more sophisticated disenchanted scholars may claim that human beings are incapable of finding what lies behind external or internal reality, that human beings are intrinsically unable to recognize the true nature of reality or find the genuine sense of being: like intelligent criminals, the disenchanted scholars use "neutralization" techniques and accuse others of imposing false consciousness on them.

INSTRUMENTAL SCHOLARS

It is necessary to stress that "instrumental" means teleological and goal oriented. It does not necessarily mean sinful, although instrumental attitudes slip easily into an ethically negative category. Nonetheless, the opposite category — those who are principled — could also be negative by their very nature. It is the evaluation of the goal that determines the final estimation of the given attitude.

Instrumental scholars are those who are agents of dogma, agents of themselves, or agents of themselves hidden behind an agent of dogma. They do not care about truth — scientific inquiry is only a means to nonscholarly goals. Instrumental scholars will do everything necessary to gain the approval of their patron (professor, dean, sponsoring agency, and so on). They do this by declaring their absolute loyalty. They seek approval in order to further their careers — they strive to obtain both material goods and power. They do not consider themselves (hidden as they are behind a veil of private ethics) to be bound by the established standards of scientific inquiry, which they regard only as pragmatic devices. Although they do not care much for the truth, they are extremely loyal to the political body that rules from above.[10] Thus, the ideal model of instrumental scholar has two subcategories: the dogma-oriented instrumental scholar and the self-oriented instrumental scholar.

Individual instrumental scholars are the product of themselves,[11] but socially developed instrumental scholars are the product of a totalitarian regime. In their early development, when Communist regimes tried to strengthen themselves, they encountered several obstacles. One of the most formidable was the bastion of men and women of science who belonged to the pre-Communist intellectual formation. In their own countries, they held the highest social prestige (this was the case in both Poland and Russia), they were basically incorruptible, and, mainly because of limited expectations, they were financially independent.[12] At the inception of the Communist system, they were needed by regimes that subsequently turned against them and built their own disciplined cadres of scholars.[13]

Regimes of this sort not only contributed to the development of individual instrumental scholars but also built institutions that were supposed to work in tune with instrumental requirements. Because the very existence of these institutions was based on corrupt principles and because social, and especially economic, life pushed people to extremes of inventiveness in an environment of "all against all," these very institutions were the training ground for instrumentality.[14]

One such institution was the Academy of Sciences in Poland. This organizational monster was created to replace an old prestigious institution that resembled a Royal Academy of Sciences. Based on Soviet pattern, the new institution created a coordinated center for instrumentalists from all categories. Here, instrumentalists (especially those in the social sciences) got a head start in cheating. They used the authority of the academy; they designed organizational tools that catapulted upstarts into prominence (some later assumed that they were indeed "geniuses"; others, convinced of their unique scholarly competence, began to rebel against the party that had nurtured them — see silhouette of Kolakowski, page 110–11); they monitored the development of socially strategic sciences (by influencing public opinion); they allocated grants; they rewarded young, ideologically flexible scholars with the funds to attend conferences; they invited "naive" scholars from abroad; they wrote what was expected of them and they published "politically correct" books.[15]

The West has its own version of an instrumental scholar; it will be discussed later. For now, suffice it to say that the Western version is based on the principles of self-promotion[16] and "publish or perish."[17] Sometimes, these principles are wielded with great imagination. For example, in order to increase his chances of getting involved in a particular think tank, one sly scholar went so far as to write a book about a "leading" psychologist of the country in which the think tank was located.[18]

Examples of servile and instrumental versions of the scholarly personality often appear under personal or political pressure, as the following three cases show.

During an international conference in Moscow, a group of East German scholars lauded the creativity and ingenuity of their Soviet colleague-masters. The Germans claimed that the Soviet research team had given them an opportunity to see social reality in an absolutely new and astonishing way, that the Soviet research had a strong theoretical bearing and very important sociopolitical implications. Everything seemed to be correct. The Soviets graciously dropped insignificant comments to the one-sided discussion; they acknowledged that their inquiry had not yet realized its full potential. It so happened that the real author of the project in question, a scholar from another satellite country, was present in the room. The Germans knew who he was — his book had been translated into German — and the Russians knew even better — they had translated the book without the author's consent and distributed it without his knowledge to a closed circle as an "inside" publication, that is, one that did not go through the normal publication process and was unavailable to the general public. When the author protested, he was rebuffed: "Are you not happy that your ideas have gained international recognition, and have become the basis for an international comparative study?"

During an international conference in France, in the middle of an informal theoretical discussion, a relatively young Japanese scholar was invited by an Italian professor to attend a follow-up conference scheduled a few days later. It was an attractive conference hosted in a beautiful Italian city, all expenses paid. The Japanese scholar was flattered and immediately agreed. At that moment a senior Japanese professor joined the group. When the theoretical discussion ended, the organizer repeated his invitation to the young scholar, clarifying certain organizational details. Now, however, the young Japanese scholar (a specialist in his own field) said, "Sorry, but I will not attend this conference." Indeed, he did not come to the meeting.

During the Communist period in Poland, a young scholar told his friend, "I do not respect our boss. I even despise him. Frankly, I regard him as a classical moron. If in my articles I quote him often, or if I write a positive review of his books, I am doing it because he is still influential and I expect him to reciprocate and support my career."

What these cases have in common is that they all describe attitudes of instrumental scholars. Rather than respect the truth, they are servile, albeit for different reasons. Obviously, servility is the opposite of an authentic scholarly stance, which upholds a duty to reveal the truth regardless of the consequences to the scholar who does so. However, servility is not unique to academic culture; it surfaces readily in various areas of sociopolitical life in totalitarian countries.

In the case of the conference in Moscow, it was evident that the attitude of dependency was generated by the obligatory patron-client relationship: East German subordination to the Russians. In the case of the young Japanese professor, the cultural notion of "seniority" was the decisive factor. In traditional Japanese culture, the truth is defined by elders on the strength of their "educated" intuition, cumulative experience, and ability to work by trial and error; access to the truth is reserved for seniors. The younger professor may assume access only if the older one gives him or her permission. The case of a conformist-flatterer appears everywhere. It is not exclusive to totalitarian countries, although it may be seen in such countries more often. Because the position of scholars, because of their incremental "professionalization," increasingly resembles a patron-client relationship, the patterns of servility and dominance are increasingly prevalent. Because I did not conduct research in this area, the examples presented here attempt only to convey the essence of these attitudes. However, it should be remembered that categories of widely repeated behavior disclose distinctive patterns of new types of social reality.

Sometimes the difference between the socialist instrumental scholar and the currently dominant professional Western scholar is subtle. The difference is essentially one of reputation.[19] The socialist scholar is mainly the agent of a dogma formulated by an obligatory ideology that exists "above" him or her. It gives him or her mandatory, general, and profitable guidance. In short, he or she is hired for his or her ideology. The socialist scholar is working for it and is praised for continually and obediently performing his or her job. The more vigorously he or she introduces this ideology into a recalcitrant and usually hostile academic and social life, the more lavish are the rewards bestowed upon him or her by powers that be.

He or she is instrumental in the sense that he or she is regarded simply as a tool, a means. He or she is as an obedient, intelligent, and creative slave to the very ideas he or she has accepted without manifest reservations. The direct and indirect gains he or she makes by working for the founders of the dogma are the primary aim of his or her performance.

In contrast to the dogma-oriented instrumentalist scholar, the self-oriented Western version is not concerned with outside authority; he or she is his or her own agent. This scholar need not work for any doctrine; his or her basic motivation is self-promotion. If he or she develops ideas, it is not to support his or her own ideology, nor is it to come closer to the truth; he or she is developing the ideas simply because he or she understands that the process of generating ideas is his or her professional job. Nonetheless, as he or she understands his or her task, his or her main ability is not to create but to produce ideas ("I was *doing* some thinking"). He or she has additional duties that are more significant from the perspective of his or her career development.

Like the repetitor and interpreter types of professional scholar, the instrumentalist ingeniously repeats the ideas of others. As mentioned earlier, this repetition is not always mechanical. Other ideas are useful when they are supported by empirical data taken from the present sociopolitical context. Sometimes they are borne out by current socioeconomic reality. These borrowed ideas often are served up in a lively, joyful, if not farcical, manner that is enjoyable for students who, in the West, understand university study mainly as a business of memorizing and digesting ideas that others present to them. In some ways, they are right: the more familiar they become with this technique, the higher the marks they receive; the higher the marks they receive, the more rewarding the job they acquire.

Another, more sophisticated skill of the Western scholar is the translation of previously generated scientific ideas into a new language. However, unlike repetitors and interpreters, instrumentalists attribute these ideas to themselves. In doing so, they "kill" history. The craftier among them avoid the ideas of their own teachers[20] (some of whom might still be alive) and reach instead for ideas that belonged to their scholarly "grandparents," their teachers' teachers. Because these people usually are dead, they cannot claim the ideas as their own. The stolen ideas belonging to foregone generations are then given a fashionable gloss. Only a few shrewd specialists can recognize the similarities between the old and "new" (and they pay little attention, because, as everybody knows, everything was said by the old Greeks). Those who are able to detect these similarities may not be courageous enough to disclose them, and they may be right: a scholar is not only a scholar but also a fighter.

Because in the West the rule is "publish or perish," another imperative is to market one's ideas. In the United States, this requirement, formally or substantially, is still binding. A teacher at Rutgers University, "X,"

Was called "outstanding," "exceptionally talented," "one of the best." But the stack of scholarly publications he submitted was described, in the precise grammar one would expect from an English Department tenure committee, as "not so thick as the usual packet for tenure." At the age of 38, X has discovered that even at Rutgers, which promotes the idea of undergraduate-friendly teaching, the only guarantee of lifetime employment at a major research institution is to have a list of scholarly credits somewhat longer than two articles, two theatre reviews, and an unpublished book. (Peterson 1995: 24)

Yet, at the present, when there are a limited number of journals and publishing houses on one side and, on the other, multiplying branches (and subbranches) of various disciplines and an enormous and constantly growing number of competitors, marketing one's ideas is not an easy task. It becomes practically impossible to say something imaginative, original, and outstanding in a way that could be recognized as such in this swelling flood of print. Therefore, it is much better, instead of proclaiming something as new, to present a conventional text in a well-elaborated, nearly perfect form. This appeals to the set tastes of "boards," "readers," "assessors," and publishers, whereas the unconventional tends only to confuse them. This manner of conforming to formal virtues does not infringe on the iron rule of evaluative mediocrity. Weber came close to formulating this rule:

The fact that hazard rather than ability plays so large a role is not alone or even predominantly owing to the "human" factors, which naturally occur in the process of academic selection as in any other selection. It would be unfair to hold the personal inferiority of faculty members or educational ministries responsible for the fact that so many mediocrities undoubtedly play an eminent role at the universities. The predominance of mediocrity is rather due to the laws of human co-operation, especially of the co-operation of the faculties who recommend and of the ministries of education. (Weber 1946: 132)

This creatively conformist skill is closely connected to another one. To gain recognition, one must not publish in specialist magazines or journals but in those that are "universally" known and, thus, prestigious. To do this, one has to know their editorial subcultures, which usually is not too difficult. However, one also needs access to them, which is much more complicated. Of course, one may send an article directly to a distinguished magazine or journal, but the probability that a nonconformist idea will be published diminishes rapidly. A good scholar has to know the right channels and utilize them, if he or she wants to be recognized.

To gain the time to gather empirical and sound data and to write books or articles, a scholar needs grants and, therefore, must know how to ask for grants. In the bureaucratic environment of modern universities, this ability alone gives him or her the chance to conduct research. Again, when the research is finished and, with luck, published, he or she needs to start seeking the attention of several prize-giving bodies. Although, as a rule, reviews are invited by boards of magazines or journals, the scholar also may try to "organize" these reviews in advance.

Additionally, a scholar needs to know how to ask for travel expenses if he or she wants to attend conferences. He or she has to know which conferences to treat as "seed" conferences by means of which he or she could be introduced into more or less significant scholarly networks and assured of subsequent publication. He or she needs to know whether to present a paper, act as a panelist or rapporteur, or organize a session. He or she should know with whom to have dinner, with whom lunch, with whom breakfast, and with whom only coffee. He or she must carefully evaluate whoever he or she is considering inviting to a party, whether or not he or she should have a party, whose parties he or she should avoid, and on whose parties he or she should bestow his or her presence. All these considerations should be recorded, evaluated, and synthesized, and it is the outcome of these calculations that decides, in the final analysis, who will be labeled an outstanding scholar. The longer it takes to cross a room at a party (the longer one is detained by people seeking one's ear), the higher is one's academic status.

How far is this from the ideal model of scholar, someone who is supposed to be a "fountain of truth"? By way of answering this question, one might say that the present conditions of scholarly life in the West are conducive to the creation of a *sly* scholarly individual.

Yet, if, indeed, the models of scholars described as instrumental, spectacular, or sly emerge so rapidly, how can space be found for the traditional scholar — the scholar who is interested mainly in truth, not subsidiary gains? Has that type of scholar become an endangered species? To what extent can the psychological factor of sheer curiosity be erased? How is the pursuit of knowledge *tout court* so easily eliminated? Is there still some place in modern society for pure, disinterested reflection? To what extent is the search for the understanding of reality and the cultivation of a long chain of deductions still treasured as the core of scholarly work? Because many of the so-called think tanks, which were originally designed to foster the pursuit of truth, seem to be nothing more than a metaniche for sly scholars, where is *pure* knowledge to be generated?

These are not easy questions to answer. Taking the present complexity of the social sciences into consideration, to what extent can problems in this field be digested, analyzed, and solved by a single individual instead of a task-oriented group? It reasonably can be argued that the perplexity of social textures does not allow an individual thinker to be wholly familiar with social problems and that this confusion forces one to seek a new synthesis-building mechanism. Such a mechanism may consist of a team working together (not working "for" somebody or "with" somebody) in a complementary manner, with no individual assuming a dominant role. The future will reveal whether teams of this sort can survive in the social sciences, not as the exception but as an ordinary enterprise. It seems likelier that any synthesis-oriented team or center would be regarded as a target by those who are instrumental or sly. Moreover, those who find authentic joy in scientific discovery would not be willing to engage in a trivial fight over the significance of the discovery, which, even when complicated, tends to be labeled as such by a relevant group of peers.

Consequently, the gap between the socialist instrumental academic model and the sly Western academic model is narrowing — all the more so since the spectacular scholar, who emerged in the East as a result of protest against the oppressive political establishment, has started to resemble the self-promoting Western scholar. In the West, there also are some who already have lost touch with social reality and academic thinking. These figures, mentally worn-out thinkers, now serve as chairs, heads of foundations, presidents, and so on. There, as gatekeepers in fact but as symbols in reality, they are supposed to contribute to the development of ideas. What kind of ideas can there be?

Instrumental scholars are a special case: they are doing something that is in direct opposition to their destiny. Although they are supposed to discover the truth, they blur the truth with their own tangle of activities. The widespread existence of instrumental scholars creates a real methodological (and even social) problem; consequently, they should be the object of increasing concern.

SPECTACULAR SCHOLARS

With few exceptions (the ex-Communist Andrei Sakharov is one), the spectacular scholar was a product of the Polish Communist regime. The mechanism for producing such a personality was surprisingly simple. In totalitarian society (it is interesting to note that Nazi Germany produced very few striking scholars like Martin Heidegger, and it is only recently that their political background has been fully revealed), the government was alienated from society as a whole, and those with power enjoyed little, if any, informal respect. This created an official void that did not provide ordinary citizens with independent guidance for determining what was true or false, right or wrong, just or unjust.

Scholars who succeeded in freeing themselves from this void, who were able to take on the role of trusted guardians, had a chance to secure the status of informal leaders. Some were pushed by events into this role against their will; others regarded it as their "mission"; still others undertook it for reasons of personal vanity (they started to believe that they were, indeed, celebrities endowed with more power than the very system that catapulted them to prominence).

Usually, the drive to become spectacular was based on patriotic motives. Dissidents regarded these scholars as convenient tools, remarkable mouthpieces. Because of their earlier achievements or their former positions in the scientific establishment, they had significant social visibility. Thus, candidates for the role of spectacular scholar were relatively safe. Representing the prestige of collective academia and having their own independent professorial status, they were difficult targets for quick reprisal. As a result of dissidents organizing public opinion in their favor, they gained even more social visibility in spite of all risks. They began to enjoy being called "governors of souls." They began to play a subtle game: how much would the authorities tolerate? How far could these scholars go without risking a crushing reprisal?

They also were involved in an additional contest: their relationship with the dissidents. Dissidents believed in and relied upon them; at least, this is what the dissidents claimed. Additionally, they became the precious pets of international opinion.[21] It became evident that their position as scholars was becoming more and more complex, and they began to find themselves without the time required for scientific work.[22] They also had to tolerate the fact that dissidents, in order to ensure their efficient role as mouthpieces, had raised their status far above sensible limits. In effect, they found themselves not in an academic realm but at the center of political turmoil and insecurity.

In the West, some once-famous scholars who have accepted positions as trustees of scientific institutions and become involved in complicated political games can be compared with the spectacular scholars from the East.

GATEKEEPERS

Gatekeepers are those scholars who have the power to determine who receives rewards for conducting research or teaching. They are professors, chairmen, deans, presidents, and members of various committees. All promotions, grants, leaves, sabbatical leaves,[23] expansion of research units, internal and other publications arrangements,[24] participation in conferences, and public recognition can be considered as rewards.

Gatekeepers can be facilitators; they also may function as censors. They facilitate by supporting and encouraging scientific work, and they censor by hindering work through the withdrawal of funds or the disbarment of technical assistance or administrative aid.

Scholars who volunteer or are nominated to personnel committees, boards (including editorial boards), institutional directorates, senates, presidencies, and vice-presidencies could belong to one of these categories.

In situations where there is a lack of credible data concerning personal motivation, one can only speculate why some scholars agree to perform functions connected with the gatekeeper's role. Could it be that, because they no longer are able to influence others intellectually, they try to influence others administratively? Is it a missionary attitude (to do something good for others), or does sheer vanity compel them to seek visibility in their environment?

The primary duty (and passion) of scientists is to seek truth. So, why would they agree to play the role of gatekeeper? Do they feel that the primary role of the truth seeker is too difficult? Are they disenchanted with the constant task of selecting between false and true, old and new, innovative and repetitive? Are they motivated to be servers whose duty is to help others? Do they believe that the role of gatekeeper involves very particular duties that they alone, on the basis of their experience, are capable of performing?

Independent of these motives, it is evident that the role of gatekeeper includes the special ingredient of power, which may be used in many ways. If gatekeepers distributing travel grants encounter the name of a friend, will they abstain from making a positive decision? If an editorial board is composed of mediocre scholars, will they be able to evaluate the paper or book of an innovator? If a department needs a vision (sometimes simply a program), can a chairman of middling ability undertake the role of leader when he or she faces peer resistance? Cases of this type can lead to power struggles that are not, or should not be, the main preoccupation of a scholarly community. Should scholars even participate in matters that deal with power, or should such matters be left to administrators who are less familiar with scientific problems but more likely to be impartial?

OPERATORS

Each category of scholars has within itself a pathological counterpart. Instrumental scholars lean close to deviancy. They are highly trained to create or to give an impression of creating by building a facade. They do this by covert manipulation and, above all, by cultivating direct links with the power center. The impression that they are authentic scholars can be substantiated because they assume, to some extent rightly, that the career of a scholar (and the perception of scientific creators) depends less on scholarly achievements than on the garnering of support that pulls them closer to the power center. This is especially true in the soft sciences, where the reputation of a scholar depends more on subjective appraisal and elusive evaluation than on hard data (the possibility of reproducing an observation or an experiment or of finding support among objective sources). The same is true for sly scholars. Gatekeepers seem to be attracted to this particular role because of the influence, if not the autotelic satisfaction, that they obtain from performing it.

When scholarly deviance appears in its plain form, operators emerge. Operators are not interested in academic work; they are not curious about the truth; they work in their particular field for reasons that have little or nothing to do with attraction to or interest in the field itself. Of course, they understand the process of scientific work, but they are not attached to the sciences: they could be equally effective as pimps, umbrella salesmen, or hotel executives. They operate in academia because they have chosen to "play the game" in this particular domain, because they know how to persuade, flatter, blackmail, or influence real scholars.

In order to be efficient, operators should be scholars themselves. As such, they know the subtle intricacies of their profession and are able to influence others more effectively. Because operators are teleological scholars, they may be oriented toward proficient manipulation of those they target.

In totalitarian countries, scholarly ability is assumed to be a precious craft because it takes many years to develop and because accumulating the work of many specialists (even generations of specialists) is their powerful capital (strategies, techniques, ways of blackmailing or flattering, collection of secret data, even quotations).[25] Consequently, the scholar needs particular handling. For example, it is assumed that making a recommendation directly to a scholar is risky (it has the flavor of a command). The scholar who does not agree with the recommendation may stiffen in a negative attitude. Hence, it seems more pragmatic to use an intermediary, someone who knows the scholar in question and who may transmit the recommendation more skillfully. The function of an operator in a totalitarian country could be quite a subtle one.

The difference between an instrumental scholar and an operator is that the operator exists to mediate between two different bodies — decision makers and academics; each has its own language and habits and, quite often, does not understand the other. An instrumentalist, on the other hand, acts alone. Operators need to be specially trained or self-trained; not only are they instrumentalists but they also need to be well-versed in that which they influence. Nonetheless, there is a continuity between operators and other types of scholars.

In some social systems, there will more operators; in others, fewer. Indeed, in Communist systems, where the prestige and stability of the scientific profession was considerable, the number of operators was higher. In social systems where the prestige of the scientific profession is relatively low (for example, where the number of years it takes to obtain an education is high and the prospects of obtaining a good salary are low), the number of operators will be limited.

It is likely that similar patterns could be noted over extended periods. For example, in post-Communist societies, where newly emerging, more lucrative professions become highly attractive, there is a remarkable shift of interest: the appeal of scientific professions drops dramatically. In Western societies, during an extended period of recession and when the attractiveness of executive positions is relatively low, the appeal of scientific work increases.

CONCLUSION

The preceding typology of scholars results from an interplay between four basic factors: creativity (with its mysterious background), sociopsychological determinants, institutional settings, and inherent requirements of various social systems including pressures from various institutions and corporations. Only the interaction among these components produces the final results. In addition to formulating an accurate and complete typology of scholars, one has to elucidate and explain the needs and requirements of various social institutions (more or less formal) that were generated to channel the advancement or recession of spontaneous scientific development. The typology might be useful for assessing the general innovative capacity of the system in question.

The following questions need to be discussed as well: How many inno-vators can a given social system accommodate? Under what conditions do innovators begin to be dysfunctional for the purposes of the system itself? How do various institutions or corporations shape the process of creating new ideas? What types of institutions or corporations are imposed (by whom? why? in which way?) in order to curb the development of ideas? What personal features (curiosity, career development objectives, personal insecurity, ambition, or arrogance) influence scientific processes? To what extent are the features of *Homo academicus* different from those of the general population (is there a greater distribution of scientific attributes among academics than among the general public?)? How can potential and authentic scientific builders be attracted to academia? Are innovators good teachers? How do the wives or husbands of scholars influence their careers?[26] Although operators seem to be destructive as scholars and have a poisonous influence inside the world of academia, do they serve to stir things up like the pike in the pond? This last question is closely connected with the following one: should theoreti-cal inquiry into scholars provide sensible devices enabling us to distin-guish "true" scholars from "deviant" ones, thus, giving some reliable prerequisites for academic selection?

4

Models of Scholars in Different Societies

Scholars can be classified from both the psychological and the social points of view. Because the world has become a "global village," it is valuable to find possible links among different types of scholars and different types of social systems. Thus, the problem is to identify which of the relations among creative (innovative) scholars working in teams (in order to build scientific schools and types of sociocultural milieux) are most conducive to the generation of scholars of that type.

My experience and research have acquainted me with the Polish, Canadian, U.S., Dutch, English, German,[1] Italian,[2] Japanese,[3] Norwegian,[4] Russian, and Chinese university subcultures. Through such avenues as teaching, lecturing, and systematic cooperation with representatives of these cultures, I have grown most familiar with the scholarly environments of Poland, Canada, the United States, and England.

This chapter presents a preliminary overview of several scholarly university subcultures. What follows is not based on any university- or government-sponsored project; it employs no replaceable methodology (indeed, it is based mainly on participant observation) or techniques utilized by a cooperating team; it intends mainly to specify the forces that sustain creative academic centers.[5]

THE BRITISH MODEL
(THE OVERLY WISE SCHOLAR)

As background to the formulation of a specific model of the current British scholar, it might be useful to present some subjective observations from my stay at Oxford.[6]

All Souls College was, at least during my stay there, an unusual place. As a rule, women were excluded from the college. They could enter into this secluded place only as low-level clerks or as strange, exotic guests three or four times a year. Women sometimes were invited to special dinners or ceremonial lunches. They could enter the college premises as special guest lecturers or as students attending special college seminars.

In principle, a fellow was supposed not only to study at the college but also to live there. In fact, only those fellows who had no family actually lived there. Visiting scholars' wives, who had to live outside the college, could not be invited to the college for lunch. Because of these restrictions, one visiting fellow, an international authority in his area, refused to attend lunches at all, protesting against stipulations that were unacceptable to him. He was surprised that his gesture passed entirely unnoticed.

Yet, it was perfectly acceptable for a scholar to come to lunch looking wild eyed, refusing to speak with his colleagues at table, and muttering incoherent orders at totally mute servants. It was understood that he was so deeply immersed in his ideas that he could not be expected to notice what was going on around him. His behavior might even be regarded by his peers as a sign of true scholarship.

During dinner, an entirely different etiquette obtained. The pecking order among fellows was strictly observed. At the head of the table sat the Warden (during my time, John Sparrow, a person with an extraordinary sense of humor) or the fellow with the highest rank (in 1971, there were eight different ranks of fellow). It was almost mandatory to prepare an interesting topic of conversation in advance. Discourses on professional matters were avoided. When a recently appointed visiting fellow tried to argue that history (the majority of the college's fellows were historians) was not a science because it dealt only with idiosyncratic facts and did not extend to nomographic generalizations, as Karl Popper maintained, he was arrogantly asked, "And who is Popper?"

A conversation about the weather was too trivial. It was best to start by discussing the shape and provenance of the silver that was lavishly displayed on the dinner tables. This could lead to serious debate about whether, for example, it was more sensible to store the college's vast silver treasure in the cellars and install an expensive electronic alarm system or to pay a high insurance rate to cover theft each year. Servants would wait for hours, slightly stooped, while participants in the discussion searched for a proper term, a persuasive sentence structure, or a convincing argument.

In the dessert room, a fellow of the lowest rank was supposed to sit at the end of the table and, at the appropriate moment, push a bottle of port along to his colleagues with a special stick. Esoteric conversation could be continued in a separate room, where the high-ranking fellow would pour coffee (visiting fellows did not have this duty [or privilege], nor were they responsible for the selection of food and wine for a given month). They also were excluded from the servant's task of pouring coffee, a job that fell, perversely, to the high-ranking fellow. Sometimes, a new fellow might be exposed to wine tasting; if, perchance, the wine was deemed inadequate, he could be asked for his opinion (in which case, the safe answer was "Acceptable, but not the best"). A hidden bell would be rung for the servants (who were not present, as a rule, in the dessert room) to bring a new shipment. Crossing the college grass at Oxford also was circumscribed by rules. Only fellows (including visiting fellows) had the right to do it. A breach did not result in visible sanction; nevertheless, the trespasser was regarded as not "belonging" (improper behavior of this type in All Souls was not a great problem, because the college was closed to the public practically all of the time).

The selection of new fellows was one of the main preoccupations of existing fellows and enormously time consuming. Although scholarly standards were nominally regarded as criteria of the highest importance, these scientific measures were set by the traditionally oriented fellows who were still in office. The best were not necessarily selected; above them was placed the outcome of the war between historians and lawyers.

The idea of engaging the "brains" of the college to discuss specific problems of current interest to the public (for example, the state of higher education in Great Britain or the make-up of British society), was regarded as offensive; it would invade the privacy of fellows and press them to display competence in matters other than those that taxed internal committees.

Of course, Oxford and Cambridge were (and are) similar in many respects. One similarity is that each has a Wolfson[7] and a Christ college. The subculture of Trinity, the best-known Cambridge college, was not altogether different from Oxford colleges. One of the most prominent Trinity scholars, Earl Russell (he used this title, as did his wives, pragmatically), published works on

Geometry, philosophy, mathematics, justice, social reconstruction, political ideas, mysticism, logic, Bolshevism, China, the brain, industry, the ABC of atoms [this was in 1923; thirty-six years later came a book on nuclear warfare], science, relativity, education, affairs, history, power, truth, knowledge, authority, citizenship, ethics, biography, atheism, wisdom, the future, disarmament, peace, war crimes and other topics. . . . Why did Russell feel qualified to offer so much advice, and why did people listen to him? The answer to the first question is not immediately obvious. Probably the biggest single reason he wrote so much was that he found writing was so easy, and in his case so well paid. (Johnson 1988: 197–98)

The uniqueness and importance of the Oxford-Cambridge subculture produces an ideal scholarly model for the entire British scholarly community. The fact that it differs from that of the scholar coming from a "red-brick" university in the United Kingdom is another story. Nevertheless, both models (Oxbridge and red brick) still have considerable, if not decisive, influence on the design of various scholarly establishments in Australia, Canada, South Africa, and some African countries. An essential feature of the British model is respect for "good manners." However, in practice, such manners are highly devalued; additionally, this model has several scientific (including methodological) and nonscientific consequences: the British social science scholars, with few exceptions, are shallow and seek mainly to make an unexpected impression.

It would be interesting to study British scholars who emigrate from Great Britain to its former colonies. Although there is a certain political tension between the center and the periphery, it does not surface readily, nor is it quite a matter of scholarly insiders and outsiders. With respect to British-Canadian, or Canadian-British, scholars, it would be particularly interesting to look at the following questions: Is it deliberate policy to manufacture second-rate scholars for export because, for various reasons, they would be unable to find jobs for themselves in the metropolis? Why are exported British scholars so often characterized by a mixture of arrogance and submissiveness?[8] Do British scholars try to hide their ignorance of "local" situations and put their new colleagues in their place with a more or less effective imitation of an Oxford accent? What percentage of British scholars returns to Great Britain after a successful accumulation of "colonial" currency?[9] Is British scholarly arrogance as displayed in Canada a characteristic element of effective teaching (to test the student by pressing him or her and compelling the student to display inherent limitations), or is it simply a display of aggression arising from unexpected difficulties in adjusting to Canadian realities?[10] Do different rules obtain in the metropolis and on the periphery?

All these quirks, so visible outside the metropolis, become even more peculiar when one takes into consideration that the Oxbridge college model is designed to produce cultivated, gentlemanly behavior. A "made-in-Oxbridge" scholar should know how to behave in all situations and treat the pursuit of knowledge almost as a private hobby. If one analyzes the other British model, the task-oriented scholar from a red-brick university, it becomes immediately apparent that this model as well is rooted in empirical reality with ingredients of sui generis meta-analysis, which tends to distance the British scientist-actor from all other scientist-actors in all other countries. Are these strange entanglements the result of an inculcated belief in the "higher-values" of British scholarly research? Do these interactions assume that the past activities in Great Britain of expatriate British scholars are superior to any scholarly activities conducted elsewhere?

The current mindset of a British scholar seems to be an eclectic amalgamation of two significant features: the well-grounded Anglo-Saxon empirical orientation and the meta-attitude of "higher value" (*besserwisser* [who knows better] orientation with an ingredient of post-Marxist shrewdness). It should be noted that the meta-attitude of a higher value seems to be significantly supported by the expedient of "invented tradition."[11] Invented tradition operates in those situations in which the status quo, in order to maintain or regain its legitimacy, needs support from rational arguments taken from the past. These arguments are built on the tradition of an established "higher" mandate. Hobsbawn, the creator of this notion, understands it as follows:

The term "invented tradition" is used in a broad, but not imprecise sense. It includes both "traditions" actually invented, constructed and formally instituted and those emerging in a less traceable manner within a brief and dateable period — a matter of a few years perhaps — and establishing themselves with great rapidity. . . . Invented tradition is taken to mean a set of practices, normally governed by overtly or tacitly accepted rules and a ritual or symbolic nature, which seek to inculcate certain values and norms of behaviour by repetitions, which automatically implies continuity with the past. In fact, where possible, they normally attempt to establish continuity with a suitable historic past. (Hobsbawn, Ranger 1983: 1)

It is not difficult to see that, although the notion could cause offence when spoken of publicly in Great Britain, "invented tradition" has its foundation in the English feeling of superiority, smartly hidden from outsiders under an ironic, mocking, and self-deprecating manner.

Some sections of the British social sciences — certainly not history but, for example, sociology — are relatively young in the United Kingdom. Indeed, British sociology, when compared with German or French or even U.S., is a newcomer. Juvenile, existing in the shadow of British anthropology, it tries to find something new and extraordinary by which to catch up to the international standards of sociology and to produce something at the level of its own ambitions.

The development of British sociology has had remarkable help from certain prestigious and internationally known publishing houses that are deeply rooted in the English tradition of clarity of language and argumentation (in the case of the publishers, Routledge & Kegan Paul, because of some excellent but invisible editors like Peter Hoppkins of the Karl Mannheim International Library of Sociology). Nonetheless, the discipline exhibits signs of what Paul Gross and Norman Levitt refer to as muddleheadedness, "a sovereign force in human affairs — a force more potent than malevolence or nobility" (Gross and Levitt 1994: 1). The time is ripe for a mature insider who is well-armed with civil courage to undertake a penetrating analysis of the pretentious but youthful and playful state of British sociology.[12]

To present an adequate diagnosis of the British scientist, not as he or she is portrayed in literary fiction[13] but based in current reality,[14] is still an open-ended task.[15] Especially interesting is the difference between the professional,[16] career-oriented attitudes of scholars coming from red-brick universities, heavily influenced by U.S. professionalism, and the unique style of Oxbridge scholars who are an eclectic mixture of amateur snobbery,[17] epistemological diletantism, and, sometimes, but not too often, authentic dedication to scientific inquiry.

THE POLISH MODEL
(A SCHOLAR TRUNCATED BY TOTALITARIANISM)

The ideal model of the Polish scholar is peculiar.[18] It is a combination of the German model and some unique ingredients generated by the specificity of Polish history. German scholarship coincides with Max Weber's view that "scientific training, as we are held to practice it in accordance with the tradition of German universities, is the affair of an intellectual aristocracy, and we should not hide this from ourselves" (Weber 1946: 134).

The Polish scholar also adopts certain patterns from the internal dynamics of German scientific seminars, such as the crucial concept of autocratic but impersonal rule that permeates traditional Polish academia, with the concept of the "chair" as its essential element (compare Znaniecki 1940: 131–34). According to this pattern, the professor is the core and centerpiece of the chair, and he or she is surrounded by his or her students (including lower-rank professors, docents, doctors, adjuncts, assistants of a higher and lower rank, graduate students, and, in exceptional cases, ordinary undergraduate students). Quite often this group is enriched by the presence of former students of the professor or students of his associates. Yet, the chair is not an autotelic unit; its major goal is to create a scientific school. In this sense, the professor personifies the drive of a specific sector of the scientific community interested in a given problem. Therefore, a new school of thought (scientific school) constitutes the main element of the chair occupied by a professor.[19]

The rules of logic may be used by those who know them and are able to apply them in cognitive processes. This involves knowing many types of reasoning and applying appropriate rules in proper circumstances. However, one also can collect various types of logical mistakes, classify them, and specify the consequences of breaking legitimate rules. Hence, the process of using logical rules can start with the application of known ways of logical thinking, but it also can start with the specification and collection of various errors and an inquiry into what rules have been violated.

Additionally, one can indicate certain existential and social situations that are prone to logical mistakes. All types of psychological or social oppression as well as authoritarian and dogmatic contexts produce an "atmosphere" that is highly prone to logical mistakes. Thus, totalitarian systems provide a cradle for illogical reasoning [20]

My interest in the social role of scholars was aroused by a seminar on the theory of law conducted by Jerzy Lande in Cracow between 1947 and 1952.[21] What was unique about this seminar was that an exceptional scholar devoted his faculties to the development of Leon Petrazycki's scientific school, which was in danger of being eradicated by the progress of an aggressive Marxist ideology.

Lande conducted three types of seminars: the basic-level seminar, in which his lectures were analyzed along with certain relevant matters (these usually were supervised not by Lande but by his assistants); the graduate seminar, in which master's theses and doctoral dissertations were discussed; and his highly coveted *privatissimum*, which I attended. During my own studies from 1945 to 1952 at the School of Law and in sociology at the Jagiellonian University in Cracow, Lande led only the *privatissimum* seminar.

Reserved for a handpicked group of students, the *privatissimum* was based on three basic principles: accumulation, continuation, and strict "gate control." The principle of accumulation was realized through successive analyses of relevant issues and problems, in which it was assumed that students absorbed the tentative findings made during the seminar. If a new avenue opened up and needed special investigation, a departure from the original direction was announced and consequently pursued. The seminar was also based on the principle of continuation. Thus, issues discussed during the seminar subsequently were treated as premises for further discussion, although, occasionally, it was necessary to return to certain assumptions that already had been discussed and accepted. This was done with the full awareness that, sometimes, additional reassessments of former conclusions were needed.

However, the seminar was not entirely exclusive. By the end of his fourth year of teaching at the School of Law, Lande became more than usually alert to the students' reactions and questions.[22] Sometimes, he even provoked comments. Occasionally, he would invite some of the "geniuses," as he called them, to join in his seminar. He once asked me to convey such an invitation to one of the students. For those who cared about theoretical matters, this was regarded as a great privilege.[23]

Lande's *privatissimum* was based on total equality of participants. The professor's role was to select the seminar topic; to conduct the seminar in an impersonal, almost "procedural" manner; to suggest the next course of discussion; and to firmly establish that each participant had only to obey the power of the arguments presented during the seminar. He made no claims to possessing a correct answer, nor did he know what the outcome of the discussion would be. Moreover, Lande saw it as his duty to try to find something worthwhile in everyone's contribution. The seminar participants always faced an abundance of absorbing issues and never were discouraged by the dead ends into which they occasionally ran.

Lande's seminar was not an aimless wandering. It had a specific goal: to develop a scientific school. However, this would-be school was not meant to revolve around Lande's ideas; it was supposed to be based on Petrazycki's teachings.

Although this is not the place to present Petrazycki's central ideas,[24] it is enough to say that some seminar participants, including myself, regarded Petrazycki as the unrecognized father of the sociology of law. A scholar who tries to develop a school in the social sciences often is tempted to use his authority to support certain ideas. Lande had no such imperial aims.[25] Although he was fond of Petrazycki personally, Lande was really devoted to his school of thought and sought to present it in the most objective way. To realize this goal, however, was not an easy task. In 1948, for example, proponents of Marxism started aggressively to eradicate all ideas that were not consistent with Marxist philosophy. Because Petrazycki regarded Marxism as something that puts economy and law upside down — "inverts all things" — he was treated as the primary target.

More than other scientific centers, Lande's original students realized the chance they encountered.[26] Some of his original students, in particular, remained politically honorable. There were some, however, who were defeated by the pressures of the totalitarian regime and others who embraced it opportunistically. Of this type, there were not too many among Lande's students. Here are presented in alphabetical order those of his students who became better known in Polish academia.

Maria Borucka-Arctowa, a non–Communist Party member, wrote several Marxist works, later took over a research center organized by someone else, and, after modifying the original research plan, conducted a study and published a book on the subject. She also turned the center into a kind of travel bureau by using grants from the Polish Soviet-style Polish Academy of Sciences to bring international scholars who were active in the law to Poland. These scholars were unaware (or could not afford to be aware) that she was a tool of the hidden, high-level political operators (like Adam Lopatka or Sylwester Zawadzki, both of whom were professors as well as ministers of the government) who wanted to neutralize the emerging and unmasking power of the sociology of law. Later, the scholars who were invited to Poland reciprocated with invitations for Borucka-Arctowa and her staff.

In contrast, Jan Gorecki, after his stay at the Center for Advanced Study in the Behavioral Study, Stanford, published a book on the achievements of the "unrecognized father of the sociology of law." The book, *Sociology and Jurisprudence of Leon Petrazycki* (1975), was published in Urbana, where Gorecki became a sociology professor. Gorecki later completed several other valuable books, some of them developing Petrazycki's ideas.

Jan Klimowski, an uncompromising Catholic activist, was oppressed politically and, in consequence, was unable to became a member of the official Polish academia.

Wieslaw Lang, who later became a party member, moved to Copernicus University in Torun, where he operated as a well-established "critical scholar" and successfully supported the existing political establishment.

Tadeusz Los, who was not a party member, was for some time the director of the Legal Bureau of the Ministry of Chemistry. He died prematurely.[27]

Kazimierz Opalek, after becoming a member of the party, was appointed dean of the School of Law at Jagiellonian University. He also was an unsuccessful candidate for the position of that university president. However, because of his close ties with the criminal activities of his colleague, Julian Haraschin[28] (a former prosecutor in cases against members of the Polish Underground Army, the AK), he also used his position to grant several masters' and doctoral titles to his own friends and colleagues from the security apparatus.

Grzegorz Leopold Seidler, originally not a party member, wrote two unsuccessful habilitation theses at the start of his career.[29] When both were rejected, he became desperate and dramatically shifted his political convictions to became a party member, subsequently writing and defending his third and Marxist-oriented habilitation thesis. Shortly afterward, he became a professor and soon was catapulted to the presidency of the State University in Lublin. In 1968, he came to national visibility when he strongly supported the contention that the autonomy of universities should be restricted even further by the political center.

Franciszek Studnicki, who was not a party member, unsuccessfully but ingeniously attempted to link cybernetics with the theoretical problems of internal operation of the law. After receiving a Ford Foundation fellowship in the United States, Studnicki returned to his former position as a professor of civil law at Jagiellonian University, where he published many valuable works. Toward the end of his life, however, he became blind, and he died prematurely.

Jerzy Wroblewski,[30] although not a party member, collaborated closely with the highest party circles and was rewarded with numerous semigovernmental positions, trips abroad, publication privileges, and the presidency of Lodz University and also of the Head Committee, which nominated all professors in the country. Although Wroblewski died prematurely of a heart attack, he published many books and articles during his career (around 700), some of them in cooperation with Opalek. In some circles, he was regarded as an authority in the area of semantic and logical analyses of law.

As for myself, my continual struggle with the political system has been described elsewhere (Podgórecki 1986). My own attempt to build a scientific school around the idea of sociotechnics (social engineering) also was presented in a different place (Podgórecki 1994: 13–35).

In connection with Lande's seminar, the question that remains is, How was it possible that such an exquisite scientific "subculture," as it was originally conceived by Lande, could harbor such diversity and, in some cases, produce such disastrous results?

Despite the outstanding example of Lande, the point must be made that the role of the Polish professor can degenerate easily, as it can in German and traditional Russian[31] academia (which was also developed under German influence). Then,[32] the professors transform themselves into people who want to be perceived as solitary symbols of central value: everything they do needs to be centered around them; they may introduce direct or indirect censorship, favoring those who flatter them, whether overtly or through their activities or writings; they may prohibit discussion of divergent points of view or demand that their own friends and enemies be adopted as such by those who "belong" to the chair.[33] These pathologies are quite common and easily recognizable.

Another essential feature of traditional Polish scholars is their anti-establishment posture.[34] As a rule, Polish scholars were representative of the traditional Polish intelligentsia.[35] As such, they were obliged to represent and defend the interests of the underdogs. Thus, in the Polish case, as opposed to the Russian, they were supposed to fight, also in their scholarly undertakings, as Polish patriots. During the nineteenth century, they were supposed to fight against German, Austrian, and Russian occupiers, although their strategies were different in each case (for example, under Austrian occupation, the war on Polish culture was organized and relatively soft).

During the period of partition (1795–1919), under the Austrians, Poles were unable to study at Polish universities. As a result, some Polish scholars went underground. In Warsaw, under the Russian occupation (the harshest), a group of Polish scholars created an underground university called the "Flying University" — "flying" because professors and students had to change apartments constantly to escape the attention of the secret police. Under such oppressive conditions, Polish scholars had no opportunity to develop their own style of teaching or research approach. Yet, the scholars' concern for independence in the humanities and social sciences persisted.

This pattern colored the model of the Polish scholar decisively. A Polish scholar alerted to the fate of the underdogs was equipped with an antiestablishment orientation. This attitude remained characteristic in the Polish social sciences after World War I and also was evident during the relatively short period of independence (1918–39). Paradoxically, it was strongly reinforced during World War II (1939–45).

Under German occupation during the war, the stakes were high: if discovered, members of the Flying University cell were liquidated, as a rule, in concentration camps. It is interesting to note that the Flying University was activated once more, in 1982, during the period of martial law imposed by Wojciech Jaruzelski.

What was more or less characteristic of the whole Communist East bloc was especially transparent in the Polish sciences, where psychological venoms dominated.[36] This concept somewhat resembles the "psychological poison" Petrazycki spoke of in his lectures.[37] Yet, it differs in that psychological poison is well-recognized as such within a given social group, its effects are recognizable, and its "carriers" are relatively easy to identify. In the case of venom, there are insurmountable difficulties, especially for an outsider, in recognizing its presence, detecting its symptoms (not only on a legal but also on a moral level), and completing the diagnosis. This venom tends to operate even when the conditions that created it disappear. Venom predominantly operates in hidden, invisible situations where conventional measures of social control can be discerned only with difficulty.

In the humanities and the social sciences, three factors reinforced the persistent operation of this phenomenon: the scarcity of attractive rewards; the lack of objective yardsticks by which to measure success, particularly in the social sciences; and the tendency to monopolize access to foreign resources. To illustrate the scarcity of attractive rewards and its effects, one need only compare the different climates in various Polish academic centers, particularly Warsaw and Cracow during the Stalinist and post-Stalinist period (1949–56). Despite similar political pressures (probably more penetrating in Cracow, with its smaller academic community and, therefore, greater transparency), the distinctions between scholars from Cracow and those from Warsaw were evident. Cracow representatives were unusually polite, even condescending, and eloquently hospitable. The Warsaw representatives were harsher, more straightforward, and more argumentative. A closer look was all that was needed to recognize that the unusually polished language of Cracow scholars contained nothing of significance and that their eloquence derived from the hypocritical gallantry of the Austrian Hapsburg court — an old heritage. This manner of speech was mainly used for public relations purposes or, sometimes, to cheat. In Warsaw, the academic community — which was not influenced by the patterns of Austrian courtesy; which insisted on creating an illusion of cooperation between oppressors and oppressed; and, additionally, which consisted, to a large degree, of first-generation intelligentsia — employed mainly a utilitarian politeness.

So, why was Cracow so much more venomous than Warsaw? Warsaw was the capital of the country, and despite (or because of) its atmosphere of political control (over scientific institutions, scientific associations, and international contacts, including scientific visitors, publishing houses, and governmental agencies), its people were more anticonformists. The situation in Cracow was the opposite: in spite of an abundance of scholars, some of them very competent, generated by the rigid canons of the university (established 600 years earlier), this community had fewer opportunities for international contact after World War II. Indeed, in Warsaw, ferocious infighting occurred over a relatively high number of international possibilities. At the same time, an ever fiercer battle, concentrated around fewer "goods," took place in Cracow.

During the state of constant political oppression, a war of all against all took place in Poland. Among the many weapons that were used, psychological venoms played an especially significant role: gossip, intrigue, and information (denunciation) were often deployed, sometimes in an extremely effective way. (Homages to decency were heard during funerals.)

The lack of an objective yardstick in the sciences, and especially in the social sciences,[38] created a tendency to delegitimize the achievements of others in order to elevate one's own. This tendency is nicely illustrated by a painting in Poznan's town hall of a devil lazily supervising sinners boiling in oil. His main responsibility is to frustrate their attempts to escape. Yet, in fact, he has no duties, because the jealous companions of those in the oil fix watchful eyes on all who are eager to flee. Those who try to escape are immediately brought back by their companions. In Poland, where it was very difficult to evaluate anyone's achievements, it seemed advantageous to diminish them. This simple device automatically bolstered one's own accomplishments: a strategy to diminish the achievements of others was used as a technique to increase one's own. This is quite a good example of the typical Polish attitude of unselfish envy.

In the Polish context, social disapproval was not necessarily connected with righteous condemnation or with unselfish envy; it was rather a perverse strategy of climbing.

Visiting scholars from abroad were (and are) regarded as a source of indirect material benefits. This was true in all East bloc countries. Poland, as the most open and liberal, was in this respect the most interesting case to observe. At the beginning of a foreign scholar's visit, everybody tried to monopolize the scholar for him- or herself. Later, the lucky one (quite often a female) would use various tactics to keep the visitor from venturing into other domains. To introduce a foreign scholar to someone else was either a gesture of the highest friendship or an act of simple foolishness. Interestingly enough, foreign scholars were ranked according to the performance of their national currency.

A different type of venom was used to monopolize the captured foreigner. Although generally effective, it had several drawbacks. It was difficult, almost impossible, to explain to visiting scholars what sort of tricks, methods, maneuvers, and devices others could use to "tame" him. Not only were they the product of an alien political system, but also they were incapable of discerning the precise nature of their new environment. During the period of "real socialism," visiting scholars caused problems with their inability to comprehend the venomous local atmosphere (which they tended to interpret simply as local differences of opinion or quarrels among "colleagues"); they did not understand the "natives'" uneasy avoidance of those who were influential and well-off and their obstinate determination to meet "true Marxists." However, the *real* danger was that the foreign scholars might inadvertently repeat to the party manipulators things that had been said to them in trust.[39]

It should be noted that the systemic change in Poland in 1989 did not automatically change the existing mental climate. Although venom is no longer used so obviously as a weapon, it still comes in handy as a device to strengthen relations with capitalist foreigners and as a tool to rebuff rivals. Consequently, the venom generated under communism counts as one of its legacies.

It was also the result of oppression and intimidation of Polish academia. Jerzy Jasinski wrote in a suggestive article: "Let's say it openly — in the social sciences, during communist domination and rule, if one was able to utter some truth, it was good; it was very good if one was able to make a truthful statement without enforced additional falsified statements. Only a few, when referring to their own books, can honestly testify, that they expressed truth and only truth" (Jasinski 1993: 7).

It must be stressed that the Polish social sciences were, to some extent, able to preserve Lande's principles of accumulation and continuation. With regard to the accumulation of knowledge, what was amassed by various scholarly centers was taken into consideration. This was the result of several factors: the tendency to collect elements that were valuable during Polish independence (until 1795 and between 1918 and 1939) and were regarded as a counter to the devastating operation of the Communist administration, the relatively large number of universities and university-like institutions that existed in Poland after 1918, and the existence of an academic community that was too large to be dispersed but small enough to establish an informal communication network. Some ideas, probably also generated to counter the process of Communist devastation, were forceful enough to persist. The fact that four generations of scholars have actively worked to elaborate the ideas of Petrazycki may serve as an example.

To summarize, after World War II, the academic situation became deeply shocking to the traditional Polish scholar. First, the instrumentality of the new breed of Marxist scholars violated the deeply embedded image of a scholar whose duty was to analyze problems impartially, to work on them in tandem with a group of dedicated coworkers, and to analyze them according to the requirements of his or her scientific school. Second, the instrumentality of the new wave of scholars violated the primary duty of a Polish scholar, which was to challenge the oppressive sociopolitical system, not to benefit from it or, worse, to cooperate with it. Third, traditional scholars began, without knowing it, to absorb the venomous environment that surrounded them.

This peculiar sociopolitical situation provided fertile ground for the development of the instrumental and spectacular models of scholarship, outlined earlier. It is necessary to stress once more that the instrumental and spectacular scholarly models generated after World War II were totally alien to the traditional Polish scholar. However, the model of the traditional Polish scholar still seems to appeal to young scholars educated under harsh totalitarian conditions.[40]

Additionally, the authoritarian experience of Polish academia pushed scholars toward a certain pathology, the result of which was the "court" structure of Polish academic centers. These centers, defending themselves against more or less deadly Marxist attacks, used to hide in small "secret societies." Once confronted with actual danger, some groups of real scholars started to create hidden alcoves, ensuring secrecy by binding themselves closely together through money, friendship, sex, cohabitation, shared vacations, shared secrets, shared crimes, or, sometimes, even oath taking. Some circles had different levels of initiation: at the center, the most secret nucleus; then the most deeply involved members; next, the "normal" members; and finally, those who aspired to membership.

Through some form of osmosis, the Marxist centers started to use analogous strategies. Although they had official university seminar meetings and exclusive party meetings (meetings that, by the way, were never sanctioned by the official state law), they started to have "private" meetings that took place in the apartments of the more active and aggressive Marxist professors.[41] The main goal of these meetings was not to develop an impartial, well-grounded, independent science but to prepare, as quickly as possible, a cadre of scholars whose assignment would be to replace the traditional scholars and, thereby, change the balance of scientific power in academia. The task of increasing the proportion of party professors relative to nonparty professors was not an easy one, because it is generally supposed to take around 30 years to produce a full-fledged professor. The breeding-ground approach of hidden subcultures was intended to shorten the process, because they have their own inertia. The practices of the secret Marxist academic subsocieties tended to persist even once their main *raison d'être* had disappeared.[42]

The pressures exercised by these apparatuses to conform to Marxist standards gave rise to a specific counterreaction: the development of scholarly civil courage. Civil courage demands that an individual should struggle for values that are not personally beneficial but belong, instead, to a certain group or to the community at large. The individual fights not for his or her own personal advantage but for the goodness of the neighborhood to which he or she belongs (or aspires). In the West, especially in academic communities, one who actively cares about the interests of his or her community might be regarded as an imposter, a person with a "hidden agenda," an unstable person, someone who is suspect. In the Polish academic community, the fostering of civil courage is regarded as a primary social and political duty that one carries out for the benefit of the dormant civil society.

Such pressures could be beneficial. Polish scholars who are able to withstand the pressures of the authoritarian social system (or its legacy) or, sometimes, just because of their fight with this system, might turn themselves into creative scholars.

THE U.S. MODEL
(A SCHOLAR OF FRAGMENTARY CONTRIBUTIONS)

U.S. scholars are a relatively young breed.[43] Despite their "youth," they wield enormous influence.[44] The richness of the United States plays an important role here, but not the only role. The dramatic growth in the number of colleges and universities from the end of the nineteenth century onward (there are presently more than 2,000) was spurred by financial support from the state and various communities. These colleges and universities, as well as certain foundations, enabled both U.S. students and those from developing countries to obtain a university education.

According to Harriet Zuckerman, there were "493,000 men and women in the United States who described themselves as 'scientists' when asked their occupation in the national census," and there are "313,000 scientists as estimated in the biennial survey making up the National Register of Scientific and Technical Personnel prepared by the National Science Foundation (1970)" (Zuckerman 1977: 9). This educational potential was, of course, strengthened by the political influence gained by the United States immediately after World War II as the strongest of the victorious allies.

The U.S. scholarly model has been heavily influenced by the characteristic features of its own society[45] — in particular, professionalism, individualism, the production of intangible goods, and a naiveté in nonmaterial matters.[46] Paul Lazarsfeld and W. T. Thielens, on the basis of extensive research conducted in 1955, succinctly portray the academic profession: "We asked our respondents [2,451 scholars were interviewed] to compare their occupations with three others: the manager of a branch bank, an accounting executive of an advertising agency, and a lawyer. These three occupations share an important characteristic with the work of a professor: none of them produce tangible goods, and all deal in symbols, either verbal or monetary. . . . It is clear that professors do not feel they are much appreciated by businessmen or congressmen" (Lazarsfeld and Thielens 1958: 11, 12).

Because professionalism appears as one of the most important features of U.S. academia, the U.S. model of scholar rejects the "high priest" aura that attaches to the European professor, whose basic privilege and duty is to "profess" the mystery of knowledge. U.S. scholars reject the vertical hierarchic and argumentative structure of the European scientific seminar, instead accepting the horizontal model based on the U.S. equality.

On the whole, Lazarsfeld and Thielens were not much impressed by the scientific achievements of U.S. academia. Little more than half of the professors they surveyed in 1967 held doctoral degrees. One of their conclusions was that: "Although in the last ten years I have visited several score colleges and, through colleagueship with Everett C. Huges, gained some familiarity with the academic rear guard, I was not fully prepared to realize that, at many institutions accredited as colleges, the faculty is by and large so little given to reading, so unintellectual if not actively anti-intellectual, that survey research would have been set back and academic instruction set forward if respondents and interviewers had changed places" (Lazarsfeld and Thielens 1958: 288).

Because U.S. scholars are professionally oriented,[47] they arrive (by car) at their office every morning and stay for the entire working day. They keep their doors half open to show not only that they are engaged in scientific "work" and are (especially if they are male) behaving (eschewing affairs with students of the opposite sex), but also, above all, that their knowledge is at the disposal of their students (because fees usually are quite high, students have a right to expect their professor to be accessible).[48] They leave their office in the late afternoon. Once home, they forget their scholarly "work" at the university, becoming at once absorbed in their private family life, or they might "escape" (from scientific work) to the cottage (which by preference is in reasonable proximity from the house) for the weekend. Their home, official, and private lives are perfectly separated. This separation is generally the achievement (even before the feminist movement) of scholarly wives, who categorically demand that their husbands give time to the family.[49]

U.S. scholars are well-aware that their primary duty is to teach. Therefore, they are alert to any invention that makes their classes more interesting, gains the students' attention and makes them happy, and helps to balance scholarly content with humor.[50] They lighten their subjects, flatter students (to develop their "egos"), and eagerly exploit any device that makes the time pass quickly. At some universities, professors are called "instructors" (indeed, this term better describes their duties).

U.S. scholars are supposed to divide their time between teaching, research, and administrative work and, thus, take part in the life of the department. At the beginning of their careers, they focus on its organic part (because they want to be noticed). They attend departmental meetings (not necessarily places to discuss mutually interesting subject matter). These administrative assemblies quite often constitute the high point of their current academic activities. Some professors prepare themselves more carefully for departmental interventions than for their lectures or seminars. The recent wave of Marxists, post-Marxists, minority-rights, or feminist arrivistes regard departmental meetings as the proper forum for ostentatious displays of rhetoric and sharp scholarly skirmishes. It is well-known that, thanks to this type of atmosphere, Reinhard Bendix left the Department of Sociology at Berkeley shortly before his death and moved to its sister department, Political Science.

At some U.S. universities (and Canadian as well), a Ph.D. has not always been regarded as a prerequisite to becoming a professor in the social sciences. Teaching skills and administrative abilities could be considered far more valuable assets. Yet, acquiring a Ph.D. often became a milestone in the life of professors who did so. They became familiar mainly with the scholarly literature published before they obtained the degree; indeed, it seemed pointless to read material that was published after, because it was no longer useful for the Ph.D. defense. Preparing for the Ph.D. also had a bearing on their subsequent material, which tended to feature literature connected to the Ph.D. and little that was not.

Generally speaking, those who work in academia are regarded in U.S. society as eggheads; they are not necessarily in the most successful profession (if one measures success by monetary achievement). To improve their financial situation, which is generally regarded as poor, scholars try either to climb higher on the academic ladder or to gain funds from additional sources. The first strategy is difficult, given the competition. The second seems to be easier for those well-acquainted with financial and administrative applications. Whether because of a desire to stimulate research or to diminish their tax obligations, many institutions donate substantial funds to academia. Scholars are, thus, inspired to use their administrative skills to compete for limited grants. It might be revealing to compare the content of these proposals and requests for sabbatical leave with the actual work achieved during such leaves, once granted.

Younger professors, despite their lack of scholarly experience, are more privileged in the distribution of scholarly advantages. The U.S. idea of equality, linked with the supporting idea of promoting individualism, is responsible for this advantage. Weighted against the demands of the system and patterns of behavior of more experienced colleagues, individual aspirations take the upper hand as a general rule. In such a system, younger professors do not gain from the opportunity to apprentice with and receive guidance from their elders, nor are they expected to; the elders are, themselves, less interested in new discoveries than in their own careers. Where younger professors have made their careers with the support or guidance of an older colleague, it is advisable for them to sever the master-apprentice relationship abruptly. Carving a niche for oneself evidently is more compelling than following up the ideas, however important, that gave rise to the relationship in the first place.

Certain trends have worked to counteract the compartmentalization of U.S. academia. For example:

In the 1950s we saw a surge of interdisciplinary studies continuing into the 1960s. Think tanks, multidisciplinary and interdepartmental institutes, joint appointments, and degree programs became fashionable. At that time the prevailing principles were (a) to put specialists from several fields together to discuss a topic or a problem, (b) to encourage infusion of extra-departmental ideas by hiring persons of other departments part-time or full-time, (c) to offer interdepartmental degree programs by combining courses from many departments, and (d) to set up institutes or departments to study generalized theories. (Maruyama 1991: ix)

However, although these ideas have had some influence on the whole, they have not prevailed.

The simplicity that typifies U.S. scholars is partially responsible for their international influence. They are proficient in finding a promotional phrase that captures, in a primitive but attractive way, the essence of their endeavor. They are less interested in the meaning of the slogan than in finding a designer label to attach to their "business research." For example, the term "pluralistic law" is currently in vogue in the sociology of law. It refers to the coexistence of two or more legal systems within the same social system. Articles, books, symposiums, conferences, and even a magazine deal with this phenomenon. Few specialists realize that the term "intuitive/living law" encompasses the same issue but in a more potent and far-reaching manner. However, intuitive/living law is relatively clumsy and inadequate as a slogan. Consequently, the theoretical context for many potentially revealing discussions on the relationships among various legal systems is deprived of depth simply because of the lack of a suitable watchword.[51]

To repeat, U.S. (but also Canadian) scholars are preoccupied mainly with their careers. This results from the fact that what they select for their research can secure for them professional success and recognition. Primarily, they want to make a mark on the development of academia to further their chances of getting a better position at their university or research center. Hence, they are not loyal to their alma maters. Although professing their loyalty, they may use an offer from another university promising higher pay to negotiate a satisfactory raise, thereby saving themselves the trouble of moving to a different intellectual environment where they would be ignorant of the local situation and initially bereft of friends and allies. Should they fail to negotiate a raise, they move.

The U.S. scholar conducts research that is strategically important to him or her. Such research is not additive; it rarely constitutes part of a larger research domain because it is not designed to prove or disprove elements of a more far-reaching theory. With little exaggeration, one might say that, if the research adds something new to an existing body of knowledge, it is an accidental result.

In the traditional European academic environment, a particular investigation was designed to prove or disprove a broader theoretical model. Currently, European science is heavily influenced by the U.S. model, in which this additive potential of traditional scientific schools is wasted, along with the possibility of the additive development of sciences.

Sometimes U.S. academia brings to mind an old and grotesque narrative: The owner of a very beautiful and unusually large pearl goes to several jewelery stores and asks their proprietors to make a hole in it. They refuse. Eventually, he goes to a store located in a shabby, isolated street. The proprietor calls his young assistant and tells him to make a hole. The inexperienced boy grasps the pearl quickly and, before its owner is able to protest, makes a perfect puncture. "Why did you give the pearl to this boy, instead of doing the task yourself?" he asks. The shop owner replies, "This young boy is stupid, he does not realize the value of the pearl; his hand wouldn't tremble."

It should be stressed again that the U.S. model presented here is highly stylized. However, to the extent that it is correct, it begs the questions of why such a primitive model yields such spectacular achievements and why U.S. academia is so influential.[52] The answer has partly to do with the sheer number of researchers and the significant number of highly competent scholars imported from Europe since the war but also with the inherent naiveté of typical U.S. scholars that blinds them to the intrinsic gnoseological obstacles and the true complexity of problems.

Thus, one may conclude that it is largely by virtue of their numbers that U.S. academics have the chance to become creative scholars and, occasionally, founders of scientific schools.

THE CANADIAN MODEL
(A SCHOLAR IN A REPLICA MODE)

The simplicity of academic life in Canada can be taken as a starting point. Canadian academia is relatively young, and its underlying influences are clearly visible; it borders the United States with its dynamic and well-sponsored universities and research institutes, and it always has been receptive to the influx of European and, especially, British ideas (sometimes also personnel) that enrich the Canadian scene with scientific approaches generated over several centuries. As Raymond Aron observed: "Nothing is more conducive to a nation's prosperity than the exchange of knowledge and experiences between universities, editorial staff, the civil service and parliament. Politicians, trade union leaders, industrialists, university professors and journalists need neither be mobilized into a single party which has a monopoly of power, nor cut off from one another by ignorance and prejudice. . . . In this respect, no other ruling class is as badly organized as the French" (Aron 1957: 221).

A look at university life in Canada presents a mixture of theoretical and practical problems.[53] They are important in varying degrees, but the practical ones can be understood better if they are placed in the following elaborated and descriptive theoretical framework.

Higher (university) education in Canada should be based on three levels of teaching: basic, medium (graduate), and advanced, which does not exist as yet. The basic is built on the principle of accessibility, which holds that anyone who is properly qualified should be accepted for education. It aims at providing whomever is eligible with the proficiency and skills required to function in society, in various professions, and in private enterprise. It is up to the individual recipients of this basic education to decide how much of it they need to enter into professional life or to try to climb further. The basic layer is regarded as a prerequisite for the medium layer, the main goal of which is to supply those who will enter into professional life with the necessary skills to operate according to certain methodological and theoretical standards that are necessary for pursuing independent research and inquiry in a given area of social life.[54] The Ph.D., which is the highest title the university can award, bestows the right to formulate independent diagnoses of given situations in the sciences or in specific areas of social life; it is a certificate of competence. In addition, it gives potential employers the assurance that its holder is recognized by the existing scientific community as fully competent in the area of his or her specialty. In short, this degree assures interested companies or institutions that candidates are adequately qualified and that they have the qualifications to develop their area of specialty according to established, obligatory standards.

This is presently the highest level of competence within the structure of Canadian advanced education. Yet, it does not motivate those who attain it to challenge and reshape the sciences or social sciences in a revolutionary way.

The accumulation and storage of essentially practical skills demanded by the present system contributes to the built-in obsolescence of the intellectual commodities being purveyed, tailored as they are to current needs. Only in an innovative atmosphere that encourages breakthrough discovery can a given social system be safeguarded against an unforeseeable future. The point is that the existing structure of Canadian higher education, although it provides individual "scholar-transformers" with the skills to make individual discoveries, is unable to open its gates to the creation of ideas and the breeding of "revolutionary" abilities.[55]

What causes this type of situation?

To begin with, at the basic level of the higher-education system, professors cannot directly supervise students because of the size of existing classes.[56] This task is fulfilled by other students who serve as "teaching assistants." Although instructed by professors, these assistants have too much discretion in guiding and evaluating students. The outcome is that it is the teaching assistants, not the students, who have a chance, and only a chance, to develop their own skills as they capitalize on the errors of those whom they supervise.

Second, students are not obliged to take the sort of once-mandatory courses — for example, in the theory, methodology, logic, or history of their chosen discipline — that would provide them with a basic intellectual structure on which to build; instead, they choose courses according to such criteria as the lenience or other characteristics of the instructor and the current vogue of a given discipline.[57]

Moreover, it is not so much intellectual "curiosity" that is treated as an independent virtue at Canadian (and not only Canadian) universities as its pragmatic value.[58] The pragmatic attitude, to some extent justified by the absence of a system (private or governmental) of widely accessible stipends (loans, bursaries, teaching and research assistantships, subsidies, and so on), has the upper hand over the *gnostic* perspective (Matras, personal communication, 1993). For its part, the graduate program, which is governed by the pressure to find jobs, does not reward those who are inherently interested in independent scientific scrutiny but forces them to adjust themselves to the existing system as fast as possible and at the lowest intellectual cost. It is partly for this reason that the dominant practice in the Canadian social sciences is to channel one's research into highly specific areas of inquiry — historical analyses of limited topics and periods, race relations in given regions, inequality (especially gender) in the workplace, ideological and practical trends in political parties, trends in welfare-state priorities, and so on — that revolve around social practices. Most such research is influenced by low-level (rarely middle-level) theory. As Frank Vallee says, "the high degree of specialization is the norm; the exception is any systematic attempt to apply high-level (or global) theory   this only rarely happens. Much of this work is left to the theologians and philosophers ('Vallee, personal communication, 1993).

With very few exceptions, outstanding former students are not interested in academic careers, because they can get more money from other occupations. This, of course, deprives the university system of fresh perspectives and applications of knowledge. The worst feature of higher education in Canada as currently structured is the lack of task-solving subcultures within the universities of the sort that have been developed in Europe under the umbrella of the chair system. Each chair is responsible for conducting education in a certain area (for example, theory, method, history of the discipline) and each generates a core of *statu nascendi* (being created) ideas: the chair is a fountain of creation of ideas. There is a crucial sui generis process of interaction and feedback between theory (research) and practice (education). Research undertakings are controlled by the educational orientation of the chair and are tested constantly through the educational process. In the former Soviet Union (and currently in Russia) and in the United States, the chair system is pathologically transformed (although for different reasons) into a variety of research institutes that are conducted, more or less, as profitable enterprises. The monstrous Soviet Academy of Sciences is a case in point. Canadian higher education is, in principle, parochial.[59] It is predominantly oriented toward the industrial and corporate situation as it exists in Canada. Sometimes it creates its own autonomous subproblems that serve as the pretext for something entirely different.[60] If it opens itself to outside influences, it does so selectively. These openings are oriented mainly to scholars imported from the United Kingdom, where the predominant paradigm of science development is still an "amateurish" one (a gentleman's hobby), or to professional scholars imported from the United States, who are dominated by the emphasis on "individual career" (discernible as pecuniary gain).[61] Therefore, until something like a "third level" of university structure gets established, the great majority of Canadian scholars should be regarded as high-level teachers. They regard teaching as their job, and that is what they get paid for.[62] However, in most universities, there is a discernible and growing tendency to assume that some of these teachers can, will, and ought to publish research-based work.[63]

What can be done to bring the necessary creativity to the Canadian higher-education system?

First and foremost, federal and provincial governments should be sensitized to social and technological changes that affect the academic milieu. This heightening of governmental involvement should not come about through scandal or, worse, crime.[64] In particular, governments must be aware that the need to establish an educational framework that fosters scientific and organizational discovery is as imperative as the need to find solutions to the problems of medicare, unemployment, the environment, and so on, because, in the long run, it is organizational and scientific ideas that have the decisive and strategic impact. This simple truth goes unrecognized by politicians and the more shortsighted activists, who do not have to pay for their own myopia.

In tandem with this first requirement, the university system should incorporate into its existing structure an additional advanced level of learning. This should be based on the concept of a continuous seminar, the main goal of which would be to stimulate the ongoing generation of new ideas. Such a seminar should include current and selected former students of the incumbent chair, his or her predecessors, theoreticians "working in practice," and emeritus professors of the field. New questions would be discussed as they arose and absorbed into the stockpile of knowledge gained over the years of the seminar's existence, supporting this scientific subculture.

In addition, there should be a countrywide network of advanced study centers (like the Calgary Institute for Humanities) and the establishment of links between these seminars and centers and the mass media in order to transmit to the public, especially to the political decision makers, the new perspectives generated therein.

If such a system were adopted, Canada could capitalize on the most creative educational approaches in the world: the German concept of the chair headed by a professor, the Anglo-Saxon attachment to empirical data, the Gallic drive toward newly minted ideas, the U.S. tendency to establish task-oriented groups, and the Nipponic concept of replicating those patterns that appear to be successful.

These reflections on Canadian university education lead to the conclusion that Canadian universities are heavily staffed by the professional type of teacher. This synthetic generalization raises the question of to what extent this particular type of teacher is conducive to the general task of preparing Canadian society as a whole for the problems of the new century and millennium. A first glance suggests that Canadian scholars and universities are not well-equipped for this task. In one of the leading papers presented during a 1994 conference on Canadian universities, Peter Emberly and Waller Newell claimed that,

According to the politically correct version of diversity, to argue this [the need to stimulate students' potential superiority of knowledge in the future] is to support "definitional autocracy" or some similar sin of logocentrism. The traditional student-teacher relationship must be replaced by a kind of transactional therapy in which all (including the instructor) share their feelings about [how] they are oppressed by patriarchy, ageism, species-ism or any kind of natural restraint. The outcome, in the post-modernist doctrine, is for everyone in the encounter group to realize that all of life is about power — you are dominated by power structures (however benignly disguised as parents, religion and tradition) and the only solution is to shatter their power and assert your own. (Emberley and Newell 1994: A13)

In sum, at the present, the chances of Canadian higher education producing innovative scholars are very, very low indeed.

THE CHINESE SCHOLAR (A SCHOLAR
YEARNING FOR HIS FOREFATHERS' WISDOM)

That sleeping giant, the Chinese scholar, currently is not well-known.[65] Marcus Brauchli notes that Cheng Kai-ming, dean of Education at Hong Kong University, said that "China doesn't really have universities in the Western sense of the term, with the culture of liberalism and critical thinking. But they need them if they want to innovate and grow." Brauchli also observed:

Under the old, centrally planned economy, students were assigned jobs for life, and theory was jettisoned in favour of specific training for specific jobs. That system has driven nearly a quarter of a million Chinese students overseas in search of more flexible education; of those lucky or connected enough to get visas to study abroad, fewer than one in five return. . . . In 1992, public expenditure on education was under 3 percent of economic output, well below the 4.1 per cent average for the developing world and half the level in some growth economies such as Malaysia. . . . The problem with China's schools is that, instead of teaching students how to think, they still teach what to think. (1994: 4)

I had exactly the same impression during my stay at Suzhou University in 1987 when I had the chance to lecture and speak with Chinese scholars. On this topic, I also interviewed several Canadian and U.S. scholars who spent varying amounts of time in China. They shared Brauchli's opinion and agreed that the current image of the Chinese scholar is definitely not clear.

On the whole, my own experience was quite revealing. Only once did I have the opportunity to meet a young Chinese scholar of the "old" school. Usually, I was surrounded by the new Chinese scholars, most of whom were "products" of Red China.

The students and professors who attended my cycle of lectures on the sociology of law were, for me, the most telling. First, when I entered the class, all the students rose to greet me, just as Polish students greeted their professors when I began my studies in 1945. Second, I realized that a fair percentage of my students (I estimated around 15 percent) understood English. Nevertheless, three Chinese professors were always present during my lectures. I should add that the sociology of law was then, and I suppose still is, a terra incognita in Chinese academia. The only available text was a translation of Leon Duguit's book *Law in the Modern State* (1919), which is now generally regarded as obsolete. Third, any questions the students had for me were filtered: they were submitted in writing[66] to the Chinese professors, who read them before translating them into

English. Questions that were written in English went through the same "censorship."[67] A substantial number of questions concerned the Polish Solidarity movement — so many that I promised to devote my final lecture to this issue and to link the lecture to legal matters that have been raised by the Solidarity movement. However, a few days before the last of my lectures, I was informed that, because of the students' examination schedule, my concluding lecture had been cancelled.

My general impression was that Chinese scholars were not interested in the specifics of the social sciences, partially because of an efficient "process of unlearning" that took place during the Cultural Revolution. Students and professors alike were capable of grasping or coming closer to theoretical and abstract points only after a relatively long and difficult process of sequential explanation. Yet, even then, they were not enthusiastic about discussing such matters. Those who were willing to discuss them displayed impressive discursive abilities and high intelligence, but in general, they tended to shift from scientific discussions to conversations dealing with private issues.[68]

Their curiosity about the conditions of scholarly life and life in general in the United States and Canada was enormous.[69] My criticism of these conditions was treated with displeasure. Even those Chinese scholars who had a chance to visit North America retained unrealistic images of the place.

There was a lot of mutual suspicion among Chinese scholars regarding "small" professional matters. Some of them had a tendency to treat "foreign specialists" as their own personal pets. I should add that visiting foreigners lived in separate, much better equipped houses and, as a rule, kept to their own circles. They were treated with high regard by the Chinese and enjoyed privileges their Chinese colleagues were not granted.

On the whole, I had a feeling that some Chinese scholars possessed enormous creative potential. Had they had access even to what by Western standards would have been regarded as modest working conditions, if their politically imposed publication bans were lifted, if they had not been weighed down with political indoctrination, their achievements certainly would have been outstanding. To substantiate this, I refer to a two-hour lecture given to me *stante pede* (immediately), richly detailed and well-situated in a comparative historical perspective, by a young philosophy professor in his own house in the tumult created by his children who were excited by an unexpected foreign guest and ignored their sick mother's persistent attempts to quiet them down.

Of course, impressions have little systematic validity. In the context of this study, they are intended only to stress the fact that the enigmatic model (ideal and real) of the current Chinese scholar has potentially enormous consequences. If the Chinese adopt (as the Japanese are doing now) the instrumental model of scholar in its former totalitarian incarnation or (more likely) if the currently popular "sly" Western scholar gains the upper hand among one-fifth of humankind, then the future of the world's scientific development, including developments in the social sciences, could be in danger. A thorough but controversial investigation that recently appeared emphasized the point that Chinese scholars, if properly understood, will, in the future, play a far more significant role in sciences than they do now.[70] According to this study, there are three subspecies of Homo sapiens, each roughly coinciding with the historic populations of Africa, Europe, and Asia. Whereas the traditional Asian population employed the K-strategy (producing fewer offspring and devoting a great deal of energy to each of them), the traditional African population employed the R-strategy (producing a larger number of offspring and limiting the amount of time spent on each). The traditional European population falls somewhere in-between. As a consequence, the Asian population is characterized, among other things, by its higher intellectual potential than the other two populations (Rushton 1995). Therefore, the current lethargy of the Chinese scholar (who conceivably has the greatest potential) is not, by any means, just a problem for China but is of vital concern to the international community of scientists, especially in light of predictions that, in 100 years, the white population will comprise only 10 percent of the total world population.

One can predict that a new type of scholar will emerge in China, a sort of hybrid: the patriotic scholar. In Western countries, these are scholars who (with artificial modesty or controlled arrogance) socialize with their colleagues not only to exhibit their own private achievements but also to show their pride in the institution with which they are associated. Chinese patriotic scholars are of a different breed: because their mother institutions tend to be low in academic prestige, they do whatever they can to improve the status of these institutions. They become patriots of their own academic workplace to elevate its scholarly standards. Of course, in doing so, they need to raise their own standards as well, intertwining them with the standards of the institution.

It is interesting to note that, in the patriotic scholar, a motivation that is not scholarly in origin influences academic standards by transforming itself into a drive to achieve high scholarly rank (that is, a heterotelic form of motivation becomes an autotelic one). Institutional patriotism can come about in various ways. It might stem from a desire to raise the academic standards of the institution with which a given scholar is associated; it might be generated by the sophisticated calculation that those who are not academically talented enough to achieve something significant of their own might accomplish something significant as a by-product of the milieu that they helped to organize; it might be an institutionally supplementary motivation; it might develop from the belief that institutional motivation alone can hasten the climb up the academic ladder. In any case, it is a primary motivation for those who assess themselves as altruistic but mediocre scholars.

For systemic reasons and because of the absence of a conducive scholarly subculture, the current model of Chinese scholar has a long way to go before it can produce builders of scientific schools. Nevertheless, ancient Chinese wisdom can be very revealing for modern (especially U.S.) scholarship. Yutang Lin summarizes some elements of this wisdom in the following way:

In speaking of a scholar, the Chinese generally distinguish between man's scholarship, conduct, and taste or discernment [interpretive insight, or, in current, more pretentious jargon, "hermeneutics"]. This is particularly so with regard to historians; a book of history may be written with the most fastidious scholarship, yet be totally lacking in insight or discernment, and in the judgment or interpretation of persons and events in history, the author may show no originality or depth of understanding. Such a person, we say, has no taste in knowledge. To be well-informed, or accumulate facts and details, is the easiest of all things. (Lin 1937: 362)

5

Scholars on Scholars: Interviews

> I am much more interested in impressing my colleagues than I am in
> impressing my students.
> > — John Merryman, Stanford University, Tape 5, Side A

Independent of the attempt to present my own ideas on scholars and their
role in contemporary society, the goal of this research was to analyze how
scholars themselves perceive their existential position in the academic
world and how society at large views the processes that mold academia.
Accordingly, I conducted interviews with 37 scholars (35 men and 2
women) at Stanford University and the University of California, Berkeley,
during March and April 1994. The interviews were based on my paper
"Different Types of Scholars" (Podgórecki 1993), which the majority of
subjects had been asked to read before our scheduled sessions. The interviews were not only illuminating but also symptomatic.

Although the majority of subjects represented the social sciences, the
seven Nobel prize winners were mainly from the natural sciences (one of
them did not authorize his interview; excerpts of that were deleted). That
so few women were interviewed is partially explained by the fact that both
the law schools and sociology departments of the two universities are
staffed primarily by males. Several women also refused to grant interviews. One professor from Canada, the president of Carleton University,
was interviewed as well.

All interviews were taped with the exception of the one with Henry
Taube of Stanford University. The tapes were carefully transcribed and
remain in my possession. The subjects were asked to authorize the tran-
scriptions of their interviews.

Although the typology of scholars served as the main stimulus for these
sessions, discussion also touched on scholarly innovation, the horizontal
or hierarchical structure of the organization of science, the place of logic
in scientific inquiry, the aesthetic dimension of scholarly research, U.S.
versus non-U.S. scholars, scholars' normative commitment, and the
professionalization of scientific inquiry. The interviews were connected
with the original typology (presented in Chapter 3) modified through
ongoing research. Although the typology provided a convenient starting
point, it was not the main objective of the interviews; rather, it was
regarded as a useful trigger for conversation on related matters. The
essential purpose of the inquiry was to discover the relationship between
various types of scholars and the different types of sociopolitical
systems.[1]

GENERAL COMMENTS ON THE TYPOLOGY

I read your paper, I liked it very much and think that you should add one more
category, that is, the scholar who is involved with social change. (Mauro
Cappelletti, Stanford, Tape 4, Side A)

I liked the paper very much, I thought it was a good typology. The only comment
that I had about a particular category was that I thought that you perhaps underes-
timated the incidence of "Instrumental" scholars in the West. In the West there
are also plenty of people who devote their energy to what you might call, you
know, sort of "political" opportunistic forms of trying to impress sources of
grants and funds. And presumably this will become even more true as research
money increasingly comes from corporations, from the private sector of one kind
or another. (Robert Gordon, Stanford, Tape 4, Side B)

Well, I think you've covered the field rather well. I would have a few minor
comments. For example, your item number five, "disenchanted scholars," I don't
see substantial numbers of those in sciences. I don't encounter that kind of person
in science. . . . Established scholars criticize each other, and a disenchanted
scholar isn't likely to be able to add anything new. It's the best scholars who can
best criticize, rather than the ones who have failed. . . . I am thinking of the kind
of person who is a good scientist in the sense that he knows a lot, and is interested
in and skillful at talking to the public and explaining to the public what science is
about, and inspiring the public in terms of what is being found out and what

science is. I think those people have an important function. . . . I guess Carl Sagan, for example, in this country, would be an example of that type of scholar, a respectable scientist in his own right, but his real skill is in interpreting science to the public and expressing it in interesting ways, and so on. (Charles Townes, Berkeley, Nobel prize winner–Physics, Tape 12, Side A)

I think it's a very comprehensive treatment, and I think it's well conceptualized in terms of capturing some key distinctions between types. There are . . . three categories that I am not sure are captured by this. One is what I call the "entrepreneur," or "consultant" type. These are people whose primary motivation is to make money for themselves, selling whatever competence, expertise that they have to the highest bidder. You see them flying around to workshops and conferences, and anywhere where they can get an honorarium, flogging their wares. They're usually very facile with words, excellent speakers, dynamic performers; they're salespersons and they are selling the expertise that they have, and their primary motivation is if they have God knows how many "frequent flyer" points. They must very seldom see their students, very seldom be at home on their campuses, because they're out making money on the side in an entrepreneurial sense, in a consultative role. . . . A second one that I have encountered that may well fit in here some place too is what I call "sympathizers" or "pastoral caregivers." And these are the people who see as their primary objective providing personal and psychological support to their students and their colleagues. They don't like to see people hurt, they don't like to see people's ideas dashed, they don't like to see people put down, they don't like the rough-and-tumble of academic debate, they're there to smooth things over, to make people feel better, to sympathize, to give pastoral care. And as a result they may save some psyches, but they may retard the development, the advancement of a discipline. The last one that comes to my mind — and again these are all people that I have met and noticed, quite distinctive types, besides some that you've listed, in applied social science fields, the "godfather" or "patron" type. This is the person who gathers around — it's typically a male; it doesn't need to be, but it's typically a male — gathers around himself a small cohort of graduate students in his field and nurtures them through their programs, carefully gets them placed in significant beginning positions and watches their development, and in a way is building up a family, like a godfather does. He'll co-author articles with them; he has a network of his own people, spread nationally, or sometimes internationally, and they owe him something. (Robin Farquhar, Carleton University, Tape 17, Side A)

When I review grant applications, you can tell immediately . . . all of these personalities you're talking about appear in the grant applications, so even when they're graduate students, you can see the "operators" and the "innovators," and the "moral imperative" people, and so on and so forth. And out of maybe a hundred, you'll find one that's driven by curiosity. Pure curiosity. And it seems to me that they're important. . . because they are rare. And they are often not in sync with their time. That is, they are not the "stylistic" people, they are people that want to know the answer to it. Or they want to understand it, or discover something. And many times they aren't innovators, but it's their curiosity that's driving them. (Laura Nader, Berkeley, Tape 13, Side A)

The one thought, I don't know where it fits, it's the role of scholars as mentors; it's related to the gatekeeping function. It seems to me that there are some scholars who serve a very valuable role as critics, as advisers, as telling/helping people, other scholars, either younger people or colleagues or even older, reshape their research. They spend a lot of time reading other people's work, attending seminars, making suggestions, and things like that. And sometimes, they're people who never publish very much who acquire a very strong reputation and are very valued in the research community for that job. (Robert Kagan, Berkeley, director of the Center for the Study of Law and Society, Tape 8, Side A)

Sometimes I feel as though I have — half of my life is devoted to evaluating other people; not just students, but people who send in papers for journals, or papers for — project proposals for research, and they say, "Well, do you think this is any good?" "You don't think this is any good?" And then, so the gatekeeper is . . . overlaps very much with academic roles, in this country, anyway; I dare say it may be more general, as well. (Neil Smelser, Stanford, director of the Center for Advanced Study in the Behavioral Study, Stanford, Tape 12, Side B)

The people — the gatekeepers, I mean. I think that's an important, important observation for the two reasons you stated. One, that they provide a critical sense, but the gatekeepers can be enormously destructive . . . in not allowing newness, or being afraid of anything new, new ideas. (Laura Nader, Berkeley, Tape 13, Side A)

Clearly Nobel Prize winners fall in the category of innovative scientists, but they represent only a small proportion. Gilbert N. Lewis and Enrico Fermi were the most innovative scholars I have known. Although he deserved to, Gilbert N. Lewis never won a Nobel prize. (Glenn T. Seaborg, Berkeley, Nobel Prize winner–Chemistry, Tape 13, Side A)

Yes, and of course, this kind of what you call "bloc," "clique behavior," is not limited to themes like "Francophones vs. Anglophone." It occurs also, especially, in the leading American universities. It's a division between those who are to some degree Marxist in their thinking, and those who are, or think of themselves, as defending more a conception which is thought of, or often labeled as, "the right." The same left-right distinction exists, and it becomes a basis for focusing and organizing people that often overrules other considerations of the kind that I think should be the ones that should be primary. And, to carry this one step further, although here perhaps it is, I mean, I consider that illegitimate as a basis for judgment. But to carry it one step further, there's a kind of division I'm not sure is illegitimate, as a basis for this kind of block behavior. Because people also become committed to, and believe in, either a certain style of work or in the adequacy or inadequacy of a certain theory or set of theories which are not chosen on political grounds. And when this happens, scholars tend to organize themselves as blocks, very frequently. To advance, not an ideological goal, in the sense of a political left-right kind of goal, but to advance one line or style of work as compared to another. Now, I would say, if I may, that this kind of dynamic is not reflected in your model. (Alex Inkeles, Tape 1, Side A)

I found myself stimulated, I found myself putting names of people that I know in each category . . . and I have a number of . . . you mentioned they are overlapping, I think that if you are talking about, for example, the three categories you put in there, the "innovators," "additive," and "synthetic builders," they get mixed up with one another, especially the "synthetic" and "additive" will mesh into one another, they're not pure types, and sometimes a person ends up synthesizing something when he thinks he's just carrying out some "building" or "additive" work. Secondly, I think you'll find that if you have any given individual, you will find a mixture; that any individual scholar will often prove to be a mixture of types, so that you think that exhausts that person. I also think that while you mention that the last four were especially associated with [a] totalitarian type of society, I would, and I certainly would find the operator and the instrumentalist to be there. (Neil Smelser, Stanford, Tape 12, Side A)

I felt throughout this section that you were a little bit insulting to people who don't happen to be Einstein, or, you know, Sir Isaac Newton, but who are doing good, careful work; the work that Thomas Kuhn called "normal science." (Lawrence Friedman, Tape 2, Side B)

I would move, if it was my project, I would move the importance of the social system, social circumstances to the very beginning and highlight, at least, your main hypothesis as to what possible institutional and cultural context might generate particular types. (Eva Morawska, University of Pennsylvania, Tape 5, Side B)

It is well-known that the conformist attitudes and behaviors that seem to be popular at any given moment often serve as a formula to gain scholarly recognition. In short, this conformist ideology may work as a self-promotion technique: because proving one's point in the social sciences is difficult, the conformist strategy often is used as a way to make oneself visible in the crowded market of academia.

However, there are what can be regarded as "collective" strategies, as opposed to individual techniques of self-promotion. Indeed, the task of individual self-promotion is a "private" matter, and only the most creative and well-established scholars are willing to admit to using it.

Yeah. I guess. I ask the question of myself many times [laughs]. I don't know. I think the first ten years of my career, I was able to do that to some extent. Then after that I found it more and more hard to do, although I suppose I did anyway, so I don't know. One hears that you have to self-promote, and I think now, I think now that one has to self-promote. (David Matza, Berkeley, Tape 11, Side A)

The collective strategy is usually more effective; it gives a cohort of scholars, however mediocre, an opportunity to attack others in the name of high ideas while quite shrewdly taking care of their own practical interests.

The following are comments on the category of scholars who voice the prevailing mood in the scientific community.

This whole group of people who were in their early years, Marxists who went in different directions but never gave up the moral and political preoccupations. I would put Daniel Bell in that category, I would put [Martin] Lipset in that category, I would put [Philip] Selznick in that category, Alvin Gouldner was in that category, C. Wright Mills was in that category. (Neil Smelser, Stanford, Tape 12, Side B)

There is no way to tell whether or not it [the typology] talks about all of the possible types of scholars. Checking that out would be to assemble lists of people who are scholars and try and see whether they fit into the typology. . . . The most useful thing to do would be to use these categories to help you think about different kinds of contribution to knowledge. (Sheldon Messinger, Berkeley, Tape 9, Side B)

For me typologies are only of modest interest, they are botany, and very important descriptive activities, but I kept wanting to know, what is the process, what are the assumptions that underlie a process that produces ideas that subsequently come to be viewed as good ideas? (James March, Stanford, Tape 3, Side B)

A scholar customarily is perceived as an individual who is equipped to undertake specialized research and to summarize his or her findings in a synthetic way. There are, however, opportunities to advance and generalize scientific conclusions.

Sometimes, there are some fields that have progressed without any single "spectacular" scholar in your sense. Rather there are a bunch of creative scholars, each one building a little more on the work of others. Suddenly, ten years later, you realize that in fact there is considerable change, people are thinking differently, without there being any one paper or book that has made the difference. It's just a lot of cumulative effort. (Kenneth Arrow, Stanford, Nobel Prize winner–Economics, Tape 7, Side A)

Thus, in the United States, the style of abstract scholarly work apparently is connected not with an individualistic but with a teamlike style of work. However:

There are many scholars (I include most of my colleagues here at Stanford) who are working on problems on their own. Nobody tells them what answers to come up with. They're not necessarily organizing or building institutions. They are not operating on behalf of the government, so they are not "instrumental" in your sense. (Kenneth Arrow, Stanford, Tape 7, Side A)

This point of view is not isolated:

I think that one thing that has happened in the social sciences is that a lot of activities have moved us in the direction of this model of what I call "normal" science. It may not be as exciting as having one outstanding figure whom everybody pays attention to, but that doesn't mean that you don't have the growth of knowledge, that there isn't actually cumulative, and definite advance made in the answers that we can give to given questions. (Alex Inkeles, Stanford, Tape 1, Side A)

It also was pointed out that the distinguished types of scholars are not clear-cut categories. These categories evidently overlap. Some considered the original model to be rather static and not sufficiently dynamic:

I suggested not "facades," but facets. A facet is a face, a side, or different phase of development, or different roles. And I was suggesting these really as substitutes for the word "type." Now, it may be that you can consider if you find this interesting, you may consider this further embellishment of one of your types. My first reaction to your use of the word "type" was somewhat negative. I found the material very interesting, and the negative reaction subsided. (Preston Cutler, Stanford, former deputy director of the Center for Advanced Study in the Behavioral Study, Stanford, Tape 2, Side B)

ON INNOVATION

Creativity appeals to all thinking individuals. As Henry Taube puts it, "Creativity, the quality that by virtue of the originality and significance of certain endeavors, sets them apart from the ordinary, is a matter of interest to every thinking person" (1994, Stanford, Nobel Prize winner–Chemistry, written statement).

Creativity is a central concept for any person who deals with scientific matters. Innovativeness is a primary feature of any scientist who intends to put an individual mark on the area in which he or she is engaged. However, creativity in its pure form rarely appears.

Independently of the circumstances, creative people will be creative. (John Merryman, Stanford, Tape 5, Side A)

Our writing is a process of continual maturation. You might say it that way. (Robert Post, Berkeley, Tape 10, Side B)

When asked what percentage of scholars are truly innovative: "Not too many." (Jerome Skolnick, Berkeley, Tape 8, Side A)

I have no words for it. I cannot explain it exactly, but I do think that the creative mind is captured by the idea. It is not something that you do, it is something that happens to you. It captures you, and you cooperate with it or you don't; you are resistant or whatever. It can be, I suspect very painful. It can screw up a career, because you get caught up in some idea that really captures you, and there you go. But it is also fun. You would be crazy to be resistant. (John Coons, Berkeley, Tape 9, Side A)

I think it's a small percentage. Ten percent at the most. (Mauro Cappelletti, Stanford, Tape 4, Side A)

Less than one percent. Very tiny. I think it's very important to note, about "innovators," that whether you recognize a person as an "innovator" has to do with the milieu within which they are innovating. (Laura Nader, Berkeley, Tape 13, Side A)

In England . . . Britain, currently, a tiny proportion. Two percent, only. Very small. Innovators of either kind, in my subject. (Michael Burrage, London School of Economics, Tape 11, Side A)

I think you have to tell me what "creative" means. My impression is that it is a very small percentage. At least, there's a lot of intelligent people in the academy, but my impression is that the academy does not really encourage that much, at least in certain fields, maybe, creativity is less encouraged in other fields. (Guy Benveniste, Berkeley, Tape 8, Side B)

[An innovator] is a person [who] in his inner being lives for ideas and for the accumulation and extension of ideas. (Martin Trow, Berkeley, Tape 10, Side A)

Well, in the strongest sense of that term ["innovator"], I am not sure that I can identify any in social science. (Sheldon Messinger, Berkeley, Tape 9, Side B)

The conditions that bring out people's creativity can of course vary. But given that a person has the opportunity to think and to have access to the necessary materials and has access to an audience of peers, of people who are interested, and who are qualified to understand and judge the work, then I don't think it makes any difference whether it is art, history, or theoretical physics, or law. (John Merryman, Stanford, Tape 5, Side A)

After their appearance and without additional tests, it is not easy to evaluate which ideas are original and creative and which are only crazy, which ideas are beneficial or harmful for society, or which are gratifying in the short or long term.

Truly innovative ideas come from the process that is not much different from the process that produces crazy ideas; absolutely useless ideas. If you try to invent a process that produces a higher fraction of innovative ideas, you extinguish fractions of crazy ideas that are good. You can increase the fraction of crazy ideas, or you can decrease the fraction of crazy ideas. When you increase the fraction of crazy ideas, you increase the number of innovators and you increase the number of disasters. . . . It is almost impossible to get a process that can distinguish good, original ideas from bad, original ideas until after the fact. So, anytime you try to make the flow of ideas better, you make it less creative. You've molded more, in the direction of received knowledge. Anytime you make it more creative, you make it worse. (James March, Stanford, Tape 3, Side B)

One problem that cropped up repeatedly during the interviews was whether scientific ingenuity is connected with a more highly developed aesthetic sense.

This is a very general and broad question. I would say, sure, that anybody who has the capacity, even in the social sciences or the natural sciences, to learn and implement the lessons of aesthetic creativity, will probably produce something that is more interesting. (Martin Jay, Berkeley, Tape 16, Side A)

So, I tend to think there's a lot of similarities between an artist and creative scientist. I don't think that there's that much difference between the two processes. What happens, it seems to me, is that the American academic training is much more narrow, focused, and therefore, for a typical American professor, art is completely unknown, eating is unknown, making love is unknown to some extent. (Guy Benveniste, Berkeley, Tape 8, Side B)

Now, to do something that's worthwhile, you have to develop a scientific taste, it's really an aesthetic judgment. Because you have to balance what's possible with what's worthwhile, what's worth doing. (Arthur Schawlow, Stanford, Nobel Prize winner–Physics, Tape 7, Side A)

A certain minimum [of artistic dimension] would be desirable, I think, for a variety of reasons. One, because it would tend to stimulate one's sense of proportion to some extent. It also would be desirable, because it would create more of a link from the abstract and obscure science to a more philosophical appreciation of one's own research. (Gregory Grossman, Berkeley, Tape 14, Side B)

Art and science, they are different approaches to the same point. (Walter Zawojski, Stanford, Tape 6, Side A)

U.S. VERSUS NON-U.S. SCHOLARS

One reason why the research on scholars was conducted at Stanford and Berkeley was that these two universities undoubtedly belong to the U.S. academic elite. Not only are their scientific standards among the highest in the country, but also scholars from these universities tend to have wide experience compared with scholars from other cultures. Because this study was not financially supported, it was more practical to choose one region with both a high scholarly reputation and a lot of international scholarly connections than to travel to various centers in Europe. Stanford and Berkeley allowed me to observe academia from one spot.

Well, I think American university people are more technicians than they are scholars, and to my mind. In this era, our universities are encouraging the production of and reward of technicians-scholars, if you want to call them scholars. (Laura Nader, Berkeley, Tape 13, Side A)

Well, I think they're quite comparable. I think scholarship is a worldwide characteristic. Of course, England, Germany, France; these countries are in good contact, have been for a long time, and so, there's a lot of interchange, and the standards are quite the same, I believe. . . . I would, however, make another comment on that [the fact that, in Poland, some scholars escaped from Marxism into formal sciences like logic or methodology]; I have seen in the Soviet Union, also effects of party pressure on intellectual people. And some people in the Soviet Union went into the physical sciences because they felt that was a way they could be freer from authority. The authorities don't know very much about physical sciences, so if you're outstanding in physical sciences, even if you don't agree with the party line, you could be accepted, well-paid, and have some freedom in the Soviet Union because the Soviet Union needed science, and these people, these very independent-minded people who object to the system, a number of them went into the sciences with that in mind, in part. They also went into the theoretical sciences because the Soviet Union did not have very good experimental apparatus. So, if you ask "what was the best of science in the Soviet Union," it was theoretical science — theoretical physical sciences. Some of the very brightest people, while they might have gone into that area anyhow, recognized that that was a good area to work in, because they would have some independence from authority. (Charles Townes, Berkeley, Tape 12, Side A)

I've always thought that the tendency for the European system to rely on long-term occupancy of "chairs" or positions, and, lower level of mobility from one institution to another, partially because of the structure, partially because of the diminished market incentives for scholars, in comparison to the United States, I've always thought, and in fact, the Europeans I talked to agree with me on this, that it's easier to become inactive in Europe, as a scholar, because you occupy a position, there's no particular advantage to moving somewhere else, there's no continuous reassessment, I mean, the one thing that makes for the American, for the dynamics of American scholarship is that the person is never regarded as ever having arrived anywhere. It's always a kind of continuous, a reassessment of an individual and what they've done recently. (Neil Smelser, Stanford, Tape 12, Side B)

I mean, better educated, first of all. I think that almost all the European countries, including the Eastern bloc, my impression is that, maybe there are fewer people who become professors, maybe it's more selective, but that there is stronger general philosophical background, more, I would say that if you applied this to American and European scholars, the Europeans would be more towards the [inaudible], you'd get a lot of all of the [inaudible]. But generally speaking, I think that, now again, maybe a selection, that people who travel, and who one meets, tend to be [preselected], I mean, we tend to get very interesting people visiting in Berkeley. (David Matza, Berkeley, Tape 11, Side B)

Martin Jay, a historian who, in some way, created the Frankfurt School,[2] presents the U.S. scholarly system in a synthetic way:

I think the American system is enormously varied. As you know, it's the biggest university system by far in the world, there are many types of universities, they are equal if not superior to any, and there are others that are rather mediocre. So, I think it's difficult to say there's one standard. But I think at the very top, American academic life is incomparably rigorous, serious, and well policed. In other words there is a public process of evaluation, which is a fairly good one. There is also, in the United States, a certain premium placed on constant evaluation through essentially anonymous means. That is to say, people are promoted by committees that are not disclosed, there's, I think that the process produces high quality work. And the absorption of European ideas that I mentioned before, has happened, I think, with a great deal of sophistication and success, not always and not in every context, but, as a result, there is in the United States, now, I think, a worldwide intellectual life in the universities. Now, France and Germany, I think the French system, is a little bit less easy to make sense of. There's a great deal of creativity in France, at least in the last 30 or 40 years, a lot of ideas which we have found stimulating. But there is also a great tolerance for somewhat idiosyncratic and sloppy talk, in which people are not asked to explain more clearly their ideas, there is a certain license for a kind of writing that is more poetic than scholarly, there is less serious evaluation of manuscripts. I think there isn't a process of judging manuscripts that's quite as severe as it is in the United States. Editors don't play as important a role in telling people they should make their ideas more explicit and clearer. So as a result, the French system often produces work that is very difficult to understand. There's a lot of creativity but also a lot of sloppiness. I'm always impressed by the quality of intellectual production when I'm in Germany. And I find there's a lot of interesting back-and-forth between the German and the American intellectual scenes these days, with a lot of Germans coming to the United States, Germans speak English. (Martin Jay, Berkeley, Tape 16, Side B)

HORIZONTAL OR HIERARCHICAL STRUCTURE OF THE ORGANIZATION OF SCIENCE

Listening to U.S. scholars on non-U.S. scholars, one finds a strong undertone of support for the values of a horizontal rather than hierarchical structure in scientific work. The traditional German or French (also Austrian, Polish, Russian, and other) scientific structures have been built on the principle of a "leading brain" occupying a chair and very closely directing and supervising all scholarly undertakings within his or her domain. The U.S. perception of an academic career is the opposite of this; it is basically and endemically "democratic." Because everyone is regarded as his or her own boss, the image of "truth" serves as the highest criterion for determining whether or not potential scholars should devote themselves to the profession. U.S. academics are strongly convinced that a democratic structure is not only the best but also the only acceptable one.

The system of having a chair and everybody else sort of clustering around the chair, to me, doesn't seem very useful. It seems to me to create divisions; to reinforce divisions that already exist. I know from our earlier conversation, that you think one can learn a lot from senior professors, and that the chair system, in some sense, facilitates that. (Sheldon Messinger, Berkeley, Tape 9, Side B)

A professor of European background, although she did not say directly whether she supported the European system, was fascinated by the European manner of cultivating the social sciences and searching for truth:

I don't know if you intend to, or perhaps already did interview scholars in Europe, but the person who should have things to say on this topic, because he has written a lot on related issues, is Pierre Bourdieu in Paris. Who, by the way, has a court of not only assistants, but a whole court of followers. I guess hmmm . . . what I missed when I came, for the first few years, is that this institution of European chairs creates a community of scholars with a leader who stimulates younger people to grow. Grow in the direction and at the pace that they would not have grown otherwise. (Eva Morawska, University of Pennsylvania, Tape 5, Side B)

Well, what I associate with Lazarsfeld was his interest in setting up a "super graduate training institution." He wanted to have his center become a training institution. Not a self-educating institution. He wanted to have senior fellows, and he wanted to have junior fellows who sat at the feet of the senior fellows. As a matter of fact during his fellowship here, there were several people whom he had sponsored for a fellowship, but as soon as these people learned that they were going to be treated just as well as anybody else, they abandoned him, and he was very much upset about that. To my thinking, he represented an attempt to transfer the European style department with a single head, who is really the "Master" of the department into America. (Preston Cutler, Stanford, Tape 2, Side B)

I think the American system, where the young faculty member can aspire to the level of the older faculty members on the basis of his or her accomplishments without any restrictions as to the number, is better. (Glenn T. Seaborg, Berkeley, Tape 13, Side A)

I'm not sure that one needs an intensely hierarchical system of academic organization in order to get the benefits of that kind of collegial interchange. That's the reservation I have about it. Also, if the holder of the chair is not a good creative person, but rather, an authoritarian and reactionary one, he can just hold everybody else back, and will in fact be challenged and threatened. . . . Well, you would be a better judge of it than I, I never had to work in such a system, and I'm actually grateful for it because I have terrible problems with authority. (Robert Gordon, Stanford, Tape 4, Side B)

This thing . . . works well if the professor is a great man, and then he can do a lot, because he has these assistants to help him. And he doesn't have to worry about getting funding for his work, it's all provided with the chair. On the other hand, all too often, the professor has just gotten his chair by being around a long time, and really is not a good leader, and he's just sort of holding back a lot of people under him. So it can work one way or the other. (Arthur Schawlow, Stanford, Tape 7, Side A)

Well, I think the American style is the one I know from personal experience and have found comfortable. The European style always seems to be very restrictive, in the sense that it gives too much power to one person, who may exercise it wisely but often does not, and creates a tremendous sense of hierarchical resentment, anxiety, jealousy, all the things that occur when people fail to reach that pinnacle. So, my experience of the European system is that it often prevents people from achieving their full potential, whereas in the United States, institutionally, everybody basically can rise to the top. (Martin Jay, Berkeley, Tape 16, Side A)

I think a collegial system is much better. It isn't that it's perfect, or that a hierarchical system doesn't have some advantages. But I think, overall, a collegial system is much better. (Charles Townes, Berkeley, Tape 12, Side A)

Here, people come from [places] like Georgia, they spend five years of graduate work here, then go off to Texas, and . . . even if I were "Herr Professor," I couldn't keep them here, there is no way to keep them, because you have to support them in some way. But I had a big project, on disputing process, and it went on for something like ten years, and when I look back on it, I don't see it as my most creative period at all. In terms of what I got from the students or what I gave to the students. And I don't consider that an enormous success, I think it was okay . . . I think what's happened since, with students attacking, not the same problem in depth, but different problems related to social and cultural control, that now it's beginning in reality — to go some place. Now, I would really love to have a cadre of students, or colleagues, working with me on these problems, because they're very interesting, and it's at a take-off point. (Laura Nader, Berkeley, Tape 13, Side A)

A sociologist comments about the genesis of the horizontal and hierarchical orientations:

The stereotype is that European scholars, some of them, have a broad familiarity with the national culture. As intellectuals, they've read novels etc., and they have a kind of broad knowledge of poetry and music etc. We have a system of mass education, so you have many scholars who come up from homes where there are no members of that essentially high bourgeois culture from early childhood. Before the war, you could not become a scholar if you didn't come from the upper middle class, because you didn't have the money to go on. They all came from privileged homes. In this country, you have a lot of people coming up from very modest working and lower class homes, where they only discovered culture when they were in university. It's a little late, and so they don't have the knowledge of the classics, the Greek and Roman classics; they never studied Greek and Latin. It is a different recruitment path. (Martin Trow, Berkeley, Tape 19, Side A)

With respect to continuous seminars, they sometimes take place, but as the exception, not the rule:

Well, they had at the laboratory, there was a physicist, who, every Tuesday or every Wednesday, I don't know what day, he had a big house and he was a Nobel laureate, and he had a running seminar. For years! Maybe thirty years! And people were invited to attend, and people were invited to give a talk, and nobody knew who was going to give the talk, and it just was continuous. And it was considered a very stimulating — Alvarez! — very stimulating. (Laura Nader, Berkeley, Tape 13, Side B)

Not only are the horizontal or vertical styles of science making connection with the administrative structure of U.S. universities and research centers, but they also are related to the U.S. style of life:

But the European academics have a different lifestyle. They go home often in the afternoon, they work in their offices at home, and so on. It is very unusual to find that around the American law school. Most of us are here most of the time. Further, the academics are more exploited in Europe, at least until they make their "habilitation," and the profs get away with it. (John Coons, Berkeley, Tape 9, Side A)

ON LOGIC IN SCIENTIFIC INQUIRY

Traditionally, European universities teach logic as an independent discipline — sometimes a subsidiary one, but always an important one. In totalitarian Poland, the discipline of logic was used by some law professors as an escape from Marxism. Those who were under heavy political pressure or who were ideologically opposed to Marxism developed an idea that logic and methodology were neglected subjects and produced several texts on them. They then started to teach the logic and methodology of the social sciences in law schools. Students who at first disliked these subjects subsequently came to appreciate them.

Although teaching logic as an independent discipline (especially in law schools) may seem shocking to U.S. scholars, it is interesting to compare the attitudes toward logic and related matters in Poland and in the United States.

Yes, logic is a tool. It's a tool which befits a high order of grace. And to be able, for a species to be able to invent the logic, it would seem to me, presupposes [being a human being]. (David Matza, Berkeley, Tape 11, Side A)

Adam, the disgrace of our university system is that we don't teach anything. We get, supposedly, the creme de la creme, you know, these people who are graduates of elite institutions, and they don't know anything. They don't know logic; they don't know methodology, they don't know any history, they don't know any history. (Robert Gordon, Stanford, Tape 4, Side B)

No, we don't try to do things systematically. I think we feel more like Percy Bridgeman. He received a Nobel Prize in physics for his work on high pressures, experiments on putting metals and other matter under very high pressure, but he also wrote some on the philosophy of science. But he said the scientific method, insofar as it is a method, consists of nothing more than doing one's damnedest with one's mind, no holds barred. (Arthur Schawlow, Stanford, Tape 7, Side A)

Our courses and activities in logic in the Anglo-Saxon tradition, if you want to call it that, tend more to be in a systematic examination and application of rules and norms of actual operations of research, which is a type of logic, but not formal logic, or mathematical, in that sense of the term. It's a continuous examination of the logic of research procedure, which is what methodology usually refers to when we discuss it. (Neil Smelser, Stanford, Tape 12, Side A)

Thus, in the United States, logic is not systematically instilled in students but disseminated indirectly, mainly by implanting it into scholarly practice.

But I think the general approach to dealing with deficiencies in analytical rigour is a, what you might call, is to do it through doing. (Robert Kagan, Berkeley, Tape 8, Side A)

You do it [teach logic] in the ordinary course of events. (Marvin Calvin, Berkeley, Nobel Prize winner–Chemistry, Tape 11, Side A)

Logic tends to offer something that is, in a cognitive sense, dependable, reliable, constant. And, I think it's a good framework to have in mind. I could probably be persuaded that if we had a core curriculum that everyone was required to take, a common first-year experience, that logic ought to be a part of it. So, I am supportive of it. (Robin Farquhar, Carleton University, Tape 17, Side A)

[Podgórecki: "In Poland logic was regarded as important. But professors don't teach it in the U.S."] "Not as much as we should." When asked whether it should be taught more, he replied, "Yes." (Clark Kerr, former chancellor and president of the University of California, Tape 15, Side B)

ON SCHOLARS' NORMATIVE COMMITMENT

Few scholars are motivated by a normative commitment to build new scientific schools or to create new scientific institutions. Instead, they are provisional innovators; they create for others the conditions to be innovators; they tend to introduce certain types of normative order into social life, or they facilitate scientific work in a general manner. Usually, they are inspired by an imperative of public service concerning what ought to be done for a given society. They are inclined to understand knowledge as a catalyst of social change. Yet, they do not suggest values; they are practitioners who use science as an instrument of a designed social transformation.

They may be inherently more interested in practical activities than in theoretical inquiries, or they may sense that they are better at theoretical investigations. If so, it may be that a desire to realize social justice has prevailed over other considerations or that other factors have pushed them in this direction. In any case, their creative endeavors in practical spheres are noteworthy.

Frank Newman said that he had spent eight years with the California Constitution Revision Commission as the chairman of the drafting committee and a member of the executive committee. According to him, those who drafted that constitution performed their work *pro publico bono*. (Newman died in February 1996. The author was unable to obtain a permission to quote *verbatim* from his interview. A reference to his statement is based on the material contained in Tape 10, Side A). This attitude is significant because it exemplifies that particular stance that treats law as not only a proper instrument to implement social, political, and economic interests but also a symbol of social and political justice. It should be noted that such an attitude is disappearing.

Before turning to your schematic approach to it, could I give you some reactions about the categories [types of scholars] that I have used, which are pretty simplistic. I was once chancellor of the Berkeley campus and the president of the university. I dealt with faculty members in all fields. I looked at scholars in a very primitive way in categorizing them. The axes on which I put people, you have different axes which are more sophisticated than what I had, but just to show you where I come from . . . first . . . of what their orientation was. Whether it was more toward truth or toward beliefs . . . (in the sciences you wanted somebody in truth, when it got to somebody in the humanistic fields, you look more at beliefs and truths). The second one that I looked at, was whether I thought a person thought vertically; you know, in a single field from basic things to advanced knowledge or horizontally across fields. . . . The third way I tended to categorize people . . . whether they are concerned with the internal logic of thinking or . . . are related more toward reality. . . . You are asking me whom I regard as the highest quality people. Well, in my field of economics, the Swedes have been excellent. . . . I would put the Swedes first, and the English second. . . . In those who are oriented toward thinking in more broader, more philosophical terms, there have been some very good people in France, in Germany.

[Podgórecki: "I was in the U.S. for the first time in 1959. At the time all Polish scholars wanted to go to Berkeley. California is not sufficient explanation. So why?"] I was chancellor of Berkeley from 1952 to 1958, and I was president of the university from 1958 to 1967 and during that period of time, Berkeley got rated by surveys of department chairmen and scholars around the country as the best-balanced [and most] distinguished university in the U.S., which meant the best in the world. They made a study of twenty-nine fields, we didn't have one of them, anatomy, but we were in the top six in twenty-eight fields.

[Podgórecki: "What have you done to elevate this university to such a high position?"] I was the chancellor at the time, and we (when I say we I mean particularly the dean of Letters and Sciences, and to a lesser extent the dean of Engineering) selected one field at a time and we would give, for example, history in a certain year, instead of distributing new positions across the board, we'd get a new chairman, we'd give history ten new appointments saying in the next two years you can hire ten new people. In mathematics, which was good but small — it was a service department to engineering and science, which is now graded one of the best in the world — we doubled them in size almost over night. So, we tried to concentrate our resources department by department, and we'd pick out individual departments and concentrated our effort there. (Clark Kerr, Berkeley, Tape 15, Side B)

PROFESSIONALIZATION OF SCIENTIFIC INQUIRY

As various factors — technological change, the growing number of scholars, scholarly competition, the increasing role of demanding sponsors (who look for sciences that can be used *now*), and the political indoctrination of scholars — undermine the scholarly "ethos," the professionalization of academia is becoming more evident. Independent of these external factors, there are internal factors that, at least in the social sciences, encourage the process of professionalization and the tendency to treat the sciences as a source of fiscal gain. These factors are connected to a disillusionment with the social sciences and the aggravation of negative selection processes that are currently employed in academia.

One of the essential features of this burgeoning professionalization is the eagerness and ability to use both natural and social sciences as additional instruments of societal control.

I distinguish "Harmony Ideology" from "Harmony." I don't know about "integrity," but certainly there is such a thing as harmony and coercive harmony. In university it means that when Adam stands up to say something, somebody puts you down. Because, they will say, if you say too loudly, it will look like we don't get along with each other. And then Adam says, but that's what a university is about. It's about debate.

The "professionals" — what you call professionals — to me is a category that overlaps with "operators," because these are what I grade between 40 and 55, today, at Berkeley, full of careerists, who want to, it is very stylistic, and they usually kill history in order to be innovators. (Laura Nader, Berkeley, Tape 13, Side A)

Absolutely. I would agree with that. The relative balance has shifted a lot. In England, we have vast amounts of funded research, which is to do things like, it's like market research, we set up a new hospital, how contented are the people with this hospital? Does it satisfy the needs of the residents? How, university students — do they enjoy their experience? There are hundreds and hundreds and thousands of projects of this kind. And they employ sociologists. They, the people who run these things, earn more than professors would. Far more. (Michael Burrage, London School of Economics, Tape 11, Side A)

So far as I can remember from the old days, I think, there was a lot less careerism in academic life than there is [now] in the U.S. Also, there were simply fewer people that contributed actively to scholarship in any field, and that made possible more serious intellectual dialogue. It made possible greater continuity of work over generations. . . . [We now face] a general decline of intellectual seriousness; period. . . . It has been happening in the Western world since, one may say, since the middle of the nineteenth century with the collapse of German idealism. The Western intellectual world is just overwhelmed by what used to be called nihilism. (Philip Nonet, Berkeley, Tape 10, Side B)

[Podgórecki: "Does international recognition influence the prestige of a scholar?"] International influence, no. This school [Law School] in particular is extremely parochial. International reputation accounts for nothing. Fame, yes, if it's the right kind of fame. (Lawrence Friedman, Stanford, Tape 2, Side A)

Social science is [not] as exciting today as it was thirty years ago . . . there was more faith in the social sciences thirty or forty years ago . . . there was, alongside of that optimism, a good deal of financial support . . . a lot of social science [has] become stereotypical now. A lot of refereed articles are almost exercises in quantitative methodology . . . in my generation, a lot of very bright young people were moving into the social sciences. . . . The best students have not been going into the social sciences, as they did in the 1950s and 60s. (Jerome Skolnick, Berkeley, Tape 8, Side A)

When the scientific competition is too fierce and when the criteria of success are nonexistent or too vague, then a new element enters into the picture.

If the competition is to be the best, to be on the top, then the only way you can ever be first in a race is by gambling. You will never be the first-ranking anything, be it an entrepreneur, a bureaucratic scrambler and so on, by following a safe route, because someone else will gamble and be lucky and beat you. So the only big winners in that kind of world are gamblers. If you want to increase gamblers, you make the rewards for being first very high. (James March, Stanford, Tape 3, Side B)

So, is it correct to say that the lack of reliable criteria and the intrusion of many irrelevant factors in current academic life tend to change scientific activities in the humanities and in the social sciences into gambling? If so, then one may say that the professional orientation of U.S. scholars currently has the upper hand over any moral evaluation of scholars. Additionally, the moral past of a scholar is of minor relevance.

Well exactly, and I think, first of all in the U.S., there is the generosity of allowing people a new start. I think that this is the way in which the U.S. works; you may make mistakes and your history doesn't prevent you from having a new beginning. You may move to the West, or to a new city. This may be a historical amnesia and may be a mistake, but I think it carries over to the way in which we accept scholars whose backgrounds were tainted, especially by communism, which was never quite as negatively stigmatized in the U.S. as fascism. (Martin Jay, Berkeley, Tape 15, Side B)

CONCLUSIONS

This survey shows quite clearly that the scholarly collective as represented in this Californian sample seems to be highly stratified. Moreover, even at the best universities, scholars are less and less concerned with solving the basic cognitive question, "what is the truth." Increasingly, they approach the sciences as efficient tools for finding a secure, accessible, professionally appropriate niche inside the world of academia — as a marketable commodity. The determined quest for instant success that is so overt in the humanities and social sciences "poisons" the situation in the sciences as well.

One can only be surprised that so few people are inclined to analyze what is going on inside academia, to speculate where this expanding scholarly nihilism (which descends when empirical proof is not applicable and when moral backbone has disintegrated) is taking society.

6

Silhouettes

To be bold, be bold.

— Bell, letter, 1995

It is relatively easy to design a typology of *ideal* scholars that supposedly exist in reality, to show that these types are produced by various social systems or by the institutions operating within them and that specified types of scholars satisfy certain needs that inherently nurture the systems themselves. However, it is harder to demonstrate that these ideal scholarly models in fact describe reality, nor is it easy to demonstrate that the preceding types were, indeed, produced by social processes.

In order to test whether the theoretical models presented here actually fit reality, I shall make a radical change in my research strategy and approach the problem from the opposite angle: several real scholars, some of them dead, will be assessed to see whether they fit the categories designed through theoretical reflection. This empirical approach may show only that reality is more complicated than the theoretical approach suggests and that real scholars must be viewed from a multidimensional perspective that encompasses various political and moral points of view, including the scholar's own. Descriptions of real scholars of the sort presented below accentuate certain aspects of their scholarly life and guess at their motivations. Secondary features may be treated as primary, and primary characteristics may be relegated to secondary status.[1]

Despite the risks and limitations of the empirical approach, the task of scrutinizing the modern scholar in depth has to be completed. The number in parentheses indicates where the scholar falls on the scale of zero to ten within the arbitrarily accepted categories.[2]

THE META-WISE OR ESCAPIST SCHOLAR:
HAZARD ADAMS (2) (1926–)

The specific features that characterize the more concrete scholarly categories are often self-evident. Such is not the case with the meta-wise, or escapist, scholar.[3]

One might expect to find this category in a pathological typology of scholars, but that is not always the case. Sometimes, the opposite is correct: in certain countries, especially England, this category is widespread and even regarded as superior because its constituents are presumed to be able to see matters from the larger perspective necessary for the preparation of much-needed syntheses. Some meta-wise or escapist scholars who are serious about their work are, in fact, genuine. They have immersed themselves in their meta-attitude so deeply that they do not realize what they are doing. When such scholars involve themselves in something substantial, their interventions can be useful and illuminating.

Yet, the majority of escapist scholars enjoy the posture of superiority they have usurped without trying to give it substance. Had they been Newtons or Einsteins, one might have studied their writings in detail, but once deprived of their masterful pose, it is difficult to take them seriously as scholars. The following is a silhouette of this type of scholar.

Hazard Adams has written several books (not always published by the most reputable publishers), visited external universities, possibly resided at institutes of advanced studies, and has held, or holds, administrative positions, such as chairman, dean, even vice-president. In short, he is an experienced scholar.

He avoids speaking of substantive matters (perhaps he is unable to) and engages, instead, in verbal acrobatics. His specialty is metalanguage, though he does not use the language of his discipline nor does he deal with the matter at hand; he does not state or negate anything in any particular area. He takes a higher stand by suggesting a proper direction for "our" discussion, indicating what is missing in our investigation(s), stating what should be done, and explaining why we have not yet achieved tangible results and what we have to do to obtain them. He is zealous in establishing new rules, new principles, and new recommendations, though they need not coincide with his personal "laws." Noncommittal, he is a master. When pressed by others or by circumstances, he escapes into wit or double entendre.

Emptiness secures his invulnerability. One of his books begins as follows: "Twelve years have passed since this book was first published. It would be, I think, a mistake to attempt minor revisions. Thus, I have let the text stand exactly as it was in 1976, with regret for anachronisms like "women's libber" (since happily replaced by "feminists") and for the somewhat dated types described in Chapter 6. My principles and anti-nomies, however, seem to stand up fairly well, and the impulse in years intervening between 1976 and the present has been but to add to them" (Adams 1988: vii).

THE INSTRUMENTAL-NARCISSIST SCHOLAR: PIERRE BOURDIEU (3)

Anatole France once composed an outstanding limerick about the title of a book he was asked to review. When politely asked about the book itself, he replied, "That's all that I can say about the volume." But for a desire to know what is behind the title *Homo Academicus* (Bourdieu 1988) and to find information about different types of scholars, I would never have come across *An Invitation to Reflexive Sociology* (Bourdieu and Wacquant 1992), because I am not particularly interested in Algerian anthropology. What an illuminating experience! How strange to encounter a grown man such bombast in. Bourdieu charms U.S. professors on sabbatical, he has his own kind of wit, and he possesses an excellent memory; he is evidently a sui generis man of erudition who takes himself very seriously. In the words of Si-tien, "There is only one way to reveal a superior man, that is to discover if he knows how to escape from serious-ness into trivia, and if he knows how to slip from froth into sincerity" (Podgórecki, unpublished).

The authors of *An Invitation to Reflexive Sociology* evidently do not know that "praxeology" (p. xvi) is a discipline created by the Polish philosopher Tadeusz Kotarbinski (1886–1981), nor do they seem to be aware that the Research Committee of the International Sociological Association has studied social praxeology since 1973 under the name of "social engineering" or "sociotechnics."

Look at some examples of the self-promoting, narcissistic statements presented in *An Invitation to Reflexive Sociology*:

It is true that *Homo Academicus* is a book that I kept for a very long time in my files because I feared that it would slip away from me upon publication and that it would be read in a manner opposite to its deep intent, namely as a pamphlet or as an instrument of self-flagellation. (Bourdieu and Wacquant 1992: 62)

I wrote a considerable number of pages which could earn me a *succes de scandale* for being slightly polemical and caustic. (65)

So in order to bring this study to a successful issue and to publish it, I had to discover the deep truth of this world, namely, that everybody in it struggles to do what the sociologist is tempted to do. I had to objectivize this temptation and, more precisely, to objectivize the form that it could take at a certain time in the sociologist Pierre Bourdieu. (65)

One can and must read *Homo Academicus* as a program of research on *any* academic field. In fact, by means of a mere mental experimentation, the American (Japanese, Brazilian, etc.) reader can do the work of transposition and discover, through homological reasoning, a good number of things about his or her own professional universe. (75)

Participant objectivization [What I have called *participant objectivization* (and which is not to be mistaken for participant observation) is no doubt the most difficult exercise of all (p. 253)], arguably the highest form of the sociological art, is realizable only to the extent that it is predicated on as complete as possible an objectivization of the interest to objectivize inscribed in the fact of participating, as well as on bracketing of this interest of the representations it sustains. (260)

Bourdieu also says, opening his seminar: "The most efficient way of wiping out errors, as well as the terrors that are often times at their root, is to be able to laugh about them together, which, as you will soon discover, will happen quite often" (Bourdieu and Wacquant 1992: 219).

If this is not enough and the reader wants to know more about Bourdieu, he should read the coauthor's appendix, "How to Read Bourdieu" (Bourdieu and Wacquant 1992: 261–64). Bourdieu does not reciprocate by informing the reader how to read Wacquant. However, it would be unjust not to grant Bourdieu some achievements. Putting together several connotations and intuitions, he introduces four meanings of "capital." Simplifying his elaborated scheme, one can present them as political capital (faculties that enable someone to operate in power elite[s]), material capital (access to financial and substantial property), cultural capital (the attributes of learning, breeding, cultivation, and so on), and social capital (a body of connections that enhance social life and facilitate access to the centers of power).

THE SEMI-INSTRUMENTAL SCHOLAR:
MARTIN HEIDEGGER (9) (1889–1976)

Instrumental scholars differ in many respects. Some of them are shaped only by their own hidden agendas. They give what is expected to the worldly authorities in order to gain space for intellectual maneuvers.

Heidegger, a Nazi collaborator, represented a particular type of instrumental scholar. His instrumentalism was based on the risky equation, "Give to Caesar what is his, and what is godly to God." He, thus, paid his dues to the National Socialist Party until 1945 and sustained his political activities as rector of Heidelberg University beyond his resignation from the rectorate. He maintained contact with Eugene Fisher, to whom he dedicated one of his books.[4] How far he was able to go may be shown in this excerpt from an interview with him,

S[piegel]: But we must — and this will be the end of this miserable quoting — still mention one more remark, one which we cannot imagine that you would still subscribe to today. You said in the fall of 1933, "Do not let doctrines and ideas be the rules of your Being. The Fuhrer himself and he alone *is* the present and future German reality and its rule.

H[eidegger]: These sentences are not found in the rectorial address, but only in the local *Freiburg Students Newspaper*, at the beginning of the 1933–34 winter semester. When I took over the rectorship it was clear to me that I would not see it through without some compromises. Even by 1934 I no longer said such things. (Wolin 1993: 96)

Heidegger also did not hesitate to write letters of denunciation[5] to Nazi authorities[6] while he continued to develop his ideas and print his books.

Upon phenomenologically entering his psyche, one would probably witness a calculation roughly as follows: "I'll pay the moral price for my own immunity in order to buy the chance to create freely." Evidently, he believed that his ideas had eternal value and, thus, decided to pay the current price for their development. In doing so, he avoided in his philosophical writings any concrete reference to existing political reality — therefore, his persistent vision that world technological advances were creating a growing monster and his subsequent condemnation of technological growth. Later, "Heidegger was satisfied to confess that his involvement with Nazism was 'a big blunder.' That was nicely put" (Ferry and Renaut 1990: 110). Apparently, he considered himself to be a neutral observer, not an involved intellectual, who was looking for consistency in his ideas and activities.

In her penetrating study of the relationship between Hannah Arendt (one of the most prominent Jewish critics of totalitarianism) and Martin Heidegger (less prominent, but, nevertheless, one of the builders of German totalitarianism), Elzbieta Ettinger said, "At twenty-two Arendt was no match for the 'fox,' as she called him later." Referring to one of Arendt's letters, she said also that "Heidegger 'lies notoriously always, and everywhere, and whenever he can'" (Ettinger 1995: 27–28). According to Ettinger, Arendt remained under Heidegger's influence and authority to the end of her life.

A SEMI-INSTRUMENTAL SCHOLAR: LESZEK KOLAKOWSKI (2) (1926–)

Totalitarian and posttotalitarian regimes are breeding grounds for clever instrumentalists. These individuals are good at derivations and skillful at hiding their own motives. They rarely, if ever, reveal their own political "development" (breeding factors). Thus, the best way to understand their convictions is to observe their behavior and confront them with their own explanations of it.

These scholars usually pretend that they are instrumental not for themselves but for a dogma of a higher order.[7] They consciously confuse their own real motives with ideas they have produced for external reasons. Leszek Kolakowski, former totalitarian collaborator with the Communist regime and later a member of the dissident movement, is a case in point. In 1989, the University of Chicago Press naively wrote on the cover of Kolakowski's original (perhaps only) book,[8] *Tales from the Kingdom Lailonia and the Key to Heaven* (1989), that he is a

Professor of the Committee on Social Thought and the Department of Philosophy at the University of Chicago and a fellow of All Souls College, Oxford University. The author of some twenty-five books, he is perhaps best known for his monumental three-volume *Mainstreans of Marxism*. Among his many honors, Professor Kolakowski was the 1986 Jefferson Lecturer, the highest honor conferred by the U.S. government for outstanding achievement in the humanities." (Flyer of the *Tales from the Kingdom . . .*). Poor Americans!

In March 1968, I was sitting in a Warsaw coffee shop with Andrzej Zajaczkowski, the real authority on Polish society and on the genesis of the Polish intelligentsia, when Kolakowski approached us and exclaimed, "Professors! You are sitting here quietly, but around you a revolution is going on!"[9] Zajaczkowski, without inviting him to sit down, replied, "Don't worry. Don't worry. We were able to domesticate you, so we will be able to domesticate them as well." Kolakowski's main treatise, *Main Currents of Marxism* (1978) is a repetition of his earlier lectures in Warsaw during the Stalinist period. In the Western edition, instead of placing a "yes" before each sentence, he blithely substitutes a "no."

During the Cold War, he belonged to the cadre of intelligent teachers with whom students used to play games. They would interrupt his lecture:[10] "Professor Kolakowski, that's interesting, what you were saying just now, but I have read an article by an American professor presenting reliable data that suggests the situation is the exact opposite." When Kolakowski responded that different sociopolitical situations lead to different conclusions, the student exclaimed, "I am sorry for this confusion, but now I remember correctly; the American professor said exactly what you said earlier."

When kicked out of the party, Kolakowski moved to the West.[11] There he was treated warmly, being regarded as an earnest scholar. It is one thing to concoct an "eminent scholar" from such material in order to score a visible political victory during the Cold War, but is it sensible to take such an individual seriously?

THE INNOVATIVE-SYSTEMATIZER AND SAGE SCHOLAR: ROBERT K. MERTON (9) (1910–)

The social sciences are in a peculiar situation: There is an overwhelming mass of interpretations, data, grand and "middle-range" theories, and paradigms that may effectively block the possibility of invention. Hence, the discipline now faces a new form of invention consisting of original systematization. In natural sciences, this predicament is healthier: scholars are constantly checked by data (and by others who check their way of testing data) and test themselves against their mistakes and pitfalls. Yet, at the same time, inventions are reduced to new combinations of old ways of thinking.

To be a genuine innovator in the social sciences today may seem impossible; there is too much information, too many conflicting ideas, too many constructions, too many theories, all cluttering the route to adequate synthesis. In the days of Auguste Comte, Herbert Spencer, Claude Henri de Saint Simon, even George Simmel, Emile Durkheim, Max Weber, and Leon Petrazycki, the store of hard reliable data was so meager and the restrictions imposed on and by it so loose that the spirit of new idea formation could fly wherever it liked (in that imprecise generalizations were not so easily disqualified).

Nonetheless, there are some remaining gaps where a synthesis of existing knowledge seems to be feasible. Merton was able to spot such generally neglected areas: the unanticipated consequences of purposive social action, nonconformist and deviant behavior, the workings of bureaucracy, mass persuasion, the social role of the intellectual, role-set and status-set, manifest and latent functions and dysfunctions, functional alternatives, and the social structure of science and its links with cognitive human structures. His findings are presented in *Social Theory and Social Structure* (Merton 1968).

A young Polish scholar, Piotr Sztompka, identifies four pervasive currents that form the basis of Merton's thought in *Robert K. Merton: An Intellectual Profile* (1986, Chap. 8). They are classicism ("balance, system and discipline"), cognitivism ("search for knowledge, enlightenment and understanding"), structuralism ("configurations, patterns and structures"), and irony ("discrepancies between intentions and consequences").

Merton is not only a builder in the theoretical sense. He also codesigned and contributed to the establishment of several scientific institutions, one of which is the Center for Advanced Study in the Behavioral Study, Stanford. The original objective of the center as conceived by Merton and his friend Paul Lazarsfeld was an innovative institution designed to group scholars at different levels of initiation; older scholars were to introduce the younger to the mysteries of science. However, the first director, Ralph W. Taylor, imposed a horizontal equality of fellows on the center's newly emerging social structure.

When asked by a prominent British sociologist for a recommendation after his stay at Columbia University, Merton told him, "I am going to give my best reference: 'When I was a student I used to go to the library at 8 am, and I was leaving it when it was about to be closed.'" Merton being an extraordinary scholar, is also a modest one. Summarizing his life, conceivably teasing a bit, he said, "For me, that review amounts to preview. It provides timely warning that any memoir of mine would surely display an even more humiliating amnesia. But perhaps, just perhaps, this slight remembrance of things past will serve in its stead" (Merton 1994: 20).

THE UNRECOGNIZED INNOVATOR-BUILDER:
MARIA OSSOWSKA (8) (1896–1974)

In humanities, only a few innovative scholars gain full recognition, and the conditions that enable them to do so are obscure. This could be because we are unable to see clearly what is close to us. In many cases, these omissions occur in situations where certain areas of reality are not fully investigated or where a loophole exists in a specific area.

Maria Ossowska was always puzzled by the question why the sociology of morals was not represented at international congresses of sociology. Originally, Ossowska wrote a book (1947) in which she analyzed the various meanings of the concept of "morality." She concluded that, because of diverse intuitions connected with this term, such a task was semantically impossible. Next, she published a study (1949) in which she tried to uncover the psychological components influencing moral attitudes and behaviors.

Her sociological approach comprised five consecutive inquiries: on bourgeois ethics (1956), on the theory of the sociology of morals (1969), on social determinants of moral ideas (1970a), on basic moral norms (1970b), and on the ethics of knights (1973). Eventually, she came to the conclusion that it was impossible to define morality as a concept that satisfied the intuitions of all. She resolved that a new cognitive category in the sociology of morals was needed. This was the concept of "ethos." It is similar to the anthropological concept of ethos in that it embraces a pattern of behavior shared by a given social group, but because moral attitudes and behaviors are perceived as individual, they differ from social ones. This allows the possibility of comparing a person's individual ethos with the ethos of his or her group. As far as the Polish situation under communism was concerned, Ossowska indicated that the value of personal "dignity," which played an important role as a legacy of the ethos of the Polish nobility, also was significant for the intelligentsia's style of life. Because communism attacked this value directly, Ossowska attempted, by developing this sociological subdiscipline, to show that the problem was not only theoretical.

When she was asked to arrange a Ford Foundation grant for an assistant professor who was working for her, Ossowska said, "Before the War [with the Soviets, 1921], when I was secretary of the Polish Philosophical Association, I used to sleep on a bench in the association office."

THE SHOCKING-SENSATIONALIST SCHOLAR: CAMILLE PAGLIA (2)

A newspaper at a high school in Vancouver characterizes Camille Paglia as "something of a renaissance woman, a Professor of Humanities at the University of Arts in Philadelphia, a verbose master of criticism, a truly imaginative post-modern intellectual. Her style is witty, engaging, full of humour and passion, and cuts to the point with awe-inspiring ferocity. At times her prose reads more like Ginsberg's . . . "Howl" than an academic essay, but this is precisely one of her strengths" (International Teletimes Authors 1994).

Martin Jay (who, as noted earlier, was able to move the Frankfurt School from obscurity to international prominence) wrote of Paglia, "'She walked into the room,' my informant sardonically remembered, 'wearing nothing but warpaint and a tampax'" (1993). This is precisely what she hoped to achieve: to present her own intellectual void as an original brainstorm.

Social systems based on the plurality of ideas, on the capitalist market, and on an orgy of mass media have their own potentially devastating but dynamic rules; those who know how to manipulate these rules can catapult an entity (including themselves) from nothingness into prominence. In this particular case, the substance, if any, of what Paglia has to say is not interesting of itself, but the style and mastery with which she manipulates fashion is spectacular. The case of Paglia is also of interest because it shows how the capitalist quest for a commodity that caters to popular demand, combined with the impact of mass media on everyday thinking, can generate a completely new, once-unimaginable type of scholar.

THE OVERTHROWN IDOL, SCHOLAR-SYSTEM-ATIZER: TALCOTT PARSONS (7) (1902–79)

There are subjective as well as objective reasons for labeling someone an innovative scholar. In the social sciences, the label is objectively applied, by and large, to a scholar who has produced a new combination of extant ideas. Subjectively, it is applied through peer consensus.

Talcott Parsons was born in 1902. During his lifetime, he reached great heights in his scholarly career, but he ended in almost complete obscurity. What lay behind this dramatic change in scholarly status?

Parsons attended Heidelberg University in Germany. He arrived five years after Max Weber's death and, thus, felt Weber's posthumous influence. Back on the U.S. scene, he was able not only to build a theory of action but also to contribute to the structural-functionalist approach, focusing on large-scale social and cultural systems. In his influential book *The Social System* (1951), he focused on various structures of society (these structures were later applied in works coauthored with other scholars). He also concentrated on the relationships among the structures themselves. Generally speaking, he maintained that the subsystems operating in a larger social system were mutually supportive and tended to drift toward a dynamic equilibrium.

He stressed the problem of order (at Harvard, among other activities, he conducted research with Lon Fuller, the most imaginative figure in U.S. philosophy of law) and analyzed normatively coordinated social change. According to Parsons, the main social processes take place within a framework consisting of adaptation, goal attainment, integration, and latency, or pattern maintenance — AGIL, as it was called. He studied various social systems as wholes and also analyzed the composition and distribution of the various social roles of separate individuals.

Despite Parson's vast knowledge, the grand perspectives he furnished — which were not always easy to comprehend — contained few of his own ideas. Why did other U.S. scholars regard him as innovative? It appears that Parsons-as-innovator was a construct of U.S. expectations. Indeed, at the time, the social sciences in the United States had no grand perspective of their own; Parson's philosophy was well-suited to fill the gap. Parsons can be categorized as a spectacular scholar, one who, although highly regarded, does not leave behind a substantive body of new ideas.

During Parson's visit to Warsaw, I went with Parsons and his wife for a tea to visit the granddaughter of Henryk Sienkiewicz (who won a Nobel Prize for literature). Parsons explained to me that he himself came from a respected family of British tea merchants.

Although almost everybody knows the main ideas of Parsons, few have heard of Pitirim Sorokin, and practically nobody has heard the name of Leon Petrazycki. However, Sorokin, a student of Petrazycki, was the first chairman of the Department of Social Relations at Harvard (Department of Sociology); he hired Parsons and later was replaced by him.

A SCHOLAR-INNOVATOR MOTIVATED BY THE IDEA OF MORAL AND SOCIAL JUSTICE: LEON PETRAZYCKI (10) (1867–1931)

Leon Petrazycki was not much concerned with others, nor was he troubled by his own affairs; he mainly was preoccupied with the stream of his own ideas. Tadeusz Kotarbinski told me that once, when Petrazycki attended one of his parties, Kotarbinski's son Adam fell off a seesaw onto the floor. Petrazycki, undisturbed by the general commotion, further developed his idea that human behavior is guided by emotion and impulsions that were generated (and then made functional) by our remote ancestors. Kotarbinski, caught between respect for Petrazycki and the condition of his child, did not know what to do for a while.

Sometimes a tribunal of peers cannot recognize that a given scholar is an innovator; alternatively, the available data may be too poor to allow for such recognition. In the humanities, an innovator is not only a product of his own creativity but also a construct of others. An innovator who is not a specialist in self-promotion should not be surprised if his or her ideas go unacknowledged. He or she should blame those around him or her.

Petrazycki's biography shows the combined effects of personal tragedy and theoretical and political turmoil. His main target of analysis was legal policy (specifically, how to change sociopolitical reality through law). To study this particular problem, he developed a new psychology, a new theory of law, a new logic, and a new sociology. He claimed that the individual psyche is governed not by three basic phenomena (cognitive components, feelings, and will), but by four: emotions (as the main motivational impulsions), cognitive data, feelings, and will. The emotions,[12] according to Petrazycki, constitute the basic element of psychic life, and the rest are derivatives. His contribution to the theory of law is the concept of intuitive (living, unwritten, informal) law. The relation between rights and duties, whether accepted by official law or only recognized by the relevant parties, denotes the most important feature of law. The function of law depends upon the complicated network of intuitive (living) legal relations and the relations between intuitive law and official law.

Petrazycki's logic consists of the idea that the basic elements of a cognitive line of inquiry rest not on sentences but on more rudimentary elements or "particles," as he calls them. In the humanities, the most important logical concept was adequacy. It demanded that everything stated about a particular subject be related to the subject and to nothing else and that what relates to areas connected with the subject be related to the subject and to nothing else.

Sociology should describe and explain the rules of social processes and the role that law plays in regulating (or disrupting) them. According to Petrazycki, all these premises are necessary to build a rational policy of law. Petrazycki's basic ideas are summarized in the book *Law and Morality* (1955). Their further development in the Polish context was summarized in *O Nauce Prawie i Moralnosci* (Wybrane — selection made by Licki and Kojder) and in Krzysztof Motyka's *Wplyw Leona Petrazyckiego na Polska Teorie i Sociologie Prawa* (1993). Petrazycki's suicide on May 15, 1931, was caused by several factors: certainly, his genius was beyond the reach of his Polish compatriots; his condemnation of some social prejudice tendencies at Warsaw University led to a backlash against him; he felt as though his inventiveness had dried up; and he was depressed by the incoming wave of totalitarianism (which he foresaw clearly). With Petrazycki, the original moral and social imperative to "serve" people was transformed into (or began, in concert with a scholarly imperative, to function as) an autotelic cognitive curiosity.

A SEMISPECTACULAR SCHOLAR:
ALAIN TOURAINE (4)

Spectacular scholars are most often the creatures of totalitarian systems, although not always. They also may be the products of psychological factors, such as insecurity, the effects of a lower-class background, and negative self-appraisal. An insecure person develops defense for dealing in advance with situations that may erode his or her fragile sense of self. Someone of obscure background may devise a range of defensive strategies to protect this particular point of vulnerability. People with low self-esteem may develop techniques to hide reality from themselves.

In his theoretical book *The Voice and the Eye*, Alain Touraine writes that subsequent volumes will deal with "the students' movement, the antinuclear movement, the Occitanist movement, trade-unionism and the women's movement" (1981: 214). It did not occur to him that, two years later (1983), he would collaborate with a team of Polish sociologists on a book about Solidarity. In this book, he maintains that, "if the movement of the Polish people has been defeated [was it?], it is Communist society which has died [did it?], and with it the central principle on which it is built: the control and direction of social life by the ideology and political organization of a Party which considers itself to be the representative of the workers and the voluntarist agent of modernization" (Touraine 1983: 188). He also maintains that "the Communist Party represented for many people the hopes of a mutilated nation which wanted to live, reconstruct, increase production and advance the education and wellbeing of the greatest number" (p. 189). Where did he get this idea?

This case illustrates the sensitivity and instrumentalism of a leading world sociologist both in his selection of issues that are currently attractive and in his precautionary inclusion of Polish sociologists on his research team. However, it also shows that Touraine prematurely discarded the notion of "post-communist society" and of post-Communist "nomenklaturas," that he failed to understand the potency of latent Communist structures, and that he was unable to foresee the spectacular post-Communist victory in the elections of September 19, 1993.

Clearly unacquainted with the Scandinavian notion of sociological intervention, Touraine and three Polish authors try elsewhere to explain the method that Polish readers should use to understand him — why? (Touraine 1981: 139–222). One of the Polish authors writes, "The way to understand Touraine's sociological intervention boils down to a test" (Kuczynski et al. 1994: 185). Later, speaking for all four, states the same author, "In its most open form sociological intervention is a method of producing sociological knowledge in the mode of negotiated interpretation. This . . . excludes the possibility of treating it as a form of a test" (p. 187).

7

Ideal and Real:
A Synthesis of Findings

Good science is what people reject initially.
—Zuckerman 1977: 231

THE CURRENT RESTRUCTURING OF ACADEMIA

The dynamic interrelations between society and academia and the internal dynamics in academia are rapidly changing the existing structure of the scholarly world.[1] The world of classical, traditional scholars[2] is shrinking, while the macrocosm of professional scholars is growing fast. Certain extremes persist: the U.S. "super-elite" of scholars, not interested in scholarly self-advertisement; the amateurish British scholar protected by a wall of good manners (the Oxford-Cambridge "nobility"), and some Polish scholars, inspired by the missionary attitude of the intelligentsia and motivated by "civil courage," who struggle against oppressive forces of various descents and remain as the last bastions of the classical search after truth. However, those who occupy extremes constantly lose ground to the increasing professionalization of science and its concerns. A closer look at the new professional type of scholar should be preceded by a reminder of the basic attributes of the traditional scholar.

THE TRADITIONAL IMAGE OF SCHOLAR

The Polish art historian Zofia Kossakowska once said, "Science is like a spring; if you want to drink from it, kneel."

It is psychologically true that the more one's own interests, predilections, or preferences are exorcized from ongoing inquiry, the likelier the inquiry is to bear fruit. This implies a need to be unassuming, open-minded, and humble before the intricate problems of natural, social, and cultural reality. It also implies that, in order to know something about human reality, one has to identify with it, and the more one empathizes with existential or social enigmas, the greater are one's chances of gaining unexpected comprehension. Because creativity is an especially elusive and ambiguous phenomenon, it seems that one can accomplish something creative only through constant emphatic approximations and subsequent analytical elaborations. If not empathy, then luck remains as a reliable companion.

A further ingredient in the creation of something significant is persistence: constant turns at the same problem in a spirit of determination, not resignation; constant attempts to check whether what is suspected is, indeed, the case; staunchness in the face of difficulties; an insolence in approaching the same question again and again; a disregard for "no" (like that of Don Juan, who repeatedly and faithfully returns to his prospective "victims"); these qualities do not furnish creativity, but they are essential to it. Not only must the brain be focused on something day and night (many discoveries are made early in the morning), but also the whole personality must become an inventive apparatus. To make a discovery, one should learn how to hunt with one's unconscious.

The potential power of the traditional thinker,[3] the armchair scholar, was based on the notion that, being "frozen" in this position, the scholar was almost forced to identify "phenomenologically" with the problem at hand. He or she was not a member of numerous committees; he or she was not challenged or bargained with by students to give them higher marks than they deserved; he or she did not have to strain his or her inventiveness to outwit peers in writing myriad application forms. Following the advice of Epicurus, he or she was "the wise man who does not take part in public affairs unless circumstances oblige him." He or she was free to think. He or she was supposed to be impartial; he or she belonged to academia; he or she did not reject the inspiring influences of its milieu. Lewis Coser stressed the influence of the academic world:

The traditional audience of the scholar was found in the community of scholars. The sense of identity of the traditional man of knowledge was largely shaped through the rewards that recognition and esteem among his peers would bring him. But once a scholar acquires a new extra-academic audience, he is subject to new influences that reshape his self-image. When recognition is bestowed by extra-academic men whose problems the academician has helped solve, a tendency may arise for the academician to seek recognition less from his peers than from decision-makers who are able to reward him. (Coser 1965: 286)

Because academia currently resembles a business, the abusive rules of trade invade its life. Scholars develop grounds for envy: they may hate themselves not only because they are jealous of others' inventive ideas or discoveries but also because, for example, they receive insufficient travel funds (or less pocket money than others) or because the chairperson that got elected was not the person for whom they voted or simply because a job was not offered to the candidate of their preference.

An old stratagem that has been tested successfully in other areas recently has found favor among professional scholars. Instrumental schol ars from the East bloc as well as sly scholars from the West have adopted this technique in order to enlarge the scope of their influence: they accumulate administrative resources, positions, titles, and other tangible splendors; they do it not only for the titles, recognition, and glory but also simply to assemble power. They tend to build their own "courts." They select, assemble, and organize younger, dependent scholars whose goal is supposed to be the creation not, as in the past, of a scientific school but of a climate of admiration for their mentors, whose wisdom they are meant to parrot. Members of this clique review their mentor favorably in different journals and recycle the reviews as articles at various congresses;[4] like a Greek chorus, they create an atmosphere of veneration around this person, who keeps a tight grip on the reins of power and controls the distribution of privileges (especially financial). If necessary, the disciples of such people would build a cement wall to protect their masters from outside influences or safeguard their demigod status. This patron-client cohabitation has mutual advantages: it ensures for the younger ones a certain security (the weaker among them rely on the direct support of the reigning scientific overlord), and allows the overlord to rely on the support of his courtiers (this norm of reciprocity takes precedence over personal sympathies or animosities; backing is required even from those who hate their boss). In the humanities and social sciences, which have no measurable criteria of creativity, this hazy atmosphere is more than powerful: the protecting milieu operates as a superpowerful structure, as an omnipresent, intangible, elastic, and overwhelming device that draws on seductive vernaculars.

THE MODERN PROFESSIONAL SCHOLAR

Professional scholars are gradually but systematically establishing their dominance worldwide. Which of their attributes have given rise to this trend?

Professional scholars are instrumental in that they are able (and willing) to use any means to achieve their goals. They may work for their "higher" cause (as a party operator), or they may be self-oriented (self-propelled operators); in both cases, they carefully differentiate between their own and others' gains, giving priority, of course, to their own. The ability of instrumental scholars to use all possible derivations was most fully developed under Nazi and Soviet totalitarian regimes.

Professionalists are sly in that they have a clear understanding of the societies in which they are living and very skillfully manipulate features of these societies for their own self-promotion. They are masters at self-advancement. Sly scholars are also the products of Western (especially U.S.) democratic society. The richness of their social fabric gives sly scholars a plethora of tactics by which to pursue, foxlike, their individual careers.

Professionalists are career oriented in that they regard their academic job with its mediocre but stable income as a more secure way of providing for their families (especially when they are tenured) than a risky business venture that could plunge them into existential insecurity. However, professional scholars, especially the British variety, apply certain manners to their work. This is because they understand, but only up to a point, the concept of "civil courage." Therefore, they would be willing altruistically to defend specific issues that may be important institutionally, nationally, socially, and so on; in other words, they would not always restrict their preferences to what is gainful for them.

The professionalism of the modern scholar manifests itself differently in different societies. Features that are specific to a given society tend to be accentuated in its products. Another important, yet invisible, factor that shapes the current model of professional scholar is the overwhelming influence of various foundations that support, subsidize, and promote the development and application of knowledge. Such foundations originally started to function in the United States (their motives — for example, the expectation of some substantial tax breaks — were at first pragmatic), but presently they operate in all parts of the world. They have, of course, specific demands; although not always clearly articulated, these demands influence their politics toward sciences and have an impact on the development of knowledge. Additionally, the foundations influence the characters of their beneficiaries. Although some countries have special semigovernmental and semi-independent bodies that distribute funds in nominal disregard of the specific expectations of industry, corporations, defense, agriculture, or other socioeconomic spheres, these bodies are, nevertheless, still influenced by the governing ideology. This is not the place to discuss such matters in detail; they require a special study of their own.

ORGANIZATIONAL DEVELOPMENT
OF SOCIOLOGY OF LAW

The following case study concerning the organizational development of the sociology of law shows not only how deftly professional scholars gain the upper hand in internal battles among scholars but also how they can take over an institution step by step and change its academic climate. The idea of establishing an international body to coordinate research and theoretical thinking in the area of the sociology of law was originally conceived during a private conversation I had with William M. Evan at his home in 1960, on the eve of my departure for Poland from the United States. The organizational consequences of that idea materialized quickly. In 1961, the Section of Sociology of Law was instituted as a branch of the Polish Sociological Association. The Research Committee of Sociology of Law at the International Sociological Association (Committee) was established in 1962 during the International Congress of Sociology in Washington. (To make the establishment of this committee easier, Vilhelm Aubert, earlier designated president by committee organizers, was replaced by Renato Treves, then a member of the executive committee of the International Sociological Association. Evan became the committee secretary, and I was made its vice-president.)

Thus, the first organizational idea to develop the sociology of law was directed at those who conducted diverse significant but dispersed and mainly empirical investigations, who represented various countries, and who were already recognized as creative scholars. Originally, the committee functioned as a small operative research group whose 18 members would meet more or less regularly to discuss their findings in order to formulate a middle-range theory appropriate for their inquiries; a broader theory of the sociology of law was envisioned as its final goal.

First Goals Replacement

In 1964, when the Law and Society Association and its major literary organ *Law and Society Review* were established, the goals of the committee were altered. It decided to remain a largely European organization (originally based on the strong Scandinavian, Polish, and Italian schools in sociology of law), which would invite only distinguished scholars from other countries to join its ranks. Philip Selznick, Richard Schwartz, Jerome Skolnick (who was young but very dynamic), and Lon Fuller became members. At that time, the committee decided to operate according to the following organizational principles: to meet every year (the organizational and theoretical skills of Treves and Judge Berio di Argentina from the International Society of Social Defence of Milano enabled us to hold several meetings in Italy); to establish working research groups that would study more specific problems appropriate for cross-societal comparisons (at first, a special working group was activated to embrace research conducted in Scandinavia and in Poland and, later, in Belgium and Holland on the knowledge and opinions of the law; Berl Kutschinsky became the head of the organizational center of this group). The committee decided not to publish reports of its studies but instead to establish a European Institute of Sociology of Law, with the main aim of publishing its findings (S. C. Versele from Belgium was the main organizer of the institute; a rule was adopted whereby committee members were not permitted to belong to boards of other international organizations of the sociology of law). Italian sociology of law was, to some degree, a reaction against the former fascist regime in Italy, while Polish sociology of law was generated as an internal academic protest against the reigning Marxist totalitarianism; the two schools have been closely linked by their antiauthoritarian political stance. This situation articulated another goal of the committee. It became clear that scholars who had experienced the fascist version of totalitarianism (including Norwegian scholars like Aubert and German scholars like Wolfgang Kaupen) or those who were still working under Stalinist totalitarianism had a distinct political goal: they tried indirectly to unmask the activities of the regimes under which they lived. Because empirical work in the area of sociology of law was growing rapidly in Europe, I suggested that a synthesis of the relevant findings could be prepared and published. Because Poland, for political and organizational reasons, did not provide the proper environment for such a venture, Treves and Jan Glastra van Loon undertook the editorial work of a volume (1968) that sought to generalize work conducted in several countries and, thus, synthesize existing findings. During the annual meetings of the committee, it became clear that a substantial amount of work was going on inside the totalitarian countries (especially in Poland and by Kalman Kulcsar's group in Hungary). This subsequently influenced the structure and the goals of the committee in a significant way. Additionally, the committee also accepted as one of its goals sponsorship of the development of sociology of law in countries that were methodologically mature and capable of conducting studies in the area. This gave a boost to the development of sociology of law in some countries in the Soviet bloc (to some degree, in the Soviet Union, but also in Bulgaria and East Germany). A major attempt to build sociology of law in countries where it had been neglected also was undertaken. Until 1972, the United Kingdom had practically no sociology of law, although British sociology, then preoccupied with courses on Marxism, was ready to sponsor the development of this particular subbranch of sociology. When, in 1972, Pauline Morris, supported by the committee, organized at Cambridge the first meeting of British and international scholars interested in sociology of law, the committee encountered an entirely new phenomenon. It appeared that the British and Scottish "scholarly markets" were saturated with competent but traditionally oriented legal scholars. Consequently, a new legal subdiscipline — sociolegal studies — was welcomed in the expectation that it might create new administrative possibilities of a novel type for young, ambitious scholars. This unexpected factor, which was even more evident in the United States, opened a new era in the organizational and theoretical development of the committee.

Gradual Professionalization and "Regression" in Sociology of Law

Under the influence of these new developments, the original academic and political goals of the committee have changed. This time, the new goals did crystallize from discussion among members and developed spontaneously. These developments led to the committee's being recognized as a convenient springboard for the professionally oriented. Some new members sought to hold committee meetings in several countries for a "variety of pragmatical reasons." These included a preference for presenting papers in a congested atmosphere that precludes the possibility of thorough discussion; an effort to exclude papers on theoretical matters; pure tourist interests; a desire of potential conference organizers to present themselves in their own countries as internationally recognized scholars; a wish to monopolize the advantages generated by such a conference and exclude another group of sociologists of law in the same country; a bid to use the forum provided by the committee to spread certain fads or fashions and to treat the committee as a market suitable for job searching; instrumental use of the committee's facilities as a vehicle to find a convenient publisher; or generally using the committee as a vehicle for advancement of one's personal career.

As it should be noted earlier, some of these new tendencies were not bad per se, but they accentuated the more instrumental and pragmatic aspects of committee activities. Thus, slowly the center of gravity started to shift toward the practical and professional aspects of developing the sociology of law. As indicated by Vincenzo Ferrari's study *Developing Sociology of Law* (1990), which continued the work of Glastra van Loon and Treves, innumerable unrelated investigations began to appear on the sociology of law forum. For the most part, these studies did not deal with issues regarded as crucial, they were not centered on issues unique to the sociopolitical culture of different societies, they were not triggered by the political problems of the given society or activated by theoretical perspectives, and they were not responsive to the questions raised by earlier studies. Rather, they constituted almost mechanical responses to politically fashionable issues.

Additionally, the professional spirit (based on administrative efficiency and oriented toward career advancement) characteristic of the enterprise-oriented academic subculture surfaced and swiftly dominated the new ideas. In this critical situation, when an idea was advanced (by E. Blankenburg, F. J. Caballero Harriet, and Volkman Gessner) to create an institution where scholars in sociology of law could have the possibility of organizing secluded seminars, a chance to work in a quiet atmosphere on particular academic issues, an opportunity to write books, and so on, the powerful law of autonomization of institutions ensured that the new institution (in Onati, Spain) started to treat itself as an independent goal and started to drift toward fiscal perspectives. It began to give courses, publish pamphlets and booklets (transgressing the originally established aims of the committee), grant professional titles, and catapult new scholars into the heart of academic life. (Almost all former scientific directors were elected to the board of the committee. As a result, administrative, not scholarly, visibility became decisive: apparently those who could not establish themselves by their scholarly accomplishments tended to enter into academia by the administrative door.) This institutionalized "regression" is harmful because it strengthens the general tendency to treat potentialities of academia as a gainful profession. It was mainly U.S. scholars (who visibly departed from the scholarly patterns established earlier by Roscoe Pound, Thomas Cowan, E. Adamson Hoebel, Karl N. Llewellyn,

Fuller, Evan [active in the committee until 1976], Lawrence Friedman, Mark Galanter, and Stewart Macaulay) who became eager to introduce such devalued patterns into academic life.

In effect, only a few scholars tend to concentrate on hot political issues pregnant with current social and economic problems and on important theoretical problems. So, who presently does continue the earlier investigation of the possibilities of the eruption of World War III? Who is studying the legal and political consequences of the time bomb generated by overpopulation? Who is studying the consequences of aborted legal arrangements to regulate the environmental consequences hanging over the world's populace? Who is studying the effects of totalitarian law and its "psychological poisons" generated by law counterfeited by the posttotalitarian regimes? Who is studying the impact of various "pathological" ethical deviations in socioeconomic legal practice? Who is studying the dysfunctionality of international establishments and the growing discrepancy between the goals and the practice of the United Nations administration? Who is studying the actual or potential pathological misuse of sociology of law as a sociopractical means for manipulation?

During the meeting of the board (Tokyo, August 1995), the president of the committee took time to thank the Japanese organizers (who, indeed, performed their task very efficiently), and she promised to devote more time to the discussion of substantial matters in 1996 in the United Kingdom (Glasgow, July). However, the Japanese hosts insisted on having a second meeting in Japan, and they knew in advance that this conference would practically exclude Eastern Europe participants (although they generously supported several participants, including students, they omitted those from Eastern Europe). In consequence, important areas remain open before the committee. There is a strong need, for political and "population" reasons, to hold meetings in China, in Egypt, or some other Arabic countries, in Israel, and in Chile; to look more attentively at the sociolegal remainders of post-Communist regimes; to scrutinize the reasons why some scholars in the West actively cooperate with the compromised post-Communist forces; to analyze the current structural inefficiency of the committee's board; to analyze more closely some potential dysfunctions of the cooperation between the committee and its offspring, the Onati Institute of Sociology of Law; to reanalyze the goals of the committee as they were consciously formulated during earlier development (1962–96) and to query whether it is reasonable to abandon those previously established goals and to dislodge them without proper consideration, thus, more or less consciously displacing the committee's goals; to state repeatedly and clearly that the committee *is not* another

U.S. type of scholarly organization but has certain distinctive goals that transcend professionalism — search for truth, antiauthoritarian stance, dissemination of sociology of law around the globe, and advancement of methodological and theoretical inquiries.

IDEAL AND REAL SCHOLARS REEXAMINED

Modern professional scholars differ from traditional scholars in that, although traditionalists were mainly interested in developing those scientific ideas that had pure, universal, and eternal values, modern professional scholars are concerned almost exclusively with detailed analyses of limited subjects that lack a broader cultural perspective. They are concerned with the pragmatic use of their knowledge and the enhancement of their own careers.

These two models, which are not far from ideal and real, interact intensely. The ideal is usually regarded as proper, as sublime and elevated, while the real is presented as sober and well-adjusted. The distinction is important: it reflects the distance between "is" and "ought." Needless to say, such interaction is dynamic, but the tensions between the two models have several important consequences. The modern twentieth-century scholar is oriented toward the development of intellectual paradigms that may help others (especially students and practitioners) to learn quickly and effectively how to put existing knowledge into practice. Instrumentality is a great asset here. Modern students look predominantly for knowledge that allows them to enter the job market and start their (not necessarily scientific) careers. Students tend to use their knowledge to find a respectable and lucrative position in society. Practitioners want quick fixes presented to them in an intellectually simplified manner. In this respect, the main function of the university has undergone a dramatic change during the twentieth century.

These changes have made a mark on the perception, vision, and shape of the new professional model of scholar. Professional scholars, by current expectations, are supposed to become effective intermediaries between the stores of knowledge and the practical demands of the market. As such, they are supposed to be equipped with a sui generis intelligence that tells them how to infuse that knowledge into practical life. In industrial and developing societies alike, there is a great pressure to produce professional types of scholars who can explore existing knowledge in practical terms. Presently, society understands the essential task of academia as a crusade to utilize in the most extensive form the existing potentialities of an accumulated pool of knowledge. In consequence, the socioeconomic conditions of modern life and social practice have put a heavy mark on the current model of scholar.

Within this situation, the professional type of scholar, with all its relevant subcategories, is rapidly gaining the upper hand. Therefore, repetitors, the erudite, classifiers, disseminators, analysts, and commentators are highly appreciated. This is visible not only in Eastern Europe but also, if not especially, in Japan and China. Those who create new ideas, who take pains with their work, who are full of hesitation, who are troubled by conditional quantifiers, and who feel themselves restricted by practical requirements are regarded as nonconformist troublemakers and are roughly pushed to the margins, while previously insignificant professional and secondary types of scholars are elevated to primary positions. They enter into ranks once occupied by the innovative scholars. Because the professionals know how to grasp what is useful, they immediately become ennobled by their new role as high priests among the disseminators of knowledge. They are not bothered by the fact that they remove the innovators from the scene; these new priests preach the value of aping others.

This new situation creates several additional strains whose psychological effects are not yet clear; more easily discernible are the social consequences that arise from incongruities between the ideal and real models. To deal with these strains, the professional scholar has developed an ingenious new technique for coping with more perplexing social and scientific matters: collective attack by allied mediocrities. The persistence of professional competitiveness has taught new adepts in the sciences and humanities, and especially in the social sciences, that individual ingenuity does not pay — hence, the alliance of mediocrities (see some versions of Marxism or feminism, postmodernism, poststructuralism). These alliances operate by creating a peculiar "jargon" that they regard as obligatory; they condemn (a common belief of others, who do not belong to their tribe; they use a sui generis metalanguage that does not refer to the issues but criticizes the assumed ideas of others; they constantly speak of epistemology,[5] with little understanding of the original meaning of this term (if they exhibit some sparks of comprehension, they do so in a distorted way); the main aim of this jargon is not to deal with reality but with meta-reality.

In consequence, the main function of an alliance of mediocrity is to provide emotional support for the cohorts of arrivistes, scholarly newcomers entering the academic market. They have five main techniques: They attempt to set themselves up as "governors of souls"; because their impotence as scientific creators can be revealed so easily, they need a leading position to frustrate any attempts to unmask them. They also eliminate the "weakest" scholars of the "older" type by bombarding them with a newly invented jargon that is understood mainly by members of the inner sanctum. They train crude and desperate candidates determined to find secure jobs in the art of entering the academic market. They develop a fashionable new legend that can mislead the inexperienced, attract the naive, and lure those who need a more appealing scholarly ideology. Finally, they create an artificial fraternity milieu composed of mutually supportive brothers and sisters. Such a milieu can be accomplished in several ways; the most effective is a specific combination of technology (jets), pathological exploitation of travel agencies (exotic places to visit), pressure on blind national institutions that support humanities and sciences (funds), and, especially, administrative skills (as developed by operators). "Jet-set conferences" (the subject of satirical novels based on fact) describes several thriving academic hoaxes. The prescription for building such a hoax is simple: find a fashionable topic, get the support of national (or international) foundations, gather a group of mediocre arriviste scholars who have come independently to the conclusion that the fast track to success in the humanities or social sciences is winning a monopoly on label creation, seduce one (or more) real scholars to the cause as token exemplars, and assemble some shrewd tactical manipulators.

The traditional model of scholar is additionally extinguished by the variety of "new" academic schools that supply their adherents with several real advantages. They present a new, sometimes revealing synthesis in the given area, and they provide help in going rapidly through preselected empirical data. They comb human reality to eliminate doubtful or useless data. They encourage the spread of their ideas to different interconnected areas to test the conditions under which these ideas can be accepted. They permit the development of a consistent strategy whereby all other schools of thought are skillfully attacked. They develop a storehouse of rationalizations, explanations, and derivations to which those who need them have easy access. They assist each other in preparing a defensive form of argumentation and search for territories in which elaborated concepts can be gainfully implemented. Independently of cognitive importance, they furnish a psychologically important sense of academic "togetherness," and they have the potential to crush discordant individuals through accumulated oppression.

Yet, sometimes, an individual encircled by schools of this type can be pushed to creativity, so that the existence of scientific schools and the professionalization of sciences, especially of the social sciences, may have more than conformistic consequences. Some unintended but positive by-products may emerge simultaneously with the overabundant array of negative symptoms. Indeed, if one has to fight so hard against the pervasive atmosphere of conformity and professionalism,[6] this massive burden of "scientific junk" triggers a counterreaction and may push one toward independence and originality. Erving Goffman's entire stream of creativity could be regarded as a phenomenon of this type.

This is why imaginative experiments like that of Stanley Milgram (1969; Miller 1986) appear so rarely. Individually conceived, highly developed, nonconformist, attacked by other scholars as morally degrading, Milgram's work was, in its consequences, unusually creative. His experiments showed that human beings have a compelling, inherent tendency to obey the orders of those who are in power, even if the orders are obviously cruel. At least four important factors contributed to the design of this particular experiment with its far-reaching implications. First, Milgram concluded his own studies at what was then the most intellectually sophisticated and socially alert school in the United States, Harvard University. Second, he was an assistant and collaborator of Samuel Asch, whose own experiments revealed in a tentative way the inherent human tendency to conform to the pressing opinions of the majority. Asch's experiments also revealed that an individual is more prone to think and behave independently if he or she is placed in the vicinity of someone who appears to agree with him or her. Milgram's experiments, thus, served as a spectacular confirmation of Asch's findings. Third, Milgram's theoretical thinking was heavily influenced by Nazi atrocities during World War II. Indeed, many scholars wanted to find an answer to the nagging question of why human beings (even in the seemingly civilized nations) were able to behave in such an "inhuman" way. Finally, Milgram extrapolated from his experiments a general sociological overview of human development; thus, "Behaviour, like any other [of] man's characteristics, has through successive generations been shaped by the requirements of survival" (Milgram 1974: 124). This important thought closely resembles the earlier ideas of Petrazycki, who developed the thesis regarding unconscious social adaptations of subsequent generations.

However, even if such experimental and theoretical pearls appear, on occasion, as impatient reactions against overwhelming conformity, they do not outweigh the general costs of professionalization.

VALORIZATION OF THE TRUTH

Postmodern epistemology runs into abstract divagations but is not mature enough to state that all human knowledge is based on value judgments. As a result, it deals in an acrobatic mixture of descriptiveness and values: it maintains that our knowledge is "descriptive," but subjectively tainted, constructed, deconstructed, and, in general, not objective. It goes even further and ridicules all attempts to find truth as such. The prevailing epistemological attitude is that, while searching for truth, one must at the same time be willing to concede that all knowledge is subjectively transformed. This inherent weakness of epistemology as it is currently comprehended greatly helps the professional attitude to sciences. In effect, it maintains that all knowledge is professionally biased.

Postmodern epistemology spreads several revelations. One is the statement that the "discovery of truth" is not the "product" of an individual scholar, not the fruit of a penetrating abstract mind, and does not result from the work of various task-oriented groups; it results, rather, from the interaction of various competing or cooperating intellectuals (religions, scientific schools, or even conflicting ideologies). All these assumptions contribute to the emergence of a new phenomenon, the valorization of the truth. One may define this phenomenon as an analytical process as a result of which notions become normatively prefabricated,[7] a process that rejects classical logic and wants to stress its limitations as merely one of many human constructs. This entirely new phenomenon, which is coming into being before our eyes, has not yet been fully identified. Although sporadic symptoms have been recognized and described, the task of distinguishing the phenomenon in its entirety has not been undertaken. The following subphenomena should be regarded as dispersed elements that contributed to its inception: newly developed "epistemologies" (as noted earlier, those who use these terms usually do not understand their meaning); material goods regarded as fetishes (they are treated as having their own inherent values, although the values are determined by the current fluctuation of the market); ubiquitous pragmatism (a point of view that evaluates something on the basis of its current "utility" and becomes, in everyday practice, the dominant criterion for assessing the falsehood or truth of that thing); new visions of reality dictated by influential normative centers (seen, almost exclusively, through the eyes of authoritarian religions or aggressive ideologies); and the influence of various branches of the academic left. Above all, the massive impact of the so-called academic left should not be disregarded in this context. According to Paul R. Gross and Norman Levitt, the U.S. left and its "critique of science have come to exert a remarkable influence. The primary reason for their success is not that they put forward sound arguments, but rather they resort constantly and shamelessly to *moral one-upmanship*" (Gross and Levitt 1994: 9).

In attempting to identify the phenomenon of valorization of truth, one should remember that epistemology (gnoseology) is a part of a philosophical *Weltanschauung* that tries to answer how, and under what conditions, human beings are able to recognize their physical, social, and cultural realities. Epistemology deals with deliberate consideration of these issues and, consequently, proposes answers that are regarded as consistent during the given chain of consideration. It, thus, builds up an elaborated cognitive system of perceiving the inner and surrounding human vision of reality as a whole. Each epistemology has its own cannons, ways of interpreting and treating this reality.

Fetishism[8] assumes that relations between human beings are based on certain objects and that certain commodities have definite properties that designate external relations that bind human beings. Thus, if objects determine relations among human beings, then they are treated as decisive; consequently, these objects normatively color the human environment. Conversely, different environmental designs shape various human ways of thinking.

Pragmatism is another component of modern (or postmodern) episte mologies.[9] According to pragmatists, true ideas are those that are attested to by their practical consequences. The problem here, of course, is what is understood by "practical." However, because all these understandings embody many possible evaluations, the evaluations *eo ipso* (in this way) enter directly into the given comprehension of truth.

There exist, as well, various sources of normative values (religions, ideologies, more or less authoritarian or totalitarian versions of cultural events) that influence or even compel people to understand reality in certain prescribed ways.

Let us repeat once again: the truth is not perceived currently, as it was according to classical definition, as something that mirrors reality, nor is it perceived as the most comprehensive synthesis of existing, reliable data. Rather, it is treated as something that is negotiated among the parties concerned. In consequence, the truth can be subjectively constructed, reconstructed, discursively authenticated, deconstructed, or just mediated among those who are interested in its understanding, application, or usage. As goods, or even services (for example, a prostitute's favors), became fetishes once they had been invested with certain properties (and, consequently, values) that now may determine their quality, so any given truth could be normatively remodeled by the particular value that is attributed to it.

The biasing impact of various normative sources should not be overlooked. Although the influence they exert should be the subject of a separate analysis, the distorting influence of the academic left has to be mentioned here. It is not easy to capture the leachlike image of this intellectual movement. Gross and Levitt comprehend it thus:

The academic left is not completely defined by the spectrum of issues that form the benchmarks for the left/right dichotomy in American and world politics, although by reference to that standard set — race, women's rights, health care, disarmament, foreign policy — it unquestionably belongs on the left. Another set of beliefs — perhaps it is more accurate to call them attitudes — comes into play in an essential way, shaping this subculture. What defines it, as much as anything else, is a deep concern with cultural issues, and, in particular, a commitment to the idea that fundamental political change is urgently needed and can be achieved only through revolutionary processes rooted in the wholesale revision of cultural categories. (Gross and Levitt 1994: 3)

Thus, through political change, new assessments and values are injected into the fabric of the academic *Weltanschauung* and academic creativity. In this way, values that are alien to scientific inquiry become essential ingredients of the "new" academic ideology and are systematically employed as scientific.

Additionally, the pure methodological requirement — that factual data have to be "organized" for outside presentation; that, in order to be comprehended, they have to be categorized; and that, in order to be used, they must be coded — deprives the former guardians of this order (scholars) of their "natural" attribute of sustaining intrinsic respect for the truth.[10] For these and other reasons, all concerned begin to seek the archetypical elements of truth in the influence of managerial factors as they organize empirical data into colonized classes.

These processes shatter the prestige of scientists searching for "objective" truth and the prestige of disinterestedness, traditionally regarded as its essential element. Because scientists are supposed to know "what is what," lay people tend to accept the understandings they offer. For such people, the scientists' labeling is solid. Only a few laymen take into consideration the fact that scientists could be cognitively lured to present normative ideas as something reified and objectified as something intrinsically neutral.

Scholars, especially in the social sciences, no longer confront reality in all its intellectually puzzling, threatening, or fascinating ramifications. They are *hired* to solve certain intellectual mysteries that seem to be important in a practical sense or especially exciting in a scholarly sense.

Thus, valorization of truth is not recognized as a theoretical principle but, in practice, is extensively utilized.

COPERNICAN LAW REVISED

In the context of this discussion, one could reformulate the old Copernican law[11] as follows: the truth of a lower order eats away at truth of a nobler origin. By this understanding, truth can be changed, obliterated, negotiated, even transformed into agreement. In other words, the truth can be swamped and the results formulated as natural. If so, one might claim further that conventionality can replace the traditional methodological rigor involved in "objective" investigation of reality. The final version of the truth, the version manufactured for mass consumption, is handed on a platter to the crowd.

In effect, these processes are tough enough to defeat any attempt to defend the last bastions of independent thinking, which, to some extent, and mainly because of its observational and experimental method of investigation,[12] still exist in a limited way in the "hard" sciences. Thus, the valorization of truth, through artful processes and pressures of a normative character, destroys the nucleus of self-sustained ideas. As a consequence, the existence of autonomous humanistic and social sciences presently is in doubt.

Two independent processes combine to produce the global effect we now face. On the most general level, the valorization of truth, as it advances, removes the possibility of grasping objective truth. On a lower social level, the professionalization of sciences spreads whatever versions of truth seem to be expedient for upholding the phenomenon of professionalization and the hidden agendas behind it. In a slightly different context, Weber noticed long ago that "The [young] American's conception of the teacher who faces him is: he sells me his knowledge and his methods for my father's money, just as the greengrocer sells my mother cabbage" (1946: 149). In sum, these two forces combined compel "true scholars" to reconsider their main role as discoverers of the truth.

IDEOLOGY OF INTELLECTUALS

Kadushin claims that, "despite or because of the many works on intellectuals, there is no adequate sociological theory of intellectuals or intellectual life" (1974: 334). Nonetheless, there are some significant theoretical investigations of this subject. One may venture to state that, although intellectuals like to have divergent thoughts, they agree on certain important, if residual, points, as follows: they do not constitute a class (like the Polish and Russian intelligentsia from the nineteenth to the beginning of the twentieth century), they are not strongly attached to their own interests, and they are not willing to defend these interests.[13] It also is agreed that intellectuals are not particularly eager to fashion a doctrine from the basic elements of their ideology (or, rather, are uninterested in doing so).

There are interesting generalizations. One is that: "If the rate and level of intellectual radicalism vary inversely with the degree to which intellectuals are occupationally and politically integrated in dominant classes and groups, then they vary proportionately with the size, level of social organization and access to resources of both radical intellectual groups themselves, and other, radical groups which can sustain them" (Brym 1980: 72). Another is that: "Intellectuals are prophets who failed because there is an inherent disparity between knowledge they have to offer and its usefulness for society; because many of their forecasts of the future on the basis of that knowledge have been wide of the mark; and because the guidance many of them have purported to offer society on the basis of that knowledge recently has not brought about the good things they promised it would, and has even helped exacerbate the problems now faced by Western society" (Etzioni-Halevy 1985: 119).

These skeptical summations are contradicted in toto by the work conducted by social engineers (or sociotechnicians), who claim that, although indeed they did not achieve much on the macrolevel (with the exception of unmasking some dubious government activities in Communist societies), much was accomplished on the mini- and mezzolevels (Podgórecki, Alexander, and Shields, 1996).

These sociotechnicians would agree that, hitherto, intellectual endeavors were connected closely with a specific value orientation; in short, they were connected with political alignment. What is new in the recently proposed sociotechnical approach is the stress on a newly developed methodology of rational and just social action and the role that is assigned to value orientation (the sociotechnical paradigm). Especially after the collapse of communism in 1989, social engineering could concentrate its efforts not so much on unmasking the activities of nongovernmental bodies and disclosing the real governmental goals behind the rhetoric but on something much more constructive — securing an environment in which such unmasking activities are ensured the maximum of operational scope, with minimum negative by-products.

THE TECHNOCRACY OF INTELLECTUALS

One may say that the general social role of intellectuals could be understood in three ways: as an international action that is performed by the political engineers; as an action propagated by the collective body of specialists, especially those in the areas of humanities and social sciences; and as an action based on the sociotechnical paradigm of efficient social action.

In Communist countries (countries that "belonged to workers"), where nobody, including workers, was willing to support Communists, certain ethically deficient intellectuals (those who were cognitively impoverished and, therefore, easier to blackmail) were "bought" in order to supply this nonlegitimized system with a semblance of legitimacy.[14] As a result, some intellectuals, if not the whole "intellectual class," were seriously politically discredited. It should be noted that various intellectuals, including very prominent ones like André Gide, Bertrand Russell, and Jean-Paul Sartre, were successively engaged, at least for a time, in direct support of the Communist camp.[15] Some of them, indirectly but systematically, started to furnish the Communist camp with derivations, rationalizations, and justifications. Some worked for the Communists through the mass media, whose real and potential influence grew rapidly after World War II.

In the East, several intellectuals, among them specialists in the humanities (or at least regarded as such), took on various functions that needed intellectual capacities. In a few cases, they volunteered, but most were pressed or blackmailed into these activities and, quite often, bought. They surfaced as editors, university professors, writers, journalists, diplomats, teachers of diplomats, politicians, administrators, even so-called priest-patriots. Having been successfully lured, they were elevated to these posts in order to contribute elements of their own intellectual work, tainted by elements of political propaganda. Their activities fueled a steadily growing condemnation of intellectuals.

In this situation, social engineers (sociotechnicians), who after 1989 intended to come out with a plan to introduce sensible social changes, faced severe difficulties. First, though deprived of power, they had the task of designing reasonable and just changes; moreover and especially, they had to perform the additional and rudimentary task of dispersing the earlier mistrust of social engineering.[16]

Because social engineers proper (those who support their recommendations with tested findings taken from the social sciences and who are conscious of the sociopolitical values they employ) had no real chance to enter into the political, economic, and social scenery,[17] the technocratic potential of scholars has been limited to two categories of self-styled propagators of rational changes: self-promoted political engineers and scholars who are not totally familiar with the existing but as yet insufficiently elaborated potential of the social sciences.

THE MAIN THESIS

Developments in Eastern and Central Europe since 1989 have greatly contributed to the process of changing the growing body of social science scholars into professionally oriented careerists. There are many reasons for this, some of which have been described above. Let us repeat the most important.

Currently, we live in a world established by the rules of the free market. Values or dogmas such as "everything has its own reward," "success is the highest measure of someone's value," and the "virtue of competition" shape the ethos of scholars, while the rules of the market heavily influence the ultimate goals and means of the academic community. This competitiveness manifests itself on many levels, not only on the lowest level, where political, economic, and social transformation occurs, but also on the level of the "ultra-elite," which develops the methods and ideas behind the processes of systemic transformation; competition occurs even in the highest scientific echelon. "It is suggested that the quality of the scientific life has greatly declined, that sensibility and cooperation are being replaced by rivalry and contention for priority, and that the Nobel prize has contributed to the general deterioration. This complex hypothesis requires better evidence than we have on historical change in the extent of competitiveness and on the further question of whether competitiveness is dysfunctional for the advancement of scientific knowledge" (Zuckerman 1977: 247).

In his study on academic man, Logan Wilson comes to very similar conclusions. He notes, "It is clear by now that the academician participates in a highly competitive social system" (1964: 157). Further, "It cannot be denied, however, that perversions of the process of competition and overemphasis of prestige values tend to make successful teaching and research commodities that are manufactured for the direct purpose of trading them for personal prestige" (p. 173).

These points may be summarized as follows: First, the exigencies of the marketplace are exerting an increasing influence on scientists. The competitiveness of the market is inherently alien to the intrinsic features of the academic milieu and destroys the fragile conditions of authentic scientific creativity. Currently, the stress is not on study but on obtaining peer review (and its effect on one's chances of getting a salary increase), competing successfully for recognition, grants, sabbatical privileges, and so on. The criteria on which these various competitions and evaluations are based have little to do with scholarly merit.

In the modern Western world and, for different reasons, in Eastern Europe, everything connected with scholarly creativity is steeped in insecurity. Political power provides privileges, not safety; material and financial supports are crucial but may be easily lost (especially during times of economic crisis) or suddenly withdrawn (as often happens when the recipients are based in Third World countries). Scholarly influence based on high bureaucratic position may be stable for a time, but it also may go astray with an election loss. Therefore, contrary to past experience, job stability gradually emerges as the scientist's chief preoccupation.[18]

Scholarly position provides tenure.[19] Unless a scholar commits a crime or displays obvious scientific impotence, this is a relatively secure arrangement. Scholars, with very few exceptions, are too smart (except for a proclivity toward sexual harassment) to be involved in a direct violation of the law. They do try to enhance their professional competence (the definition of which becomes increasingly narrow and overspecific). Scholars also are not beset by the litigiousness that increasingly characterizes certain more lucrative professions (principally the medical profession in the United States but now even the presidency). Hence, the scholarly profession emerges as a comparatively attractive, quiet, moneymaking device.

This general trend (the search for material security) appears in various countries and does not seem to be restricted to any particular social system; as shown, it emerges as the dominant feature within the academic community. It does not affect so much the hard sciences, where, in order to achieve something, one has to produce solid data.[20] In the soft sciences, however, careerism has generated crisis.[21] This situation undermines respect for those who try to develop ideas in solitude and try to synthesize existing data into a coherent whole.[22]

Second, the vast bottleneck of dispersed data increases the difficulty of assimilating the data, while the growing number of theories, packaged into small and "middle" range conjectures, leaves limited space, if any, for grand theories.

Third, the explosion in the number and influence of sly and sensationalist scholars in the West and instrumental scholars in the East (and the influx of the latter to the West) blurs any vision of "who is who" in sciences. This makes room for all possible ethical and political suicidal acrobatics and provides an atmosphere that militates against the development, testing, and dissemination of new and pure scholarly ideas. This peculiar process, with all its inflationary characteristics, affects not only individuals but also the whole tenor of the scientific world.

Fourth, the ubiquitous resort to tricks aimed at strengthening one's own career creates a situation in which valuable books, articles, or papers are smothered beneath piles of junk. To rectify this situation, two opposite types of action are required: one to clear a space for creative undertakings or for presentation of undertakings that are really creative and the other, strangely enough, to create.

Fifth, because it currently is very difficult, if not impossible, to test vigorous assertions in the social sciences, the acceptance of a given thesis quite often is accomplished by circumvention. Those who achieve positions of academic superiority have a chance to impose their theses in a manner that renders even the possibility of rational argumentation spurious. Therefore, circular strategies for gaining scholarly and dominant positions are deployed as means to secure the scientific appropriateness of the thesis that one is defending. It seems strange that a real scholar would be willing to undertake the complicated, and sometimes highly responsible, administrative chores of a chair or dean.[23] This is also why a position as foundation administrator or evaluator appears to be attractive. Why would real scholars be willing to spend several hours evaluating someone's clumsy bid for travel reimbursement or a grant to conduct an inquiry if not because they like to feel they have power over other people's affairs? (Can one assume that they want this power in order to influence developments in the given area of scholarly discipline?) Why would a real scholar travel to foreign countries to spend many hours participating in tedious discussions of fiscal and administrative matters and, additionally, seek time-consuming positions in those administrative bodies if not because they are greedy to show themselves? (Are they really interested in influencing the course of studies and pushing it in directions they regard as proper?) Why would real scholars want to evaluate someone's paper or manuscript if not because they want to have even anonymous power? (Do they, indeed, want to influence the course of the inquiries conducted in that particular area of social sciences?)

In the absence of objective evaluative criteria, subsidiary standards are developed and used by administrators or evaluators to elevate their influence over their peers. If their particular area of inquiry also starts to gain a more widespread interest, their scientific prestige goes up and the probability of their building a network of their own rises accordingly. The principle "if you scratch my back, I'll scratch yours" takes precedence. All types of strategies and tactics may be utilized to enhance one's own dominance. Overdevelopment of these positions may not only lead to an absence of loyalty toward the place of work (university, institute, research center) or colleagues but may also prompt the shrewd search for places that are regarded as neuralgic. If you land in such a place, you may be a moron, but its prestige is doing the job for you. The statement "one should be in the right place at the right time" is especially valid for the sciences.

There is a desperate drive among scholars to set themselves on pedestals.[24] However, what is said from this height is not evaluated according to its merit. Few care about the content of the message; instead, people attend more to where the message comes from. If the message is from the president, if it is delivered with a simulated Oxbridge accent, if it comes from a well-known publisher, and if, additionally, it is enhanced by the halo bestowed by the mass media, the message is presumed to be true and significant. Few are aware that to play the role of president is time-consuming; few are aware that, in Oxford and Cambridge, there are gullible operators at work who poison these places with their own specific subculture.[25] The inner wisdom of this strategy is quite clear: instead of trying to find something new, creative, and significant, why not disseminate something trivial from a position of authority? The trick of recycling worn-out ideas is used more and more often and with growing success.

One more conclusion can be drawn from these reflections. It pertains to two independent and parallel tendencies, both of which point to the present destiny of the world army of intellectuals and scholars.

The first tendency affirms the possibility of scientific progress in the domain of hard sciences. It is well-known that scholars in these sciences have the chance to test (by a sequence of experiments and other repetitive measures), accumulate (by adding new data to those that already have been amassed), precede (by using the existing store of knowledge as a point of departure for further investigations), and, in consequence, establish hard denominators commonly accepted in these sciences.

The second suggests the inherent impossibility of reliable progress in the humanities and the social sciences. These sciences do not have the possibility to test, accumulate, and precede. They are cursed by an intrinsic, whimsical type of epistemological subjectivity. Human beings cannot cognitively identify with an object (and, thus, have a chance to penetrate it by cognitive abilities), whereas the same human beings, although they can unite themselves with other human beings through values, meanings, or symbols, cannot trespass the physical boundaries of human experiences.

If one accepts the thesis of spreading professionalization in the sciences, one additionally should be aware that professionals, slowly but consistently, are gaining the upper hand over the deepest and most sacred human values; if one acknowledges that, in the hard sciences, progress is made perpetually and that the destructive potential of these sciences is constantly growing, one may find the escape only in despair; the moment when those without any inbuilt restrictions (or those influenced by a mad ideology or a madman) can grab the unlimited potentialities of annihilation is moving closer and closer.

Thus, the main thesis of this work can be formulated in this way: There is an inherent antagonism between the human lifespan and the lifespan of a scientist. Although the big discoveries in mathematics, physics, and chemistry take place in the early phases of a scientist's life, the average (pedestrian) scientist needs much more time to reach creative maturity.[26] This discrepancy creates a gulf between the careers of those who are outside academia and those who are inside it. Therefore, those who are inside and who are alert to the standards of life existing outside (a peculiar type of status inconsistency) have a strong temptation to use artificial[27] or administrative measures to accelerate (improve) their careers. Because this artificial acceleration is impossible to achieve without the employment of outside grants or administrative positions like chairs, deanships, presidencies, and various categories of gatekeeper, an element alien to the nature of the scientific inquiry intrudes into academia at an ever-increasing rate. This element multiplies barriers between real scholars and those who are artificially catapulted to academic positions (of higher rank) and contributes nothing essential to the development of general scientific knowledge. It also systematically "enriches" the pool of academic wisdom with ersatz material.

An additional conclusion of this work is the assertion that sciences in the twentieth century have acquired a potential such that they cannot exist autonomously. For example, the possibility of using a nuclear bomb (a contribution from pure physics) or the possibility of using "dark" social engineering on a macrolevel (a contribution from the latest development of the social sciences [Podgórecki, Alexander, and Shields 1996: 63–79]) compels humankind to link (bind organically) independent research to its basic ethical ideas. Applications of science have to be guided by present philosophy and, therefore, should have guidance from global ethics.[28]

FUTURE VISION

If the synthesis presented above is correct, a general state of crisis should be announced and rapid and decisive action undertaken. However, how should it be undertaken, and what should be its underlying assumptions?

Because the present situation of existential chaos directly violates the uplifting spirit of world community, it also shatters the conviction that the task of finding the truth is the responsibility of the whole human community. This conflict, thus, violates the nucleus of global ethics. However, is global ethics now the only hope and guide for collective human behavior?

How did humankind survive a similar crisis during the Middle Ages? At that time, an oppressive — for some, unbearable — weight of religiously shaped values and rigorously prescribed patterns of behavior gave rise to unifying patterns of conformity. Now that Western and Eastern European societies are deeply secularized,[29] these unconsciously man-made conformist safeguards are disappearing. This contributes to the growing scientific professionalism[30] and to some sort of universal skepticism, but more importantly, it does not bestow on this professional conformity[31] any measure of ethical control. This phenomenon is perilous, because in modern (and postmodern) times, the Western tradition has proved unable, with the exception of civilizational prosperity for some, to generate patterns of socially and culturally unifying behavior. In this situation, a global ethics is needed even more.

GLOBAL ETHICS

First, what is the meaning of "global ethics"? It is quite clear that the diverse ethical understandings that currently exist around the globe do not adequately explain, help, solve, or satisfy the existing needs and expectations of all cultures, nations, tribes, and minorities. A cry for a new, more comprehensive religion is everywhere visible. Yet, a closer analysis shows that not so much a new religion[32] as a more extensive and inclusive ethics is required. Indeed, the need for a global ethics, an ethics that would encompass the whole planet, is ubiquitous.

Second, one may summarize the postulates of this emerging ethics in the following manner:

1. Living creatures should not be engaged in constant war but, rather, should unite their potentials.
2. Not all creatures are equal in their capacity to understand the meanings and ways of consolidation and alliance. Hence, the greater (more influential) one's position on the planet, the greater should be the scope of responsibility attached to that position.
3. Human beings have a duty to be reliable sponsors[33] for all other living creatures. Because human beings, individually and collectively, are destroying the planet's environment at an accelerated rate, they face an aggravated

responsibility to preserve it. Therefore, they should use their rational capabilities to develop and implement cognitive plans and strategies to counteract the destruction of their habitat.

One may go even further and say that

4. All living creatures are responsible for the whole environment and the universe they share. These responsibilities should be assessed according to their powers of destruction and reconstruction.

Recently, the rapid and dramatic development of environmental movements has shown that human overpopulation poses one of the most urgent threats to the survival of the globe. Human beings, as the only creatures who are able to recognize the consequences of limitless population growth as well as formulate and subsequently implement imperatives restricting such growth, are burdened with an exclusive and collective duty to sustain life on the planet. It is not important under what circumstances this idea has been conceived, but again, intellectuals and scholars bear the main responsibility not only to spread awareness of the ramifications of approaching disaster but also, if possible, to undertake appropriate measures to counteract them.[34]

5. Global ethics, which is not organically tied to any religion or ideology, shows that certain ideas or religious beliefs are outdated, having been formulated when the problem of finding a solution to potential global destruction was not yet well-enough recognized. According to global ethics, a human being should not be treated as the "lord of other living creatures" but as a cohabitant on the same planet. Thus, human beings have a triple responsibility generated by their ability to create the means of global annihilation, to diagnose the present situation from a global point of view, and to forecast the process of decomposition and destruction. (Podgórecki 1993: 77–79)

Third, the inner tension between the rising trend of global ethics on one side and the destructive powers of professional scholarship on the other does not reveal which part of this feeble equation is going to gain the upper hand. Therefore, the survival of humankind (and, consequently, of most other species) is strangely balanced between the potentially negative power of truth and the visible but fragile tendency to unite human behavior into a global trend leading toward global preservation. So, the final answer depends on an assessment of whether some internal human powers are able to stop this farcical sorcerer's apprenticeship that is developing before our eyes.

After this excursion into the related problems of global ethics, let us go back to the main issue. Generally speaking, there are now, on our planet, three types of societies: totalitarian, developing, and democratic. Because totalitarian societies, as I tried to demonstrate, produce scholars whose work is not conducive to the development of ideas of justice and truth and because developing societies, as a rule, replicate the types of scholars that are generated in democratic societies, scholars in democratic societies are (and should be) the main concern of the study of academia. Additionally, in democratic societies, scholars can be subcategorized in many ways. Most broadly speaking, they fall into three categories: members of the ultra-elite (outstanding scholars, such as Nobel Prize winners), pedestrian scholars, and auxiliary scholars.

To narrow the target of inquiry even further, if pedestrian scholars follow the patterns of the ultra-elite and if auxiliary scholars ape the pedestrian scholars, then the ultra-elite are the appropriate target of a study of the whole community of scholars. Hence, the creative ultra-elite of scholars from a democratic country should be the aim of an investigation into the decisive intellectual forces determining the future of humankind.

The above considerations, let us hope, make it clear that the development of sciences (natural and social and the humanities) depends not only on individual discoveries but also on the functioning of scientific schools (which have not degenerated into pathological scientific milieux) — solidly grounded scientific schools.

If creative scientific schools led by ultrascientists are the strategic element and if there is a way to avoid the pitfalls of the existing chair system (which could transform such schools into feudal courts), then there is, indeed, a basis that might support attempts to build a unified system of science. If one assumes that such a possibility exists, it must also be assumed that it would materialize under several restrictive conditions.

A scientific school with a noninstitutionalized structure may furnish a theoretical frame useful for the primary assessment of an innovative idea, may serve as an appropriate forum to discuss whether a particular concept is worth further discussion,[35] and may facilitate an investigation into the possible theoretical and practical implications of the idea in question. Thus, a scientific school could exist mainly as a pure meeting of minds, an institutionalized arrangement that allows the possibility of debate and dispute and serves as a forum for the final examination of certain scientific conclusions. The scientific school may have a permanent head or may change heads successively.[36]

Of course, it is difficult to predict the future direction of human development in this area.[37] The hitherto prevailing observations of the strength and dissemination of values and strategies guiding human history do not seem to indicate that its tragic end could be avoided.

Scholars remain as the only social group whose responsibility (actual and potential) for others is growing. Around the world, politicians are regarded increasingly as cynical,[38] self-oriented infants or as priest-entrepreneurs (in concert with the rapidly progressing secularization of religion). Even their bureaucracies are ridiculed by the "Blondie" comic strip in such a remote place as Papua New Guinea. Therefore, scholars by default remain the sole group that could take over the difficult collective role of reliable sponsor in ethical and practical activities.

Thus, in the final analysis, the future shape of the scholar depends on three essential features: the development of global ethics as a guiding force for humankind, the spirit of academic culture (based on the development of scientific schools),[39] and the development of the ideal model of creative scholar and its placement at the head of scientific schools.

How to alert scholars themselves to their responsibility is a subject for separate analysis.

Notes

ACKNOWLEDGMENTS

1. At Stanford Law School (one of the main targets of this study), 13 female and 43 male professors were employed in 1994–95; none of the Nobel Prize winners residing at Stanford and Berkeley at the time were female. The main reason for the scarcity of female respondents to this study was that female scholars either were not willing to be interrogated (because they did not have time) or, in some cases, failed to send written comments concerning my paper "A Typology of Scholars," which summarized the basic ideas of the study).

INTRODUCTION

1. Although the empirical material presented in the book refers mainly to sociological and legal studies, the intention was to formulate theses valid for all sciences.

CHAPTER 1

1. Here, Znaniecki speaks about theoretical practitioners who historically were the main core of those who had advised the real practitioners. He is not speaking about modern sociotechnicians ("social engineers"). He says:

There seems to be, indeed, some justification in making social scientists responsible for the lack of a technology in their field which could be distantly compared with that found in engineering or medicine, for the explanation of this fact is to be sought, we believe, in the specific variety of social roles which social scientists have performed almost exclusively in the past and with a large number of them still performing. . . . During the last century and a half, some scientists studying cultural phenomena have broken away from this traditional pattern and begun to develop a theoretical knowledge independent of practical social purposes, expecting that eventually a new type of technologist will apply the results of their investigation to social practice. Those people who now demand that such scientist make themselves useful for having their knowledge serve social aims and ideas probably do not realize that they demand the perpetuation of that very pattern of "social scientist" which has hitherto prevented the development of a really useful social technology. (Znaniecki 1940: 63–64)

2.   In Polish literature, an attempt was made to deal with these issues (Gockowski and Kisiel 1994).

3.   Galtung remarks, "It is based on impressions and intuitions, written down on paper and in my memory during many years of travels and stays in various intellectual climates around the world" (Galtung 1981: 817).

4.   This concept will be discussed later. Here, suffice it to say that "intellectual" is not exactly a pejorative word in North America (nor in Great Britain), but it does not have the favorable connotation that it has in many European countries.

5.   For a discussion of the intelligentsia, see Podgórecki (1994). Here, it is enough to say that the intelligentsia is a specific social stratum that does not have its own interests but has a definite ideology. The essence of this ideology is that the intelligentsia serves as a subsidiary social body dedicated to the goals of its own nation or to the well-being of other, less articulate strata of its own society. It is appropriate to add that, if, after the contributions of Isaiah Berlin (1969) and Aleksander Gella (1976), people do not distinguish between intelligentsia and intellectual, they are ignorant or want purposely to destroy trees.

6.   Nevertheless, Daniel Bell has different opinions on this subject (1973: 375).

7.   Intellectual and politician Vaclaw Havel understands intellectuals in the following way: "To me, an intellectual is a person who has devoted his or her life to thinking in general terms about the affairs of his world and the broader context of things. . . . That is, their principal occupation is studying, reading, teaching, writing, publishing, addressing the public" (Havel 1995: 36). Here, he is not consistent with his claims that intellectuals also play a missionary role.

8.   The pressure of public opinion, the pressure to better understand what they did to others through their cooperation with communism, and a feeling of individual guilt or personal shame should have compelled them to do this. However, as recent history has shown, they did not reveal their own cooperation with communism but immediately started to play the role of metajudges, those who would be able, on the basis of firsthand involvement, to explain to others, and especially to Westerners (who are not empathic to these issues), the nature of the inherent evil of Communist systems. One notes also that the more intelligent

and vicious former Communists or Communist cooperators who foresaw more quickly the collapse of communism started, after their defections, to denigrate communism. It is quite clear that Western public opinion had a vested interest in supporting them. For what strange reasons are they praised even now? For example, see the treatment of Czeslaw Milosz and Leszek Kolakowski in an otherwise interesting article by Michael D. Kennedy, "Eastern Europe's Lessons for Critical Intellectuals" (1991).

9.   None of these denunciations has the power of Arthur Koestler's *Darkness at Noon*.

10.   These perspectives are summarized succinctly by R. Radhakrishnan (1990: 57), who states, "On the one hand we experience, more urgently than ever before, the need to posit a common and solidarity humanity that faces global threats of unprecedented magnitude. On the other hand, our situation is characterized by an unbounded heterogeneity of subject positions, each of which is a world unto itself insofar as it is informed and semanticized by its own macropolitics." See also C. Charles Lemert (1991).

CHAPTER 2

1.   The concept of creativity can be analyzed from various points of view, but the following are perhaps the most viable: originality, or whether something existed earlier in the suggested form; synthetic potential, or whether parts can be brought together into an unprecedented form of a whole; genesis, a question of bringing into being (for example, investing something with a new rank, function, or position). Synthetic potential seems to be the most meaningful because, although many things already have been said and a progenitor can be found for most existing ideas, the problem is to find an idea that is laden with significant repercussions.

2.   L. C. Repucci has prepared an appendix to Calvin W. Taylor's article "Various Approaches to and Definitions of Creativity" (Taylor, in Sternberg 1988: 118–19). Six understandings of creativity are specified here. The first refers to definitions that emphasize the concept of Gestalt. According to M. Wertheimer (1945), creativity is the "process of destroying one gestalt in favour of a better one." Definitions from O. A. Keep (1957) ("the intersection of two ideas for the first time") and of A. Duhressen (1957) ("the translation of knowledge and ideas into a new form") accentuate the same feature. The second understanding of creativity is derived from the end product or innovation. Lindsey Harmon (1955), for example, describes creativity as "any process by which something new is produced — an idea or an object, including a new form or arrangement of old elements." The third is described as "aesthetic" or "expressive" and stresses the need to express oneself in one's own unique manner. W. J. Lee (1957) defines this as the "ability to think in uncharted waters without influence from conventions set up by past practices," whereas G. C. Lange (1957) states that "the creative process is God, the creator, working through his creation,

man." Brewster Ghiselin (1955) defines creativity as "the process of change, of development, of evolution, in the organization of subjective life." The fourth understanding, characterized as "psychoanalytic" or "dynamic," is enmeshed in the terminology of id, ego, and superego. Using this terminology, C. Bellak (1958) claims that all forms of creativity are permanent operant variables of personality, while the creative ego must regress to enable the preconscious or unconscious elements to emerge. Definitions from H. H. Anderson (1959), Ernst Kris (1951), and Lawrence Kubie (1958) stress similar features. The fifth group of definitions belongs to the solution thinking category. For C. Spearman, creativity should be defined in terms of correlations: creation takes place when the mind sees the relationship between two objects in a way that generates a third object. According to Dunker (1945), in order to elucidate a problem, one must move tangentially from common types of solutions. The sixth group, because there is no definitive way of characterizing it, is called "varia."

3. "Only one characteristic of personality and orientation to life and work is absolutely, *across the board*, present in *all* creative people: *motivation*" (Rothenberg 1990: 8).

Findings, at present, are largely limited to psychological factors. Possible physiological determinants are not taken into consideration because "(1) so little is known at this time about the biological facets of creativity; (2) the impulse to analyze the biological basis of creativity and giftedness has been a controversial issue, partly for good reasons" (Gardiner in Sternberg 1988: 298).

4. In great detail, Seidler presented Jules Henri Poincare's report on one of his mathematical discoveries. Albert Einstein did not reveal that his discovery, which gave him fame and a Nobel Prize, was earlier invented by Poincare, but Poincare was less interested in self-promotion than Einstein. Jerzy Giedymin concludes his thorough study on the matter with the following: "In 1895, 1900, 1902 and 1904 Poincare formulated the principle of relativity in terms of the impossibility of detecting by any physical methods the absolute velocity of the earth or in terms of the invariance of physical laws in all inertial frames." He adds, "Since Einstein read Poincare (1902), it is possible that the prediction turned out to be self-realizing in that it prompted and encouraged Einstein to set up a new theory along these lines" (Giedymin 1982: 188–89).

5. William Evan presents the most comprehensive analysis of the concept of global ethics in his paper "Human Rights and Global Ethics" (1994); see also Podgórecki (1993).

6. Implicitly, this statement assumes that an important discovery is the result of a collective effort and that the discoverer mainly gives voice to the "spirit" of the group. It simply articulates the wisdom generated by the processes that take place inside a given scholarly, artistic, or ethical milieu.

7. Arnold J. Toynbee rather eloquently made this point in a letter to C. W. Taylor: "It would follow from this, if I am right in my diagnosis, that new educational philosophies and new institutions of learning need to be constructed to provide an opportunity for creative individuals to enhance their talents in schools.

If the American people, or any other people, are unwilling to change their minds and hearts to remould their educational establishment in ways that foster creative talents, they cannot expect to be able to persist in this negative attitude with impunity" (Taylor in Sternberg 1988: 113).

8. Mediocre persons tend not to quote their sources; these are revealed only where they are obvious or where a source is used that might be understood as a kind of homage.

9. In its political version, Marxism has always been (and is) related to dogmatic, crude, and commanding appeals to the "lowest residues" of human beings even in its most sophisticated theoretical elaborations.

10. In the Western (mainly French) way, "cooked" Marxism appeals to frustrated, politically minded, but socially inexperienced scholars who quite often are motivated by a philosophical vision of social justice.

11. Poststructuralism is the oddest mixture of various ambiguous elements: the reaction against formerly inhuman structures developed by the enlightened Marxism of the Western type (which was, however, blind to Stalinist terrors); the proficient arrogance of the new-generation scholars (hungry for professional success); and the generalized reflection of deficiencies of technocracy in everyday modern life. From all these features, only the last seems to be cognitively legitimate and appropriate for analysis, but as yet, it has not been studied enough. Indeed, this particular feature of poststructuralism should be studied meticulously, not as a subject worthy of study in itself but as a symptom of things much more important: technocratization of present everyday life, the teleological sophistication of youngsters (including small children), and the instrumental dehumanization (not reification in Lukasc's sense) of the modern self. Poststructuralism appears to be more symptomatic than Marxism. In the case of Marxism, it was clear, at least in Eastern Europe, that those who supported it wanted to gain politically, because its hidden agenda was to catapult those who were ideologically possessed, gnostically arrogant, or basically ignorant to the pinnacle of academic life. Paradoxically, they were rewarded even when safely converted to the ideology of the West. The main function of poststructuralism has been to propel an entire class of individuals to the surface, leaving them to fight among themselves.

12. One of the worst plagues of modern academia (including postmodernism or poststructuralism) is the widespread conviction that those who develop their own jargon are original scholars.

13. Thus, the U.S. concept of academic equality is based on the wrong premises, which is why it cannot generate an original academic school.

CHAPTER 3

1. Because the problematic of intellectuals (or even members of the intelligentsia) is very complicated, it might be useful to accept an arbitrary definition of "scholar" in this book. A scholar (Coser's "academic intellectual" or "men who

never seem satisfied with things as they are" [1965: viii] or Bourdieu's *"Homo Academicus"* [1984]) is understood here as a person teaching and conducting research at a university or another institution at the university level. Thus, intellectuals are individuals who are professionally engaged in the creation and disbursement of theoretical knowledge. "Intellectual" includes scholars, scientists, writers, and some journalists. The concept of intellectuals and scholars is not inclusive: as noted earlier, not all scholars are intellectuals, and not all intellectuals are scholars. However, because scholars create science and because science's role in social (and, to some extent, political) life is so important, they should be investigated as an especially portentous social group. That they are a massive, homogeneous group that is relatively easy to identify makes the task easier.

The typology as it is developed in this book does not serve as a set of purely descriptive labels. It is used mainly as an heuristic device that is applied to specify various roles of scholars in different social systems and to suggest hypotheses of lesser or greater generality.

2.   In this book, "scientific" is not limited to "natural sciences" but intends to encompass all investigations concerning physical and social reality conducted on the basis of systematic and recognized methods.

3.   The term "scientist" is understood here to mean one who is engaged in developing sciences (humanities, social and natural sciences) and who is not necessarily intent on making a remarkable discovery.

4.   At this point, the problem of overlapping types of scholars and of a scholar's dynamic transmutation from one type to another is omitted. This matter will be discussed later.

5.   Some very well-known and respected people have, nevertheless, attempted generalizations. Simon Wiesenthal says: "I keep sentiment for Poland. I was brought up on Polish and Jewish culture; these two cultures have a lot in common. In particular, they respect tradition, they search for truth and esteem justice. The whole Jewish elite has Polish antecedents. So many Nobel Prize winners have been Polish Jews. We don't have that any more. Before Hitler, Jewish scholars created an elite of knowledge and culture. Now we have only an aristocracy of money" (Wiesenthal 1995).

6.   In 1972, Seymour Martin Lipset told me that, in his view, to be competent in the social sciences, a scholar should read at least 150 pages of professional material daily.

7.   Those who are overwhelmed by the mounting task of reviewing existing empirical data apparently reject this task on the grounds of a different understanding of the very concept of knowledge. Quite conveniently, therefore, some of them reject as "positivistic deviation" the scientist's duty to be familiar with empirical generalizations accumulated in his or her branch of science.

8.   Dirk J. van Kaa, the former director of the Netherlands Institute for Humanities and Social Science, turned my attention to this category of scholars.

9.   Many scholars are inexorably shaped by their own Ph.D. This experience often marks the high point of their academic career. In fact, they know only what they learned while obtaining the degree; once involved in the repetition of knowledge they have already acquired and the consuming benefits of their position or academic infighting, they are unable to go beyond this enchanted threshold.

10.   Traditionally, an instrumental scholar "licks the shoe" of his or her professor, to use a German expression, while in a Nazi or Communist system, he or she does the same with the abstract "shoe" of political authority.

11.   Compare Podgórecki (1993: 19–22).

12.   According to Znaniecki:

There are many examples of scientists who were recognized as bearers of impractical knowledge, but who nonetheless enjoyed high honour. Remember the Chinese mandarins whose prestige and power were entirely based on knowledge of the classics. Among orthodox Jews, a poor student of the Talmud has greater prestige than a man of wealth. In France, if a member of the Academy of Sciences is invited to dinner, he is given the place of honour at the right of the hostess. In Poland, before the present invasion [in 1939, by the Germans], the official rank of full professor was one below that of the undersecretary of state and equal to that of the governor of a province or a brigadier-general. (1940: 92.)

13.   The following anecdote is more telling than a long treatise on the subject:

An officer at the rank of lieutenant colonel enters the party office and says, "The war is over. My task in the army as a political officer is completed. Thus, I submit myself to the party's disposal. What should I do?" He was asked, "Comrade B. B., do you know anything about philosophy? Do you recognize the names Ajdukiewicz, Ingarden, Kotarbinski, Ossowski, or Tatarkiewicz?" He replied with some indignation, "No, I don't know them." "Good! Very good! So, you are assigned to an accelerated course for philosophy teachers." Colonel B. B. responded, "But did I make myself clear that I was totally ignorant in this matter? Before the war I worked as a tailor's apprentice." "Yes, yes. This gives you an advantage. You will not be prejudiced." Currently, B. B. is a well-known scholar in the West. In some circles, he is also a highly respected scholar in Poland.

14.   According to an astute observer of Communist scientific life, an instrumental attitude can change even an individual character. Korchak writes:

This duality of commandology [activity caused by a command] often requires outstanding diplomatic abilities and even artistry. In reality it is a mere demonstration of two spheres of consciousness: a personal and an ideological one, which function in different fields of existence. If such a functionary reads an original source, he learns only those things that correspond to his actualized demand and serve his changing goals. On the other hand, artistry and diplomatic skills which were so important for survival in a totalitarian organization gradually become traits of his character. Both these "acquisitions" gradually "grow into personality" and impart to it a two-faced character. (1994: 201–2)

15.   In fact, they originated the idea and practice of "political correctness."

16.   Logan Wilson connects this scholarly attitude with the following background factors: "There is a common sentiment that the professor who devotes considerable energy to promotional activities must fall into one of three categories: (1) he is trying to compensate for incompetence in or indifference toward his own specialty; (2) he would rise on the basis of personality traits or 'pull' rather than technical competence; or (3) he is mistakenly permitting himself to be sidetracked from the 'true' ends of scholarship" (1964: 176).

17.   In the East, one has to publish in order to be "socially visible."

18.   "Volleyball is a serious sport at the NIAS [a Dutch think tank in Wassenaar], and the NIAS Selection Committee naturally makes sure that most of the scholars it invites are good volleyball players. Jan X was invited twice on these grounds, and proved that his play was worth the money spent on him (the favorable exchange rate between the Dutch guilder and the Polish zloty also helped). If the proposed international tournament between all the world's Advanced Study Institutes indeed takes place, then Jan X is tipped to be the NIAS team captain, together with a Dutch professional, Theo Kuipers" (Zielonka 1994: 52).

19.   Richard Abel, the well-known sociologist of law, said during the American Conference of the Law and Society Association held in Toronto (1995), "Reputation is our only capital, and its value constantly fluctuates."

20.   Those who do not simply may take up residence in another country.

21.   For example, Adam Michnik, a mediocre and controversial historian but also a well-known dissent activist (*New York Times Magazine* 1996).

22.   Scientific work here is understood as all those achievements that are accomplished when somebody purposely tries to uncover the truth.

23.   A British scholar who was employed at a Canadian university quickly discovered that, at this particular university, one could take not just one but two sabbatical years in a row (although the salary for the second year was somewhat reduced). It was not easy to get this privilege, but he succeeded. He, then, with his entire family, went around the globe presenting the same (though gradually improved) paper at many universities. Colleagues from his department were impressed with his ability to use the collective agreement with the university in such a skillful manner, but they also were envious that he, as a "novice," had so quickly discovered how to exploit their own university. On his way around the world, one small university, impressed by the sequence of his successes, wanted to hire him on better terms. He quickly terminated his contract with the Canadian university and moved. Nonetheless, he soon found that good financial terms could not compensate for the relatively amicable atmosphere of Canadian academia. So, he applied again to his old university, arguing that several of his students had pressed him to return. However, his colleagues, well-recognizing his instrumental abilities, voted against him.

24.   One of the mediocre scholars was unable to publish anything. His articles, reviews, and manuscripts were rejected constantly. When, as the result of his

academic "impotence," his university existence was threatened, he invented the following method, which provided him with the possibility of unlimited publication. First, he stopped cultivating his own interests or areas of competence. Then, he started to observe the present trends in publication to determine which topics were "hot" on the academic market. After careful consideration, he would take issue with one of the questions and assault one or more participants in the ongoing discussion. In short, he would select a narrow, specialized topic and attack violently. In effect, his contributions would be published as an interesting element of the debate. Later, he would look for other, similarly vivid areas of academic controversy and use the same stratagem. He repeated this strategy until, eventually, he emerged in the ideas market as an established scholar who was frequently asked to express his ideas. Privately, he would call himself a "mugger."

25.   In the former Soviet Union, a certain scholar had a collection of quotations from Marxist classics. He was ready to sell appropriate citations to those who needed them.

26.   This interesting question needs independent investigation. Here, one should note that there are many types and subtypes of scholarly wives and (increasingly) husbands. For example, there are those who pave the road for their spouses, working for them as secretaries and promotion agents; aides de camp, who take care of all problems as they appear; KKK spouses (Kuche, Kirche, Kinder), who take full responsibility for the kitchen, church-related issues, and children; competitors, or those who are employed in the same or a related area and suffer heavily when their spouses are more successful; Greek chorus types, who repeat, rephrase, accentuate, and exaggerate what is going on; "disposable" spouses, those who have had the "honor" of accompanying their husbands or wives during the difficult period of career building and child rearing but who subsequently are abandoned or replaced once their life partner is established; psychiatric spouses, who have the ability to listen to all the important and trivial details of their partner's academic adventures, vigilantes, who keep constant watch on the proceedings and alert their partners to all approaching good or evil; spouses with "broken careers," those who have sacrificed their own careers in order to help their partners; and superconscious spouses, who play the role of superego for their partners.

CHAPTER 4

1.   Among others, I have had an opportunity to observe the life of a "transplanted" German academic chair. This was the chair, transferred from Germany to the United States, of Max Rheinstein (the follower and translator of Max Weber). When I attended his seminar in 1959 in Chicago, he invited me to his home, where his students, friends, and colleagues met for scholarly and social gatherings. There, I had a chance to discuss the peculiarities of the structure of academic life in Germany (which influenced Poland, Russia, Austria, and other

countries). Since then, I have discussed these matters with Rheinhard Bendix and Lewis Coser as well (both of them prominent followers of Weber).

2.   Where I coorganized some conferences with Renato Treves and met several of his collaborators.

3.   Where I coorganized two conferences (1975 and 1995).

4.   Where I coorganized several conferences and met Johs Andernaes, Vilhelm Aubert, Niels Christie, and Thorstein Eckoff.

5.   Additionally, this classification omits German and French scholars. Nonetheless, I preferred to limit my study to areas of which I had more or less reliable firsthand knowledge.

6.   My participant observation of British academic life started in 1971, when I was a visiting scholar at All Souls College, Oxford. Later, in 1977–78, I was able to continue my Oxford observations when I was appointed senior fellow at Wolfson College and a special research fellow in the Center of Socio-Legal Studies (as a "sort of" codirector of this center). I visited Wolfson College again in 1979, 1989, and 1991. During these visits, I resided at Beechwood House, All Souls College. Currently, Wolfson College lists the following categories of fellows: emeritus, extraordinary, governing body, honorary, junior research, librarian, ordinary, professorial, research, supernumerary, and visiting.

I also spent the second half of 1987 in Cambridge, residing in Churchill College.

7.   Isaac Wolfson was a U.S. industrialist who gave Isaiah Berlin £3 million to build a college at Oxford. Berlin became its first president.

8.   Are they arrogant because they are dealing with their former "subjects"? Are they submissive in order to gain a favorable reaction from former subjects through flattery? Are they arrogant and submissive because, in fact, they do not know how to behave?

9.   It is interesting to note that Frank Vallee once quoted a statement by a distinguished Canadian scholar relating to "the typical one thousand mistakes of British scholars in the 1950s." He was referring to the double prize of crossing the Atlantic. The first crossing was caused by the relatively high Canadian salaries, the second by personal defeat (disappointment with Canadian life in comparison with a now-distant and mythologized British reality).

10.   Especially interesting is a subcategory of British ex-Communist Party scholars working abroad. They are frustrated to the highest degree, and they channel this frustration into an aggression directed not only against their faculty colleagues but also against the students. What is characteristic of their party heritage is their persistent drive toward the most significant (neuralgic) administrative tasks in the department. Without fail, one can find them on personnel committees and publication committees.

11.   In the United Kingdom, at least, this operates as a tradition appended to real tradition. Recently, British scholars invented an additional device: instead of supporting themselves on the shoulders of giants (Newton, Merton), they tend to

support themselves on the shoulders of their former students, the latter repaying old favors by serving as an "image-building clique."

12. British scholars invented the institution of "seminars based on grants." In some sense, these seminars open the way to creation of new scientific schools. In my view, W. Garry Runciman or Anthony Giddens, both from Cambridge, would be the best candidate for the job of giving the comprehensive synthesis. In his book *Confessions of a Reluctant Theorist* (1989), Runciman provided outside observers with some taste of such an analysis.

13. See, for example, C. P. Snow, *Strangers and Brothers* series; see also Malcolm Bradbury, *Rates of Exchange* (1983) and *History Man*.

14. The past superficiality of British sociology was inadvertently disclosed in a book that undertook a diagnosis of European sociology: "A specific case is British sociology, which for a long time remained hostile toward the theoretically alien continental sociology and which in recent decades has flourished greatly, probably due — to a certain extent — to the influence of such distinguished immigrants from the continent as K. Mannheim, K. Popper, N. Elias, G. Poggi, R. Dahrendorf, and Z. Bauman" (Kapciak 1994: 259). British sociology could not have been very profound if the intellectual products of scholars like Zygmant Bauman or Giafranco Poggi were supposed to have deepened it.

15. The current situation of British scholars seems to be very poor. The accuracy of the signals given out in the press should be investigated.

In September I shall pack my bags and return to research and teaching in Britain. Quite frankly I am dreading the return to a university system in which market mechanisms (there is nothing "quasi" about them) have been fully internalized and institutionalized. I antici- pate returning not to "a vibrant and responsive system" . . . but to a nasty, brutish compet- itive environment in which presentation is all, where there is insufficient concern for the substance of teaching and research, where the free exchange of ideas seems a quaint anachronism and (a few designated super producers excepted) to mainly overworked, poorly-paid, and demoralized colleagues. (McNeil 1995: 9)

16. British sociology has had the advantage that it was able, using the English language as a carrier, to capitalize on the great advantages of the Americans. A great disadvantage was that the red-brick universities, not being immune to Cambridge and Oxford subculture, easily absorbed U.S. professional- ism.

17. This meta-attitude, consistently manifested toward everything and everybody, deeply resembles the Polish meta-stance. Whereas in the Oxbridge milieu this attitude has been generated by an authentic posture of superiority (sometimes justified), the Polish meta-stance has a different source. It stems on one side from an authentic feeling of superiority (justified or not) and on the other from a genuine underlying inferiority combined with insecurity.

18. Znaniecki provided an excellent description of the scientific and organi- zational structure of Polish academia as it existed before World War II (1940: 131-33). For an outsider, especially for an American, it might not be easy to

comprehend that, after the Soviet-totalitarian period, Poland varied from other former Soviet Union republics or Russia itself. In my book *Polish Society* (1994), I tried to show basic social and political differences; here, I want to outline these differences as they apply to the academic world.

I have had a chance to study the peculiarities of Polish academic life as a participant-observer first, during my law studies (1945–49) and my sociological studies (1948–51) at Jagiellonian University in Cracow, and second, since 1957 at the University of Warsaw, where I started to teach methodology and logic and where in 1972 I became a professor of sociology. (Although, at the beginning of 1977, I was ousted from the country, I still remain a professor of this university — under Polish law then, it was easier to evict someone from his country than from his university.) Finally, I was secretary of the Polish Sociological Association, president of its Warsaw branch, president (and founder) of the Section of Sociology of Law, and president (and founder) of the Sociotechnical Section of this association.

19.   A description of Jerzy Lande's seminar is presented later in this book. I also attended the seminars of Maria Ossowska (theory and sociology of morals) and Tadeusz Kotarbinski (logic; gnoseology [epistemology]; reism, according to which only matter and human beings exist; and praxeology [the theory of an efficient general human activity]). These seminars were organized according to the same principles: truth seeking, a democratic regime of rational argumentation, and an attempt to build a scientific school as it was understood by the professor leading the seminar.

20.   This observation was also made by a Chinese philosopher Si-tien in his unpublished story. "Si-tien, although I try to be reliable, always something small and unpredictable spoils my plan. Don't tell me that I should follow the rules of logic, I do; don't tell me that I should study geometry, I do; and don't tell me that I should unsew from myself, strong feelings, I am doing it," asked the scholar Yan Pin. "You assume that everything is based on logic," replied Si-tien, "but some types of reality are run by logic of a different kind." "What kind?" inquired Yan Pin. Answered Si-Tien, "A mischievous one."

21.   Lande was Leon Petrazycki's student. He was one of the outstanding followers of the well-known "Warsaw-Lwow" logical school, and he was devoted to the idea of "social help for underdogs." After his release from the German concentration camp in Sachsenhausen, he worked in the "Secret University" (organized during World War II); many who were involved with this university were sent to concentration camps, usually Auschwitz, or killed by the Germans on the spot. Lande also was instrumental in organizing secret shelters for Jews. He was an example of intellectual decency and of unusual tolerance.

Here, I also want to follow the track established by my friend Vilhelm Aubert in his book *Continuity and Development* (1989), which opens with "An Autobiographical Introduction." I am using this chapter as an opportunity to present, on the basis of my participant observation, a picture of totalitarian scholars in action, a picture totally unknown in the West.

22. Toward the end of the period 1945–49, the political climate in Polish universities became quite uneasy. Once, I met Lande in his favorite coffee shop, where he was sitting with his friend Klara Pigwa. In amazement, he told me the following story: "Recently, 'they' [Party officials] discussed the 'case of Lande.' So, an official came to Cracow directly from the Central Committee of the Party at Warsaw to participate in these deliberations. They were confused. Two plans were developed: the first was to 'send Lande to early retirement,' the second to leave him one abstract course for fourth-year students." Lande smiled and added that, by then, students were immune to his heresies. However, the mysterious official remained silent, and because they did not understand what this meant, they began to drift toward the first proposal. Finally, the party representative spoke up and recommended that Lande should not be "touched" in any way. When Lande finished his story, he smiled again. "Really, I do not know who is behind this strange mandate. It might be Jerzy Licki (Jerzy Finkelkraut), who is presently high in the Party, and thinks that he owes me something, or it could be Czeslaw Rudzinski (Sawa Frydman) for whom I was able to find shelter during the German occupation. I don't think I will be able to solve this puzzle."

23. The number of those wishing to belong to Lande's seminar was relatively large. The political climate of the years after 1945 was not conducive to one seeking a career as a lawyer. Grades, for example, were not noooooarily the most accurate indicators of an individual's potential, and the accumulation of those who were unable to study during World War II (universities had been closed by the Germans during the war) had swollen. Consequently, the gnoseological and political problems connected with jurisprudence and the social and political role of the law were regarded as hot topics. This was one of the reasons why Lande's seminar was considered so attractive.

24. A good summary can be found in Ian Gorecki, *Sociology and Jurisprudence of Leon Petrazycki* (1975).

25. Apparently he did not take into consideration the newly emerging style of academic discourse, a style that was not so much an expression of one's own opinions as an articulation of ideas that were, one way or another, obligatory. "In Gramsci's own conception there is no question of intellectuals becoming themselves historical agents; their social weight consists in their ability to link themselves with "real" agents, namely classes" (Aronowitz 1990: 11).

26. The names of the most significant participants of this seminar are listed by Adam Podgórecki (1966: 14): Maria Borucka-Arctowa, Jan Gorecki, Jan Klimowski, Wieslaw Lang, Tadeusz Los, Kazimierz Opalek, Adam Podgórecki, Grzegorz Seidler, Franciszek Studnicki, and Jerzy Wroblewski.

27. His death probably was the result of the conflict between his roles as a legal scholar, a practitioner of unusual ability, and a decent human being and the acute demands of his high administrative position.

28. Julian Haraschin was the chief military judge for the south of Poland. He passed more than 100 death sentences against Polish patriots fighting during World War II. He was also head of the extramural division of the law school.

29.   A habilitation thesis, in the Polish postwar system as in the German university system, was higher than a doctoral dissertation; it was the necessary step to a professorship. One of them was published in 1946 and reprinted in 1995 (Seidler 1995).

30.   His name is included in *The Philosophy of Law: An Encyclopedia* (Gray in preparation).

31.   A literary description of the internal structure and processes involved in the chair can be found in Irina Grekowa's novel *The Chair* (1983). This insightful work was based on participant observation. The author's real name is Elena Ventcel. She was a professor of mathematics in one of the higher technical schools in Moscow.

32.   In Poland, during the period of "real socialism," two terms were coined in connection with the general and, to some extent, neutral term "scholar": *naukowiec* and *pracownik naukowy*. *Naukowiec* is an ugly term denoting people who work in sciences, earn their living from it, and try to contribute something to their particular areas. *Pracownik naukowy* has the same meaning, although it accentuates the fact that someone is *working* in sciences. These terms differ sharply from the traditional word *uczony*, which now is reserved exclusively for those whose contribution to sciences is regarded as essential.

33.   One Polish professor, of the Marxist breed (Jerzy Sawicki), demanded from each of his graduate students a positive review of his book in one of the criminal law magazines. He claimed that this helps students to learn how to write a good review: according to Sawicki, a good book itself structures a good review.

34.   This attitude also was present in the natural sciences, although to a lesser degree. After World War II, several scholars were working in areas connected to the military establishment and could be sent to the Soviet Union to meet with Soviet scholars or to find a direct application for their work in the military-industrial complex. Consequently, they were alert to the political implications of their scholarly activities.

35.   As was indicated in the study *Sto Lat Sociologii Polskiej* (One hundred years of Polish sociology), the majority of Polish sociologists came from the nobility (Szaki 1995).

36.   It is useful to employ such extreme language here, because only a few Western scholars perceive the motivations of the former Communist scientific gang in a true light. Gross and Levitt describe this gang in the following way:

In the earlier days, Marxism, in the form of a disciplined Communist movement, lured intellectuals by offering them the illusion of membership in a priesthood, an inner circle of initiates privileged to understand, by means of esoteric doctrine, the secret inner workings of the world, a coven of hierophants signalling to each other in an arcane jargon impenetrable to outsiders. It was the promise of numinous power, inherent in arcane doctrine and obscure lexicon, that convinced instinctive radicals that Marxist communism alone had the potential to purge the world of its indwelling evils. The melancholic chronicle of Communism in America, and its horror-laden history in those parts of the world where it has at one time or another actually held power, have by now demolished its intellectual prestige beyond hope of resurrection. (1994 : 73)

37. In his lectures, Petrazycki employed the term "psychological poison" to convey the content of human attitudes (not behaviors) that, invisible and difficult to identify, had the ability to spoil, if not destroy, people's relationships in moral and legal life.

38. In Poland, the historical fact of centuries of political danger generated a peculiar ethical measure of integrity. The Poles have (or, at least, had) a tendency to judge people on the basis of their entire lives. No biographical gaps were accepted. For people entering new social surroundings, nothing less than a full elucidation of the past, supported by reliable credentials, was accepted as proof of their decency. The otherwise-true phrase developed by Marxists and party members that "only a cow does not change her ideas" should, from this point of view, be regarded as a shallow and ridiculous mockery.

39. During the worst part of the Stalinist regime (1950–53), a small group of scholars (now professors), Jan Gorecki, Janusz Maciaszek, Jan Steczkowski, Jacek Wir-Konas, and myself, used to go to the remote parts of the country (mountains, lakes, forests) and discuss various political issues in complete isolation. This was one of the ways in which we and several other close-knit groups of friends tried to keep our mental sanity amidst the terror of organized irrationality.

40. Edmund Wnuk-Lipinski, one of the best sociologists of his generation (he finished his studies around the end of the 1960s) and a former Communist Party member, says, "I do not support egalitarianism in sciences; that's not the area of social activities of the state, but an area where this one is better, who more adequately discovers truth in physical or human worlds, and who better elucidates these worlds and who better explains them" (1995: 4).

41. For example, Julian Hochfeld, a former adviser to Wieslaw Gomulka and a professor of sociology who was regarded as a humanist, had private seminars in his home. His well-known Marxist lieutenants (people like Zygmunt Bauman, Maria Hirszowicz, Wlodzimierz Wesolowski, and Jerzy Wiatr) were the show products of this seminar.

42. The section on Polish academia was expanded in response to Daniel Bell's suggestion to rearrange the book into a more detailed and picturesque description of the "socialist scholar."

43. I have had a chance to observe U.S. academic life during my several visits to this country as a Ford Foundation fellow (1959–60), visiting professor at the Northwestern University law school (1967), visiting distinguished professor at the University of Pennsylvania (1972), fellow at the Center for Advanced Study in the Behavioral Study, Stanford (1972–73), and, in the spring of 1994, at Stanford University and the University of California at Berkeley, when I conducted the empirical research for this book.

U.S. academia is based on the principle of organizational continuity. Yet, this continuity is not supported by an institutional memory of ideas; if it is sustained in any way, it is only by institutional memory; it registers unusual administrative events: the car accident of a new director; a foreign fellow's marriage to his secretary; the cleaning lady's triumph on the lottery. U.S. scholars do not remember (they do not feel a need to specify) what has been developed in the old organizational setting. Any ideas they do develop are generated, for example, by reading books or articles, through attending conferences or maintaining personal contacts, or writing reviews (of published or unpublished manuscripts) but rarely through correspondence. The concept that the atmosphere of a given institution may germinate certain innovative thoughts is alien to U.S. academia. Also, they do not feel (or sense any need for) loyalty toward a given institution. For U.S. scholars, institutions are totally neutral (perhaps with the exception of the Stanford University community): useful if convenient, worthless if not.

The U.S. scholar is an enormously complicated creature. He or she wears too many hats; he or she may come from Europe or may be indigenous but often is too difficult to identify. Therefore, the model presented in this subchapter is taken from Weber's "library." Careful observation of the European among scientific immigrants (with some exceptions, like Max Rheinstein) eventually reveals a common thread, a genuine U.S. stamp. I have undertaken the ungrateful task of describing some of its main elements.

44.   This model is, to some extent (and of necessity), exaggerated. Of course, there are scholars who stand like watchtowers on the horizon of U.S. academia. On the other hand, one cannot avoid noticing a sea of mediocrities.

45.   Gross and Levitt present not only a keen description of the U.S. academic left but also a succinct and sharp diagnosis of current U.S. society as a broader framework for the development of academia in the United States.

We emphasize again that the underlying grievances that ignite their [change-oriented thinkers' and theoreticians'] anger are by no means wholly imaginary or capricious. Racial bigotry and the deification of greed have clogged cities with ruined men and women, and have come near to turning crime into a rational career choice for tens of thousands of young people. Unprovoked brutality with no apparent cause against women is a continuing fact of our culture as, of course, of others. Easy as it is to mock the self-righteousness of scholarly bluestockings in their academic sinecures, we must keep in mind the real fear of violence that attends the life of any woman, no matter how privileged. The crime of rape remains a brutal expression of power, not only over women, but over other — vanquished — men. Matters of sexual taste and private choice that a true civilization would cede ungrudgingly to individuals remain subject to an intolerance that is sometimes expressed as violence and is never less than humiliating. And when we contemplate the mess and the real, if invisible, dangers that are at times created by the frenzied processes of industry and technology, we are once again faced with the mordant power of greed, with the shortsightedness that can offend the landscape in aid of a few more years of cheerful annual reports to stockholders. (1994: 216)

46.   Some more perceptive U.S. scholars describe themselves as "childish."

They even perceive themselves as "more childish than children." Strangely enough, these scholars live in a society that does not appreciate them, that does not even like to keep them in their own boundaries. Nevertheless, U.S. scholars pretend not to notice their internal alienation, communicating mainly among themselves.

47.   Professionalization is most visible in the humanities and social sciences, in which the measures of scholarly success are not easy to discern. Palliatives are applied by means of an elaborate formalism to hide (or artificially replace) the inherent impotence and emptiness of this professionalism. Thus, although it often is very difficult, or impossible, to discuss something on a substantive level, decorous battles often are fought at a lower level; one person scores over another person's linguistic, literate, or erudite weakness and then persuades a larger audience that these deficiencies equal substantive incompetence. This type of palliative gives rise to a variety of formalistic requirements, especially in reviews of books and articles, scholarly promotion evaluations, various scientific assessments, and so on. When the substantive argumentation is demanding, time-consuming, and complicated, discussion on a low and conventional level seems to be self-indulgent: then someone proves to be efficient or fails the test. If he or she fails, an impressive psychological (but not logical) jump demonstrating his or her adversary's incompetence becomes the weapon of choice; in logic it is called an argument ad hominem (appealing to personal features), or better, *ad personam.* An ability to substitute open-ended argument with a confusing contest between formalistic criteria has been one of the modes of modern eristics (a semilogical dialectical play introduced by the Greeks to tear someone down in a humiliating and cheap manner). These eristic styles of scientific discourse, cultivated mainly in practice, seem to be undergoing a revival in academia, especially when it is not so much the search for truth as the desperate drive toward any form of personal and scholarly success that is at stake. In contemporary political sciences, which are well-known for their shallowness, these duels reveal an impressive emptiness. In sociology, they tend to be transformed into statistically unintelligible deductions. Even in history, they might be presented as an accumulation of facts according to a priori preconceived formulas. In philosophy, professionalization manifests itself through excessive inquiries of a linguistic-analytical character; these inquiries are preoccupied less with substance than with one or another version of the research epistemology.

48.   This does not mean that, among U.S. intellectuals and scholars, some do not work nights and weekends, ignore their wives and families, do not work in their offices all day, and are not preoccupied with avoiding the impression that they are making sexual advances to students, and so on.

49.   A majority of (male) U.S. scholars give thanks for the "patience" of their wives in acknowledgments.

50.   At one U.S. university, a European professor was advised by his chairman to attend the lectures of a colleague who was regarded as a great teacher. The only contribution of this master professor was a video of a final train journey,

before the line was closed, and tape-recorded conversations of the last passengers. Nonetheless, he was apparently a real maestro at dancing: he was able to mime the behavior of the last passengers impeccably.

51.   After my stay in 1959–60 in the United States, a prominent U.S. couple visited me in Poland; he was a political scientist, and she was an internationally known politician (the former head of the United Nations Children's Fund). In the Europejska Coffee Shop in Warsaw, after a few niceties, they told me,

Adam, we came her to propose that you join us in an international study concerning *leadership*. This topic is very important: we already have sufficient funds to conduct it, and we need an insider from a "socialist" country. The next conference will be conducted in India, the following one in Yugoslavia, and the one after in the U.S. We plan to publish several reports on this subject. You may connect the study to your own scholarly interests in the sociology of law. Could you prepare a draft of interviews with people at the highest level and specify how we might reach some prominent dignitaries, including Gomulka. Please suggest strategies and names.

I was not sure whether they were serious or joking. They answered, first, that they did not need to spend time and money to travel to Poland to be witty; second, that they regard this research as especially important for enhancing international understanding; third, that further delay (he was seriously ill) was working against them; fourth, that several prime ministers and presidents of Third World countries already had agreed to be interviewed (some of them owed deep thanks to Betsy for the help they received from the United States after World War II; and fifth, for political and theoretical reasons, they could not omit the Communist world from the study. They added that their central idea was to compare the basic values of leaders in different political and social systems.

I asked whether they had tried to employ someone to do a content analysis of Gomulka's speeches, mentioning that, in the Polish academic world, it was absolutely impossible to attain such heights and that if he (Gomulka) agreed, he only would repeat the last of his public orations (which were usually five hours long). They asked me to be serious. I replied that the whole thing could only be a farce unless they secured access to the insignificant ranks of local government, given that this study was being conducted by someone politically trusted. To make a final point, I suggested they approach Professor W. in Poland, who was internally, and perhaps internationally, known (for falsifying the results of his field studies). Either the irony escaped them, or they pretended that it did. We parted.

Eventually, they did approach Professor W. This was the beginning of their "famous" Communist extension of research on local leaders, in connection with which several politically oriented Poles published articles and books and got invited to various conferences; some who were directly linked to Polish security organs became internationally known scholars. Currently, this study is widely respected by those who value pseudotheoretical sophistication or those who never had the opportunity to check its empirical base and the comparability of the key research notions.

In 1995, the Canadian university at which I was a professor wanted to invite a scholar of this type to summarize the findings of the group and to lecture on democracy in Poland. During a board meeting I protested against the invitation but was overruled. I then wrote to the dean as follows:

Dr. O. was for several years (in the 1970s), the head of the Section on Science of the Warsaw Voivodeship Communist Party Committee, which was charged with full control of academic life in the region. The Section headed by Dr. O. was overseeing such areas as promotions of academic personnel (especially professors) scientific publications and academic travel abroad. Given that the Warsaw Voivodeship represents the highest concentration of academic institutions and scholars in Poland and influences scientific life in the whole country, the ideological control exercised by the said Section was of immense consequence. Dr. O. used the power of his office without hesitation, implementing authoritarian policies that subjugated all post-secondary education and scientific activity to the omnipotent Communist Party. Eventually, he was rewarded for his vigilance with a promotion to the Central Committee of the Communist Party. Subsequently, he was appointed as an official to the United Nations in New York. It is disturbing to see someone so adroit in muzzling scientific thought in Poland invited to teach Canadian university students about the merits of democracy. Moved by the irony of this situation and its incongruity, several Carleton and University of Ottawa professors of Polish descent, familiar with Polish social and political reality, have asked me to convey to you their protest against the announced lecture. They believe that it is a travesty of democracy to ask a stellar member of a totalitarian system to lecture here on democracy in Poland.

The names, affiliations, and home telephone numbers of the nine professors concerned were appended.

The director of the institute responded as follows:

I appreciate your making me aware of your objections to this lecture and hope that I can answer some of your concerns. Dr. O. is visiting Canada on his own and was proposed to me by a colleague in Montreal as a potential speaker. I reviewed his CV and publication resulting from the research project on local government in which he is involved. I am also familiar with the work of his collaborators on this project (Henry Teune, Adam Przeworski) and have myself engaged in joint research with and have high regard, as I believe you do as well, for the colleague responsible for the project in Russia. On this basis, I concluded that this lecture might prove interesting to our students and faculty. I do not know Dr. O. personally and have never worked with him, so I acknowledge that I can hardly claim to be aware of the way he carried out his functions during the communist period. In inviting Dr. O. to speak, this was in no sense an expression of approval of any actions taken in the communist structure; I am aware that many of our colleagues from the region held prominent, sometimes potentially powerful, positions in the old structures. These facts can make them controversial and objectionable to some, particularly to individuals like yourself who experienced the brunt of the repressive apparatus. I certainly regret that our invitation to Dr. O. is offensive to you and that the invitation may elicit memories of unpleasant episodes; I do not, however, believe that it is feasible to reject speakers on the basis of such considerations, unless there is a very clear and compelling reason to do so. My own personal conviction is that, except in extreme cases, it is more constructive to react to individuals on the basis of their present activities, rather than trying to make judgements about past actions. I think it is instructive for our students to be exposed to a variety of speakers and perspectives; at the same time, disagreements about which speakers are desirable or preferable are probably inevitable. I should emphasise that Dr. O. will not be instructing our students about "the merits of democracy"; rather he has been invited to give a talk on his research work which does relate to processes of democratization and local governance in Eastern Europe. Dr. O. talk is, as you know, a public lecture; you and our colleagues from Carleton University and the University of Ottawa are welcome to attend, to address questions to Dr. O., and to engage him in dialogue about his research work. I would hope that this work would be judged on its own merits; of course we also need to maintain the discussion on the level of scholarly discourse appropriate to the objections which have been made to his appearance here. I again express my regret that the invitation to Dr. O. has engendered discomfort or has offended you and your colleagues mentioned in your letter; I can appreciate your concerns and hope that you will accept my assurance that my decision to maintain the lecture as scheduled in no way reflects any disregard or disrespect for your opinion. I am certain you are quite right that those of us who did not experience firsthand the brutalities of communist repression may appear naive or insensitive at times, but I would hope that the distance we have from the subject matter we study will also help assure that all voices are heard, as these societies and the international community of scholars try to analyze and understand both the communist past and the present dilemmas of the transition. Respectfully.

The dean and, later, the president approved the director's decision. Not even the statement by one of the signatories that "here we have a direct analogy with a situation in which a SS officer would be asked to present his opinions about the Holocaust" shattered the internal "loyalty" of the administration.

52.   This can serve as an example of how some U.S. scholars are treated. A Canadian university organized a conference on community, modernity, and religion (University of Saskatchewan, June 25–27, 1995). The rationale for this conference was the revelation, attributed to U.S. sociologist Robert Bellah, that we are currently witnessing "the collapse of meaning and the failure of moral standards."

53.   Social science and humanities scholarship in Canada — especially in English Canada — has been influenced by the historical experience of being, first, a British colony and, later, a U.S. one. Some Canadians, nevertheless, managed over the years to establish distinctive subschools (Northrop Frye in literary studies, Harold Innis in political economy, Marshall McLuhan in culture and communication, George Grant in political philosophy, John Porter in the global understanding of Canadian society, to mention a few). However, significant innovators have been rare.

54.   "Students believe that going to school will help them find future employment, but mostly because they will have a university diploma, not because of anything they will have learned," says Neil Postman. He also indicated that the average North American high-school graduate will have spent 13,000 hours in school and 19,000 hours watching television (1994: A1, A2).

55.   There are some voices demanding change. In an article entitled "How to Improve Universities," David M. Bishop (1994) states that the main role of the professor is "to discover new knowledge and to pass it on." However, he focuses exclusively on the practical orientation and comes to strange conclusions. For example, some students "would like to practice a profession in which they use their acquired knowledge but they have no desire to create new knowledge themselves. They could well be taught in a less expensive institution by people who are like-minded. . . . The latter are the ones who, in four-year honours research programs or graduate studies, benefit most by being taught by motivated practitioners of the discipline."

56.   John Perry (1991) suggests that the drawbacks of large classes can be offset with a few simple techniques. Thus, "Eye contact with students, voice quality, physical movement and humour — all play a part in ensuring good professors who have . . . a profound impact on students." His "empirical" research shows that "voice intonation and physical movement are two most important qualities teachers can bring into a classroom."

57.   The point that the social sciences are different from natural sciences is well-established. The crucial point here is that the social sciences are characterized by an understanding, human coefficient, or *verstehen*. Nonetheless, the basic feature underlying the various methods and humanistic strategies — historical, psychological, sociological, and anthropological — seems to be overlooked. This is to say that practically nobody has analyzed the problem of social empathy, which is basically different from individual empathy. Individual empathy is concerned with penetrating the psyche of another human being in a way that makes it possible to disclose the unique disparity between the observer and the observed. The observers identify with certain attitudes, values, and feelings of the people they observe without losing their own identity. Social empathy, on the other hand, is concerned with the social setting in which the observed person is situated. Therefore, to see them properly, the observer should not focus only on the features that may characterize a given individual but should try to "enter" into their particular ethos. One must not only enter into their gnoseological (epistemological) life frame but also try to understand their unique approach to basic human issues; not only enter their hierarchy of values but also comprehend how various life matters are perceived from an entirely different point of view; not only link oneself with the life tradition of the social position of the given person but also acquire a feeling for how certain matters are evaluated and viewed from a life perspective of human beings who occupy different social positions and places in the life of the whole social entity. Here, one should be able to jump into the self of a different person and also into the whole atmosphere surrounding that person.

58.   The heavy stress on teaching apparently is caused by an understanding of universities as institutions that are supposed to be instrumental in finding a profitable job. Znaniecki noted this trend as early as 1940: "The whole career of a scholar depends on his activity as a scientific contributor, helping to maintain and

develop recognized systems of absolute truth which the school transmits to successive generations by the process of teaching. Nor is there any fundamental difference in this respect between the structure of European and that of American universities, except that in comparison with scientific work in the latter teaching is relatively more emphasized than in the former" (1940: 133–34).

59.   However, this is true not only in Canada; some patterns come from the United States. For example, the well-known theoretician Bernard Berelson said, "The graduate school should aim at training the skilled specialist — not . . . at producing the 'educated man,' the 'cultured man,' the 'wise man' (nor, for that matter, the 'mere technicians,' either)" (1960: 124).

60.   Canadian writer Margaret Atwood describes it in the following way:

It will be a good lecture, good enough — her lectures are always good enough — but as time goes on she comes to feel, at these events, more and more like a talking dog. Cute, no doubt; a clever trick, a *nice* dog; but nonetheless a dog. She used to think that her work was accepted or rejected on its own merits, but she's begun to suspect that the goodness of her lectures is somehow not the point. The point is her dress. She will be patted on the head, praised, fed a few elite dog biscuits, and dismissed, while the boys in the back room get down to the real issue, which is which of them will be the next society president. (1993: 123–24)

61.   Apparently to strengthen the instrumental professional orientation, Canadian universities recently started to hire ex-Communist scholars from Europe (including Poland).

62.   Canadian universities resemble grocery stores more than factories. "For Norm Wagner, former president of the University of Calgary, the problem is that universities do not resemble Wal-Marts nearly as much as they ought to. He called retailers 'a good model for how to deliver better services' in Alberta's universities. Wal-Mart claims to deliver great customer service, cheap. So should universities and other public institutions" (Vandervlist 1995: A20).

63.   This situation creates a new type of tension. Because all professors are treated in an equal way, then professor-creators have the same access to photocopying facilities, secretarial assistance, and financial help as the professor-teachers do. In this particular case, the idea of equality plays some backward function.

64.   Scientific activities sometimes can bring out the pathologies of those engaged in them. The scientific community should be alert to the possibility and beware of creating conditions conducive to their appearance. A case in point is the murder of four colleagues by Valery Fabricant of Concordia University in Montreal. Fabricant accused his victims of having stolen his research and sabotaged his chance of getting tenure. The report commissioned after the event says:

Some of those accused by Fabricant had been involved in conflict of interests with industry or did not follow guidelines in dealing with outside research. Engineering professors used university facilities to fulfil private research contracts without reimbursing Concordia. . . . Universities need to re-emphasize learning rather than the pursuit of research grants and industrial contracts. . . . "Too often, university honours, research grants and industrial contracts are awarded on the basis of publications rather on their quality and significance." . . . Concordia, like other universities, must develop procedures to make sure faculty devote themselves primarily to teaching and "the disinterested pursuit and dissemination of knowledge." (Bull 1994: A5)

65. During my first visit as a tourist to China in 1962, I had no chance to observe academic life at Chinese universities, which were almost completely suppressed at that time. During my two months' stay in 1987 at Suzhou University, Jiangsu Province, the situation was different. Although this visit was short, my observations were enhanced by studies I had undertaken earlier on the Chinese academic situation and by the cooperation of other "foreign specialists" who were willing to share their experience.

The Chinese, it seems, were able to grasp the meaning of "scholarship" before anyone else. Yutang Lin writes, "Wang Ch'ung (A.D. 27–c. 100) distinguished between 'specialists' and 'scholars,' and again between 'writers' and 'thinkers.' I think a specialist graduates into a scholar when his knowledge broadens, and a writer graduates into a thinker when his wisdom deepens" (1937: 388). Apparently this approach is based on Confucian wisdom. Confucious said, "He who learns but does not think, is lost; he who thinks but does not learn is in danger" (Wing-Tsit 1963: 24), or, in Lin's translation, "Thinking without learning makes one flighty, and learning without thinking is a disaster" (1937: 364).

66. I think this was done partially for pragmatic reasons: in this way, they were easier to translate into English.

67. I know this because I grabbed those questions and was not willing to return them to the "authorities" (the professors).

68. Still, there was the possibility that they were not eager to discuss sensitive matters with a stranger, even an enthusiast of Chinese culture.

69. One of the "foreign specialists" (a teacher of the English language) told me that one of her students insisted that everybody in Canada has their own helicopter. This student persisted in his request to be adopted and, in this way, to obtain Canadian citizenship.

70. Nazi ideology and its criminal practice (its genocidal policy toward Jews, Gypsies, Catholics, and so on and its systematic persecution of Slavs and other minorities) generated an extremely cautious environment for any discussions linking intelligence and behavior with social or national background. Yet, studies about the origins, forms, and consequences of intelligence and behavior abound.

CHAPTER 5

1. I did not change the grammar of interviews; additional remarks have been introduced in only a few instances where the text otherwise may have been misunderstood. These remarks are presented in square brackets.

2.   Apparently there were many scientific schools, but because they were not described or acknowledged and promoted as such, they are not recognized as independent schools. To be a scientific school, at least three conditions are necessary: a group of scholars has to create a body of new ideas, different from the existing body of knowledge; there must be adequate funding for research in the given area; and the scholars have to be recognized as an independent element. Polish schools of "sociology of law" or of "sociotechnics" were not originally recognized as independent schools, and, therefore, they do not figure on the international map of scientific centers. By publishing his book *The Dialectical Imagination*, Jay provided several scholars with the label "Frankfurt School" and, in some way, "created" this school. In Poland, there were several scientific schools, some of considerable interest (for example, the Lwow-Warsaw Logical School), but nobody worked to elevate them to the rank of an internationally recognized scientific school.

CHAPTER 6

1.   The scholars portrayed in this chapter were selected for their resemblance to the scholarly types described above. They were not selected on the basis of their intellectual capacities: from one point of view, they are well-known because of their real or alleged achievements, and from another, they are known because of nonscholarly factors. They come from the social sciences; I cannot claim sufficient competence in the natural sciences.

2.   This evaluation inevitably has a somewhat childish character.

3.   Adams does not distinguish between meta-systems and meta-systems interventions. The first one is spurious and pointless. The second is justified: if someone eats many poisonous mushrooms, then any expectation that the body (a system) will get rid of the poisons (or notions) without outside help is nonsubstantiated. In such a case, the person must have a gastric purge.

4.   Fisher was a former director of the Institute of Racial Hygiene. As minister of education in 1935, he put his name forward for the deanship of Freiburg University.

5.   About Eduard Baumgartner, he has written: "During his tenure here, he was anything but a National Socialist. . . . I regard Baumgartner's becoming a member of the teaching staff as improbable as his joining the SS" (Ferry and Renaut 1990: 26).

6.   There are striking similarities between Nazi and Soviet totalitarianism. A highly respected Polish scholar (the head of the National Professors' Promoting Committee) mentioned in this book wrote a negative opinion about a colleague, blocking her from obtaining a professorship. He was not a party member himself but was a member of the high-ranking nomenklatura (those who occupied a high position in the governmental hierarchy and were individually approved to keep these positions by the personnel section of the Central Committee of the party). He wrote that Hanna Waskiewicz, "accepting the views

opposite to that of Marxism, and not even taking Marxism into consideration, *ex definitione* should not be considered for the professorial position." These facts became known in Poland when the political climate changed in 1989, and some of the relevant documents kept in personal files were released.

7. Apparently this is enough to absolve their sins!

8. The publisher did not indicate that the book was a collection of essays written each week in mockery of the Bible. The essays were written in Poland when he was a loyal party member. Its main objective was to ridicule the religious beliefs of the Polish people.

9. He was referring to the brawls instigated by secret police (in the first phase, when head of police Mieczyslaw Moczar wanted to take power from party head Wladyslaw Gomulka, and in the second phase, when students protested legitimately against aspects of the totalitarian regime).

10. In the same way, Kolakowski used to interrupt the lectures of Wladyslaw Tatarkiewicz, accusing him of not being Marxist and of spreading false, harmful, non-Marxist ideas. Later, Tatarkiewicz was not allowed to teach at the university.

11. Before that, he appealed his ouster before the highest party organ, the party congress. His appeal was rejected.

12. A recent book by Daniel Goleman, *Emotional Intelligence* (1995), supports this point. Goleman presents an accumulation of well-analyzed physiological studies that substantiate even more the emergence of the theory of emotions. However, evidently, seduced by a one-dimenional mono-U.S. perspective, he does not know that the theory of emotions as the central factor of psychological life was established in a flash of genius by Petrazycki almost one century ago.

CHAPTER 7

1. After all that has been said thus far, these conclusions may sound quite trivial, but such may be the case with all summaries. The Chinese sage Si-tien asked, "What separates an outstanding invention from trivia?" Certain that no one would come up with a proper answer, he added, "The moment of its formulation."

2. Here, the term "traditional scholar" is not introduced as a new descriptive category. To clarify its meaning, keep in mind that, in Europe, this term was used to refer to a scholar who was not practical, who was abstract (if not absent-minded), was detached from reality (especially from social reality), and was devoted to books or to the close circle of friends who were interested in similar matters. A German scholar was a good example of this category: he or she loved music (classical), did not care about his or her dress, started each lecture with a joke (in order to invoke a positive atmosphere), told another joke in the middle of the lecture (to wake up those who were asleep), and finished the lecture with a joke (to leave the audience with a good impression).

3. The traditional should not be accepted as good merely because it is traditional, but at the same time, it should not be rejected without thorough evaluation. It should be given sufficient chance to display its merits and flaws.

4. Apparently no one was admitted to the graduate seminar of Jerzy Sawicki (former professor of criminal law at Warsaw University and party member) who did not write a positive review of one of Sawicki's books.

5. Here, I propose a cognitive revolution. Its assumption is that it is not "purely" descriptive statements (or departures from such statements) that should be taken as elementary epistemological elements. Instead, values should be regarded as points of departure. If values are the basic epistemological elements, then the descriptive statements are only shortcuts of value pronouncements. A statement that a particular paragraph or chapter of a book is logically consistent and unfailing means that it positively appeals to the sense of order and integrity; a statement that a painting is beautiful means that its content arouses emotions of desire and appeal; a description of a given behavior as propitious and authentic conveys that this behavior encounters a positive appraisal. In effect, the whole superstructure of descriptions portrays a vast pool of existing and accumulated emotions. Thus, epistemology is designed by values.

6. It is necessary to stress that, in the United States, whose scientific potential decisively shapes the predominant methods and subjects of inquiry in the natural and social sciences around the world, there are two layers of scholars: the "professionals," who are aggressive and imperialistic, and the high-class scholars, who resemble "traditional scholars" (scholars searching for truth) and who are almost invisible. Because the mighty category of professionals is on the run and because this category both shapes the features of the scientific market and designs the preferred scholarly profile, its representatives play a decisive role in establishing the dominant picture of current scientific life. Also, because the high-class scholars, a tiny membership layer, are interested almost exclusively in developing their own areas of scientific work and because, being oriented to task solving, they have no interest in promoting their own personalities, the professionals in effect retain a monopoly on shaping the vision of contemporary scientific life.

7. One has to distinguish valorization of truth in two forms: pure valorization of truth and instrumental valorization of truth. Pure valorization of truth is an approach by which one perceives cognitive notions as derivatives of evaluative ones. "Instrumental valorization" indicates that many epistemological versions are preferable to some political or social movements: feminism announces a change in the comprehension of various epistemological notions but is unable to call attention to anything other than psychological differences in intuition or empathy, and movements of the "left" claim that they introduce revolution in epistemological perspectives by elaborating those notions that seem to be suitable for further subjugating the oppressed. Only the first understanding should be regarded as a philosophically legitimate change of the epistemological perspective.

8. The term "fetishism" was introduced in a cognitively aggressive manner by Karl Marx. Because it is understood in various ways, all of them politically loaded, it seems reasonable to turn to one of the best specialists on Marx for an interpretation. Jon Elster puts it in this way: "The fetishism thesis can in fact be stated as follows: relations between men appear as relations of comparison between objects. Even more sharply: they appear as external relations, since the properties by which the objects are compared do not appear to have a relational component (i.e. to embody a reference to the relations between men), but to inhere in the objects as natural qualities" (1985: 96).

9. Created mainly by William James (1842–1910) and Charles S. Pierce (1839–1914).

10. Scholars can organize data, consciously or unconsciously, in ways that represent the interests of those who employ these scholars; although quite well-known, this is a different problem. This remark is intended to stress only an additional source of skepticism toward the objectivity of scholars.

11. Drawn up in 1525 (but published in 1816).

12. They are consecutively pestered by a different pressure: those who have power, more or less legally, assign to themselves the truth belonging to others.

13. Robert Brym summarizes the ideas of Karl Mannheim in the following way: "Intellectuals in the modern world are 'relatively classless.' Because intellectuals are recruited from various social classes, and because they are educated in a milieu which encourages them to view social and political problems from numerous perspectives, their ideas are, Mannheim submitted, not so class-determined as are those of, say, workers or entrepreneurs. The relative classlessness of intellectuals may enable them to arrive at a pragmatically valid set of solutions to pressing social issues — solutions which express no particular class viewpoint" (1980: 12–13).

14. A similar process took place earlier in fascist Germany, but the processes concerning intellectuals and the intelligentsia, despite the illuminating works of Hannah Arendt, Zbigniew Brzezinski, Carl Friedrich, Franz I. Neuman, and others, are less well-known. The Frankfurt School, which was supposed to be "critical," was, indeed, analytical, sometimes even derogatory, but mainly toward other sociological orientations. Recently, there have been some attempts to elucidate the nature of the relation between the humanities and power in this area (see, for example, Wolin 1993).

15. It is interesting to note that these came almost exclusively from the West. No prominent and authentic intellectuals from the East would support this ideology.

16. Etzioni-Halevy presents this point of view in the following manner. "In contrast, I argue that such deleterious effects [those originated by science-based technology] no less than the beneficial ones, are inherent in the very nature of scientific knowledge and its practical results, *as well as* in certain social arrangements which exacerbate the problem" (1985: 45).

17.   In Poland, the first democratic government of Tadeusz Mazowiecki did not ask sociotechnicians for help but, instead, nominated as head of a government-expertise team the eloquent ex-Communist Waldemar Kuczynski, who converted to the free market way of thinking during his self-imposed exile in Paris.

18.   The scientist in social sciences and humanities does not risk much, unlike the engineer. He or she can teach students any type of stupidity, because the damage this does is invisible!

19.   "The academician enjoys an unusual degree of freedom because, unlike most men, he receives a guaranteed salary that is not tied to the offering of particular products on the market. Or, to put the matter somewhat differently, the salary for his teaching furnishes the economic foundation for his free research and general scholarship" (Coser 1965: 291). Of course, this protection becomes very precious when academic freedom is at stake — when an inventor could fear dismissal by a group of mediocrities who do not understand his or her achievements or when someone pronounces ideas contrary to conformist values. However, this protection also may be quite harmful, giving those who like a "quiet life" a feeling of comfortable security that defends their laziness.

20.   This does not mean that a tendency to "steal officially" somebody else's achievements is not growing in the hard sciences. (Compare the Fabricant case [Bull 1994]).

21.   It was not my goal to propose recommendations on how to deal with the recognized crisis. Nonetheless, it is hard to escape the nagging question: what is the general remedy suggested by this study? The basic recommendation would be to introduce a sharp distinction between those universities (university schools, departments, or scholarly branches) that are structured and targeted toward transferring certain practically oriented skills into technical, economic, and social life and those university branches that develop high abilities and general theoretical considerations. These two tracks could be vertically structured: after studying on the lower level (oriented toward praxis), a gifted and theoretically oriented student may enter into a higher theoretical university branch (here, he or she may enter into the theoretical world of generalizations); a practically oriented student may continue his or her original track, chosen after entering the university, toward subsequent studies oriented toward applicability.

22.   At the present moment, it is much easier for a scholar in the social sciences to undertake a "grant project" than to make a scientific discovery. First, it is not easy to define what subject of study is prone to discovery if objective criteria for doing so are lacking. Second, peers accustomed to the existing standards, even if they are not envious, may have some trouble in agreeing whether this particular thesis is, indeed, a discovery. Third, not everybody is aware of his or her discovery, and not everybody is able to fight efficiently for its recognition. Fourth, the pressure to be successful may not lead to "discovery"; it accentuates only the need to make a career.

Additionally, it is difficult to make even a small invention that would secure professional success. In fact, it is easier to get a grant that would lead to publication, recognition at one's own university (because this university takes part of the grant for its own purposes), and positive professional evaluation. In other words, short-term rewards seem to be much more available and attractive than long-term rewards, which are remote and intangible in their ramifications. Thus, in the social sciences, the short-range strategy seems to be more attractive: it is relatively easy to acquire the skills to carry it out if one has to learn how to prepare a grant proposal, and it is risky following a path in the hope of making an attractive discovery.

23.   Of course, there are some exceptions, like scholars who, under the pressure of circumstances, need additional budgetary resources, scholars who are truly dedicated to the development of their particular branch of social sciences, scholars who are politically motivated, scholars who like to influence praxis by developing a "theory," and so on. The main observation deals not so much with those exceptional circumstances but with the main currents of behavior presently typical for scholars engaged in social science research and teaching.

24.   Probably this is the cumulative result of exposure to two generations of mass media. It is now common knowledge that it is the well-educated who are most heavily influenced, not so much by the written word (which once so strongly impressed peasants) as by what is said on radio and, especially, on television.

25.   Once, during lunch at one of the youngest Oxford colleges, I was sitting at the same table as scholars belonging to the college's power elite. One of them, whose accent was distinctively non-Oxford, tried to make a good impression on his colleagues. I was amazed to realize that he was one of the most hated sharks of Polish Marxism and his wife was a prosecutor who became known during the tragic Polish political trials. (She prosecuted a group of Polish World War II heroes; they were officers on Polish submarines and cruisers who spent the war in England, fighting together with the British fleet. Upon their return to Poland after the war, they were arrested and persecuted by the Polish authorities as British spies. Most of them were sentenced to death and executed; some were rehabilitated). Nonetheless, the scholar in question was quite successful in his endeavors. Now he is a respected fixture of the Oxford scenery.

26.   To finish a study in the given area involves 11 years of ordinary school, 4 years of university, 2 years to prepare a master's thesis, 5 years to write a doctoral dissertation, and about 10 years to finish an apprenticeship. Thus: $11 + 4 + 2 + 5 + 10$ (in the social sciences and humanities, where cultural empathy — knowledge of different societies, their cultures, life styles, unique cumulative experiences — is a sine qua non of real competence) $= 38$. Full academic maturity (around 40 years) is, therefore, reached exactly at the point when a career in most other professions is winding down.

27.   The following anecdote reveals quite clearly the "spirit" of an artificial fix that people sometimes attempt to apply to science. "Euclid, who opened a

school of mathematics at Alexandria in the reign of the first Ptolemy, was once asked by that sovereign whether he could not explain his art to him in a more compendious way; to which Euclid made the celebrated answer, that there was no royal road to geometry." Upon this Dr. Johnson has observed: "Other things may be seized by might, or purchased with money; but knowledge is to be gained only by study, and study to be protracted only in retirement" (Timbs 1858: 162).

28.   The situation is exacerbated by the recent shift of interest in the sciences from discussion of theories, explanations, interpretation of facts, and so on to the lobbies standing behind individual scholars. These lobbies become decisive forces that shape not only the careers of scholars but also the visibility and validity of various scientific ideas and theories.

29.   Even in Poland (where the Catholic worldview has an unusually strong traditional backing and where the Catholic religion served effectively as a battering ram that destroyed the rigid structures of Communist totalitarianism), the deeper layers of society, under pressure by those hidden Communist structures, gradually became secular. Presently, the victorious pressure of the Catholic church keeps these secular tendencies under the surface, but one may venture that they again will erupt with force.

30.   There are several pressing reasons for professionalism. One is the selectivity of professionals. Norman Davies says: "Historians often think of themselves as the most impartial of commentators. I have my doubts. There are several failings to which they are susceptible. One is their ultra-specialization. They tend to pick part of the subject during a very short period of time and to ignore everything that was going on around it. The body of historical knowledge is now so enormous, they feel incapable of reaching for broader perspective" (1995: 7). Among the lower echelons of professionally socialized scholars, this situation of ultraprofessionalization coupled with the erosion of basic human values leads to total nihilism.

31.   Additionally, a professional orientation deprives scholars of the sense of humor essential for keeping a distance from imposed ideas, anti-ideas, or fictions. U.S. scholars especially seem to be affected by this shortcoming. W. G. Runciman noted, "[But] I was still more surprised when a professor came up to me at the cocktail party afterwards [after a lecture] and said 'You must allow for the fact that American audiences are not very good at recognizing irony.' I said, 'But I wasn't ironic,' which merely confirmed him in his view that I was. But I wasn't. And I'm not now" (1989: 235).

32.   With all its elaborated paraphernalia and theatrics.

33.   The idea of "reliable sponsor" is taken from Tadeusz Kotarbinski's ethical philosophy.

34.   It is quite unfortunate that so spectacular a figure as the present Polish pope, John Paul II, does not understand the scope of this danger and, thus, aggravates it.

35.   In Poland before World War II, the Lwow mathematical community kept a book in which everybody belonging to this community wrote their ideas.

These ideas were treated as a community pool that could facilitate discussion on any given subject. Ideas recorded in this book were anonymous. Strangely enough, after the war, when some professors from the mathematics circle were moved to Wroclaw, the habit persisted. Again, as earlier established, everybody was entitled to record their idea(s), pick an inscribed idea, comment on it, reject it, or develop it. After some elaboration, the idea could resurface as the product of an individual or even an anonymous group; later, on the basis of these processes, anyone could call a meeting to discuss the transmutations and implications of the idea.

36.   If a given school decides to keep a head, the power of the head should be restricted to administrative issues: its discretion should, in no case, affect the content of the disputed matters. The strong points of this type of noninstitutionalized scientific school are that it is an open-minded group of specialists interested in the given subject; it is immune to any pathologies connected with the potential use of intellectual or administrative power; it is based on the principle of continuation (because the school assembles and consists of a core of ideas and, with time, develops an intellectual memory of previous discussions and accumulated solutions and conclusions); and no one is able to use the school as an instrument of domination. Scientific schools of this type also have drawbacks, principally that their structure restricts the possibility of continuous apprentice training as well as the possibility of furthering the ideas of a scholar who may be so far ahead of his or her colleagues that they might not see the innovative potential of his ideas. In short, this structure works against those who are either too little or too greatly advanced.

37.   Because one cannot exclude the unpredictable influence of sporadic events — wars, natural catastrophes, man-made disasters — all those events that, according to Leon Petrazycki, can turn the history of humankind in unforeseen directions; such events are not regulated by "tendencies of development."

38.   A scholar and practicing lawyer known, among other things, as a Polish connoisseur of European operas may serve as an example of how expediency is sometimes more important than perfection. In the conclusion to a book she wrote (supported for publication by the American Council of Learned Societies and also by the Foundation of Stefan Batory in London), she does not show the best of taste: "Maturity, as well as time, is required for noble wine and exquisite cheese. The same with a constitution, which matures with the awareness of those who have to create it, who are going to apply it and whom it should serve" (Lentowska 1994: 145).

39.   Vaclav Havel adroitly captured the fate of scholars with a rhetorical question: "After all, who is better equipped to decide about the fate of these interconnections, who pay the greater regard to them, who take the most responsible attitude toward the world as a whole?" (1995: 37).

Bibliography

Abel, Richard. Plenary Session: "Being, Doing and Remembering: The Practice and Promises of Sociolegal Research at the Close of the Twentieth Century" (June 1, 1995, Toronto, Canada; written statement, meeting of the Law and Society Association).

Aron, Raymond. 1957. *The Opium of the Intellectuals*. London: Secker & Warburg.

Aronowitz, Stanley. 1990. "Intellectuals." In *Regulating the Intellectuals: Perspectives on Academic Freedom in the 1980s*, edited by Craig Kaplan and Ellen Schrecker. New York: Praeger.

Atwood, Margaret. 1993. *The Robber Bride*. New York: Talese.

Aubert, Vilhelm. 1989. *Continuity and Development in Law and Society*. Oslo: Norwegian University Press.

Barron, Frank. 1968. *Creativity and Personal Freedom*. Princeton, N.J.: van Nostrand.

Barron, Frank. 1965. "The Psychology of Creativity." In *New Directions in Psychology*, vol. 2, pp. 1–134. New York: Holt, Rinehart and Winston.

Berelson, Bernard. 1960. *Graduate Educated in the United States*. New York: McGraw-Hill.

Berlin, Isaiah. 1969. *Four Essays on Liberty*. London: Oxford University Press.

Bishop, David M. 1994. "How to Improve Universities." Ottawa *Citizen*, December 9, 1994, p. A11.

Bourdieu, Pierre. 1986. "The Forms of Capital." In *Handbook of Theory and Research for the Sociology of Education*, edited by Jacques G. Richardson. Westport, Conn.: Greenwood Press.

Bourdieu, Pierre. 1984. *Homo Academicus*. Cambridge: Polity Press.
Bourdieu, Pierre and Loiec J. D. Wacquant. 1992. *An Invitation to Reflective Sociology*. Chicago: Illinois University Press.
Bradbury, Malcolm. 1983. *Rates of Exchange*. London: Arena.
Bradbury, Malcolm. 1975. *History Man*. London: Secker.
Brauchli, Marcus. 1994. "Mao's Thought Still Hangs over Education." *Globe and Mail* (Toronto), November 16.
Brym, Robert. 1980. *Intellectuals and Politics*. London: George Allen & Unwin.
Bull, Rob. 1994. "Concordia University Report Supports Killer's Allegations." Ottawa *Citizen*, June 8.
Chomsky, Noam. 1978. *Intellectuals and the State*. Dortrecht, Holland: Het Wereldvenster Baarn.
Coser, Lewis.1965. *Men of Ideas: A Sociological View*. New York: Free Press.
Cross, William M. 1985. "The Sociology of Creativity." Paper presented during the meetings of Illinois Sociological Association, Chicago, October 18–19.
Davies, Norman. 1995. "The Misunderstood Victory in Europe." *The New York Review*, 42(9), May 25.
Duguit, Leon. 1919. *Law in Modern State*. New York: Fertig.
Elster, Jon. 1985. *Making Sense of Marx*. Cambridge: Cambridge University Press.
Emberley, Peter, and R. Newell Waller. 1994. "Universities under Assault." Ottawa *Citizen*, May 27, pp. 10–11.
Ettinger, Elzbieta. 1995. *Hannah Arendt Martin Heidegger*. New Haven, Conn.: Yale University Press.
Etzioni-Halevy, Eva. 1985. *The Knowledge Elite and the Failure of Prophecy*. London: George Allen & Unwin.
Evan, William. 1994. "Human Rights and Global Ethics." Paper presented at the World Congress of Sociology, Bielefeld, June 18–23.
Ferrari, Vincenzo (Ed.). 1990. *Developing Sociology of Law*. Milano: A. Giuffre.
Ferry, Luc, and Alain Renaut. 1990. *Heidegger and Modernity*. Chicago, Ill.: University of Chicago Press.
Feuer, L. 1963. *The American Intellectual*. New York: Basic Books.
Galtung, Johannes. 1981. "Structure, Culture and Intellectual Style." *Social Sciences Information*, 20, pp. 820–34.
Gella, Aleksander (Ed.). 1976. *An Introduction to the Sociology of Intelligentsia*. London: Sage.
Giedymin, Jerzy. 1982. *Science and Convention*. Oxford: Pergamon Press.
Gockowski, Janusz, and Kisiel Przemyslaw (Eds.). 1994. *Patologia i Terapia Zycia Naukowego* (Pathology and therapy of scientific life). Kracow: Universitas.
Goleman, Daniel. 1955. *Emotional Intelligence*. New York: Bantam Books.
Gouldner, Alvin W. 1979. *The Future of Intellectuals and the Rise of the New Class*. New York: Seabury.

Gorecki, Jan (Ed.). 1975. *Sociology and Jurisprudence of Leon Petrazycki.* Urbana: University of Illinois Press.

Gray, Christopher B. (Ed.). In preparation. *The Philosophy of Law: An Encyclopedia.* New York: Garland Publishing.

Grekowa, Irina. 1983. *The Chair.* Moscow: Sovetsky Pisatel.

Gross, Paul R., and Norman Levitt. 1994. *Higher Superstition: The Academic Left and Its Quarrels with Science.* Baltimore, Md.: Johns Hopkins University Press.

Harvey, O.J. *Experience Structure and Adaptability.* New York: Springer.

Havel, Vaclav. 1995. "The Responsibility of Intellectuals." *The New York Review,* 42(11), June 22, pp. 26–30.

International Teletimes Authors. 1994. *Gazette,* 3(4), May.

Jasinski, Jerzy. 1993. "Jak by sie nic nie stalo" (As nothing happened). *Arka* 48(6): 20–27.

Jay, Martin. 1993. "The Academic Woman as Performance Artist." *Salmagundi,* (Spring–Summer): 28–34.

Jay, Martin. 1973. *The Dialectical Imagination.* London: Heinemann.

Kadushin, Charles. 1974. *The American Intellectual Elite.* Boston, Mass.: Little, Brown.

Kapciak, Alina. 1994. "British Sociology." In *European Sociology in Search of Identity,* edited by Brigitta Nedelman and Piotr Sztompka. New York: Walter de Gruyter.

Kennedy, Michael D. 1991. "Eastern Europe's Lessons for Critical Intellectuals." In *Intellectuals and Politics,* edited by Charles C. Lemert. London: Sage.

Kolakowski, Leszek. 1989. *Tales from the Kingdom Lailonia and the Key to Heaven.* Chicago, Ill.: University of Chicago Press.

Kolakowski, Leszek. 1978. *Main Currents of Marxism.* Oxford: Clarendon.

Koestler, Arthur. 1941. *Darkness at Noon.* New York: Macmillan.

Korchak, Alexander. 1994. *Contemporary Totalitarianism: A System Approach.* Boulder, Colo.: East European Monographs.

Kuczynski, Pawel, Marcin Frybes, Jan Strzelecki, and Didiera Lapeyronnie. 1994. *W Poszukiwaniu Ruchu Spolecznego — Wokol Sociologii Alaina Touraina* (In searching for a social movement — Around sociology of Alain Tourain). Warsaw: Oficyna Naukowa.

Lazarsfeld, Paul, and W. T. Thielens. 1958. *The American Mind.* New York: Free Press.

Lemert, C. Charles. 1991. *Intellectuals and Politics.* London: Sage.

Lentowska, Ewa. 1994. *Po co Ludziom Konstytucja* (Why people need constitution). Warsaw: Exit.

Lin, Yutang. 1937. *The Importance of Living.* New York: John Day.

Mannheim, Karl. 1936. Ideology and Utopia: An Introduciton to the Sociology of Knowledge. New York: Harcourt.

Manturzewska, Maria. 1995. "A Biographical Study of the Life-Span Development of Professional Musicians." In *Psychology of Music Today,* edited by Maria Manturzewska, Kacper Miklaszewski, and Andrzej Bialkowski. Warsaw: Fryderyk Chopin Academy of Music.

Manturzewska, Maria. 1969. *Psychologiczne Warunki Osiagniec Pianistycznych* (Psychological conditions of pianistic accomplishments). Wroclaw: Ossolineum.

Maruyama, Magoroh (Ed.). 1991. *Context and Complexity.* New York: Springer-Verlag.

Matejko, Aleksander, and Guy Germain. 1993. "The Role of the Sociologist as Scholar and Citizen." *Guru Nanak Journal of Sociology* 14(2) (October, 1993): 47.

McNeil, Maureen. 1995. "U.K. Is No Nirvana for Academics." *CAUT Bulletin,* 42(5) (May 1995).

Merton, Robert. 1994. "A Life of Learning." Occasional paper No. 25, Charles Homer Haskins Lecture, American Council of Learned Societies, Philadelphia, April 28.

Merton, Robert K. 1968. *Social Theory and Social Structure.* New York: Free Press.

Milgram, Stanley. 1974. *Obedience to Authority.* New York: Harper & Row.

Miller, Arthur, G. 1986. *The Obedience Experiments.* New York: Praeger.

Motyka, Krzysztof. 1993. *Wplyw Leona Petrazyckiego na Polska Teorie i Sociologie Prawa* (Leon Petrazycki's impact on Polish theory and sociology of law). Lublin: Redakcja Wydawnictw Katolickiego Uniwersytetu Lubelskiego.

Ossowska, Maria. 1973. *Ethos Rycerski* (The ethos of knights). Warsaw: PWN.

Ossowska, Maria. 1970a. *Social Determinants of Moral Ideas.* Philadelphia, Pa.: University of Philadelphia Press.

Ossowska, Maria. 1970b. *Normy Moralne* (Moral norms). Warsaw: PWN.

Ossowska, Maria. 1969. *Sociologia Moralnosci* (Sociology of morals). Warsaw: PWN.

Ossowska, María. 1956. *Moralnosc Mieszczanska* (Bourgeois morality). Wroclaw: Ossolineum.

Ossowska, Maria. 1949. *Motywy Postepowania* (Motives of behavior). Warsaw: KIW.

Ossowska, Maria. 1947. *Podstawy Nauki o Moralnosci* (Foundations of a science of morality). Warsaw: Czytelnik.

Parsons, Talcot. 1951. *The Social System.* New York: Free Press.

Perry, John. 1991. "You Can't Just Go In and Do a Johnny Carson Routine." *University Affairs,* June/July 1991: 14–16.

Peterson, Ivor. 1995. "Professor?" *International Herald Tribune,* May 10, 1995, p. 24.

Petrazycki, Leon. 1985. *O Nauce Prawie I Moralnosci* (On science law and morality), edited by Jerzy Licki and Andrzej Kojder. Warsaw: PWN.

Petrazycki, Leon. 1955. *Law and Morality.* Cambridge, Mass.: Harvard University Press.

Podgórecki, Adam, Jon Alexander, and Ron Shields. 1996. *Social Engineering.* Ottawa: Carleton University Press.

Podgórecki, Adam. 1994. *Polish Society.* Westport, Conn.: Praeger.

Podgórecki, Adam. 1993. *The Trivia of Si-tien and Si-tien: The Unknown Chinese Thinker.* Ottawa: Carleton University.

Podgórecki, Adam. 1986. *The Story of a Polish Thinker.* Koln: Verlag fur GesellschaftsArchitectur.

Podgórecki, Adam. 1966. *Prestiz Prawa* (Prestige of law). Warsaw: KIW.

Podgórecki, Adam, and Maria Los. 1979. *Multidimensional Sociology.* London: Routledge & Kegan Paul.

Postman, Neil. 1994. Ottawa *Citizen,* May 30, pp. A1, A2.

Radhakrishnan, R. 1990. "Toward an Effective Intellectual: Foucault or Gramsi?" In *Intellectuals,* edited by B. Robbins. Minneapolis: University of Minnesota Press.

Rothenberg, Albert. 1990. *Creativity and Madness.* Baltimore, Md.: Johns Hopkins University Press.

Rothenberg, Albert, and Bette Greenberg. 1974. *The Index of Scientific Writings on Creativity.* Hamden, Conn.: Archon Books.

Runciman, W. G. 1989. *Confessions of a Reluctant Theorist.* New York: Harvester Wheatsheaf.

Rushton, Philippe. 1995. *Race Evolution and Behavior: A Life History Perspective.* New Brunswick, N.J.: Transactions Books.

Sadri, Ahmad. 1992. *Max Weber's Sociology of Intellectuals.* Oxford: Oxford University Press.

Seidler, Grzegorz Leopold. 1995. *O Istocie i Akceptacji Wladzy Panstwowej* (About essence and acceptance of governmental power). Lublin: Wydawnictwo Universytetu Marii Curie-Sklodowskiej.

Smith, Gudmund, and Carlsson Ingegerd. 1990. *The Creative Process.* Madison, Wis.: Madison University Press.

Sternberg, Robert. 1988. *The Nature of Creativity: Contemporary Psychological Perspective.* Cambridge. Cambridge University Press

Szacki, Jerzy (Ed.). 1995. *Sto Lat Sociologii Polskiej* (One hundred years of Polish sociology). Warsaw: PWN.

Sztompka, Piotr. 1986. *Robert K. Merton: An Intellectual Profile.* London: Macmillan.

Timbs, John. 1858. *Curiosities of History.* London: Kent.

Touraine, Alain. 1983. *Solidarity Poland 1980–81.* Cambridge: Cambridge University Press.

Touraine, Alain. 1981. *The Voice & the Eye.* Cambridge: Cambridge University Press.

Treves, Renato, and Glastra van Loon (Eds.). 1968. *Norms and Actions. National Reports on Sociology of Law.* The Hague: M. Nijhoff.

Vandervlist, Harry. 1995. "Wal-Mart Has Nothing to Do With Universities." *Globe and Mail,* September 24, 1995, p. A20.

Weber, Alfred. 1925. *History of Philosophy*. New York: Schreiber's.

Weber, Max. 1949. *The Methodology of the Social Sciences*. New York: Free Press.

Weber, Max. 1946. "Science as a Vocation." In *From Max Weber*, edited by H. H. Gerth and C. W. Mills. New York: Oxford University Press.

"Who's Who." *The New York Times Magazine*, April 14, 1996, Section 6, p. 66.

Wiesenthal, Simon. 1995. "Ciagle Jest Ze Mna Smutek" (Sorrow accompanies me constantly). *Tygodnik Powszechny*, February 5, 1995, p. 7.

Wilson, Logan. 1958. *The Academic Man*. New York: Oxford University Press.

Wing-Tsit, Chan. 1963. *Chinese Philosophy*. Princeton, N.J.: Princeton University Press.

Wnuk-Lipinski, Edmund. 1995. "Psucia Ciag Dalszy" (Continuation of spoiling). *Tygodnik Powszechny*, May 21, 1995, pp. 2–3.

Wolin, Richard. 1993. *The Heidegger Controversy*. Cambridge, Mass.: The MIT Press.

Zielonka, Jan. 1994. *22 1/2 Years of NIAS*. Wassenaar: Netherlands Institute for Advanced Study in the Humanities and Social Sciences.

Znaniecki, Florian. 1940. *The Social Role of the Man of Knowledge*. New York: Columbia University Press.

Zuckerman, Harriet. 1977. *Scientific Elite: Nobel Laureates in the United States*. New York: The Free Press.

Index

ABOUT THE AUTHOR

ADAM PODGORECKI is Professor of Sociology at Carleton University in Canada. He is the author of over a dozen books, including *Social Oppression* (Greenwood, 1993) and *Polish Society* (Praeger, 1994).

ISBN 0-275-95616-4

EAN

HARDCOVER BAR CODE